the Many Presences of Christ

EDITED BY TIMOTHY FITZGERALD

AND DAVID A. LYSIK

LTP

LITURGY
TRAINING
PUBLICATIONS

Acknowledgments

This book was edited by David A. Lysik. The production editor was Audrey Novak Riley. The design is by Anna Manhart, and the type-setting was done by Kari Nicholls in Sabon and Gill Sans. The cover photographs are by Victor Aleman, Eileen Crowley-Horak and Antonio Pérez. This book was printed by Webcom Limited in Toronto, Ontario.

THE MANY PRESENCES OF CHRIST © 1999 Archdiocese of Chicago: Liturgy Training Publications, 1800 North Hermitage Avenue, Chicago, IL 60622-1101; 1-800-933-1800; orders@ltp.org; fax 1-800-933-7094. All rights reserved.

Printed in Canada.

Library of Congress Cataloging-in-publication Data
The many presences of Christ /edited by David A. Lysik.
    p.   cm.
    Includes bibliographical references.
    ISBN 1-56854-313-1
    1. Catholic Church—Liturgy.   I. Lysik, David A.
BX1970.M285   1999
264'.02—dc21   99-25798
                                                                                        CIP

ISBN 1-56854-313-1
MANY

Contents

Timothy Fitzgerald

Introduction

When Christ gathers us together as a visible sign of his presence, when he gathers the church together to pray "through him and with him and in him," what happens to us? What gets changed? Even more profoundly, who gets changed? What is the relationship of the church to the eucharist? What is the relationship between the church as the body of Christ and the eucharist as the body of Christ? What, to borrow Nathan Mitchell's fine words, is the relationship of the body of Christ on the table to the body of Christ gathered at the table?

When the Second Vatican Council addressed these questions a generation ago (1963) in its *Constitution on the Sacred Liturgy* (CSL), it reiterated the ancient belief of the church: There are many ways Christ is present to the church in its liturgy and its life, so that the church might become Christ present to the world. This ancient belief of the church animated the *Constitution on the Sacred Liturgy:*

> Christ is always present in his church, especially in liturgical cel-
> ebrations. He is present . . . in the person of his minister . . . in
> the eucharistic species. . . . [and] in the sacraments so that when
> anybody baptizes it is really Christ himself who baptizes. He is
> present in his word since it is he himself who speaks. . . . [and]
> he is present when the church prays and sings. . . .

> The liturgy, then, is rightly seen as an exercise of the priestly office of Jesus Christ. . . . In the liturgy] complete and definitive public worship is performed by the mystical body of Jesus Christ, that is, by the Head and his members.
>
> From this it follows that every liturgical celebration, because it is an action of Christ the priest and of his body, which is the church, is a preeminently sacred action. (CSL, 7)

When this passage first appeared, some read it with consternation, believing that it altered and diluted the narrow focus of preconciliar Roman Catholic language and practice concerning the eucharist. In our day, however, we are blessed to rediscover the immensity of the great mystery—that Christ is present to the church and the church is present to Christ when the church gathers with Christ to give thanks and praise to God.

The insight of this conciliar text was a favorite of Pope Paul VI, who often expounded on the many presences of Christ. In *Mysterium fidei,* his 1965 encyclical on the eucharist, he embraced the language of paragraph seven of the *Constitution on the Sacred Liturgy* and pressed it further. The church gathered, he said, is the first and foundational presence of Christ.

> All of us know well that there is more than one way in which Christ is present in his church. . . . Christ is present in his church when it prays, . . . [and] as it performs works of mercy . . . [Christ] is present in his pilgrim church longing to reach the harbor of eternal life. . . . (#35) [Christ] is present in the church as it preaches. (#36) He is present in his church as it shepherds and guides the people of God. . . . (#37) Christ also is present in his church when it offers the sacrifice of the Mass in his name and administers the sacraments. (#38)

The 1967 instruction *Eucharisticum mysterium* urged the wisdom of the conciliar text upon the whole church:

> [T]he faithful should be instructed in the principal modes by which the Lord is present to his church in liturgical celebrations. He is always present in an assembly of the faithful gathered in his name. He is also present in his word . . . present both in the person of the minister . . . and above all under the eucharistic elements. (#9)

In the celebration of Mass the principal modes of Christ's presence to his church emerge clearly one after the other: first he is
seen to be present in the assembly of the faithful gathered in his
name; then in his word, with the reading and explanation of
scripture; also in the person of the minister; finally, in a singular
way under the eucharistic elements. (#55)

The Notre Dame Center for Pastoral Liturgy convened its 1998
pastoral liturgy conference to address the questions: How is Christ
present to the church in its liturgy and its life? Even more profoundly,
how is the church present to Christ? The conference raised up again
the wisdom of the tradition, the "various modes of Christ's presence," to a church whose experience with its liturgy continues to
change. People from forty states and eight countries gathered, people
from Roman, Anglican, Reform and Evangelical traditions. The first
two people to register (via the Internet) were Reform pastors from
South Africa.

We know all too well how the Christian churches pick and
choose among the "modes of Christ's presence." Some have claimed
that Christ is present primarily (even solely) in the word; some that
he is present only in the eucharistic food; still others that he is present
ultimately in the assembly or in the ministers. But the ancient belief of
the church, echoed in the *Constitution on the Sacred Liturgy* a generation ago, has startled all of us, all the churches, and has opened
our eyes to our selectivity. For if each of the churches has held to
some of the truth about Christ's presence with us, each had also forgotten or ignored some of the truth. Now in this generation the
churches have the opportunity to learn one from another that part
of the wisdom about Christ which they held onto and cherished, so
that all might be enlightened and changed.

The issues, circumstances and dilemmas facing the present generation of disciples are completely different from those earlier gener-
ations of Christians have known. Readers of the following chapters
will quickly agree. Yet our foundational belief remains exactly the
same: The Risen One stands always in our midst to nourish and to
surprise and to strengthen us. He who gathers us, who announces
the good news to us, who teaches us how to pray and prays with us,
who calls us to table and opens our eyes and touches our hearts—the

one who does all this—is the Lord. Slowly, surely, truly, in the gathering and the announcing, in the giving thanks and in the breaking of the bread, in the intercessory prayer and in the sending forth, the church becomes the living body of Christ.

Some 1600 years ago, Saint Ambrose expressed well the mystery of our faith to the neophytes of Milan. We now use his wise words to express what is more easily experienced than explained: "Where the church is, where the mysteries are, there Christ richly provides his presence." (*De mysteriis,* ch. 5, no. 27)

Gilbert W. Ostdiek, OFM

Response to the Michael Mathis Award

Thank You

The Michael Mathis Award is something I would never have imag-
ined receiving. Because this honor is so unexpected, it is all the more
precious to me—a sheer gift. I offer my heartfelt thanks to the Notre
Dame Center for Pastoral Liturgy; to its director, Sister Eleanor
Bernstein; and to the Center's staff and board of advisors. It is a great
honor to receive this award named after Father Michael Mathis, CSC,
a giant in the liturgical renewal whose pioneering work just prior to
the Second Vatican Council strikes so many resonances for me: his
promotion of a fully participative liturgy, his vision of programs of
liturgical theology and catechesis wedded to celebration, his interest
in the architecture of worship spaces, and his work as a translator
for the first English edition of the Roman Ritual in 1953. I commend
the Center for cherishing and carrying on his legacy. And if I may be
so bold as to speak on behalf of pastoral liturgists from across this
land, I thank you for the gift you have given all of us in the renewal
of the liturgy.

I wish to extend special thanks to my family, who have taught
me at our family table and gatherings the meaning of sharing, presence, and belonging. I am also grateful to my other family, my
Franciscan brothers, who have helped me to understand the good-
ness of all God's creatures and that creation is only a thin veil

between us and our God, not an impenetrable barrier. And finally, I offer my thanks to all my colleagues in pastoral liturgy. We are co-workers in the vineyard of the liturgy. We need each other more than ever now, when the renewal hangs in the balance. At an earlier time in the renewal, there were giants in the land and we could stand on their shoulders. So many of them are gone from the scene. We may not be of their stature, but we are more numerous now and we need to take turns standing on each other's shoulders as we carry on their work. I humbly accept this award in solidarity with and respect for all these colleagues.

Response

It is to these colleagues in the ministry of pastoral liturgy that I now address my formal response to the Michael Mathis Award. Four principles that were characteristic of his work in the renewal of the liturgy serve to frame my remarks.[1] These four principles, translated into our current context, have perduring value for the work of renewal.

First, for Michael Mathis, the goal of the renewal of the liturgy was to realize the liturgy's full potential for the pastoral enrichment of the members of the church. He is noted for his determined efforts to provide for worshipers of his day as rich and full a celebration of the liturgy as possible.

The *Constitution on the Sacred Liturgy* (CSL) is equally clear and emphatic on this score: "In the reform and promotion of the liturgy, this full and active participation by all the people is the aim to be considered before all else." And that is only fitting, for such participation, the *Constitution* continues, "is their right and duty by reason of their baptism." (#14)

The liturgical richness that Michael Mathis envisioned in a more restrictive context must now be extended to text and silence, to symbol, space and song. There is a special urgency for crafting a second generation of texts to meet the needs of a fully inculturated liturgy that draws on the genius of the English language to address the faith and religious imagination of the assembly. The principles that Mathis helped his committee to formulate in 1953 as it translated the Roman Ritual compare well with those of Rome's 1969 *Instruction on the Translation of Liturgical Texts*.[2] "Accurate"; "not slavishly exact or loosely free"; "clear, idiomatic, eloquent, simple dignity" — such are the words and phrases Mathis' committee uses.[3] Language marked by hospitality and inclusion for us all and by a beauty that invites us to look beyond ourselves to the Risen One who walks with us on the way: these are the hallmarks of good prayer. But this is now at risk. "Correctness" of whatever sort threatens to usurp the priority of the assembly's ability to enter into the prayer and make it their own.

Faced with efforts to revert to a style of language more concerned for literal fidelity and theological precision than for the prayer of the people, we can take consolation in something we have known in our Catholic bones for centuries. Liturgy does not rely solely, or even primarily, on words. Liturgy speaks in many voices. The multivalent languages of symbol, gesture, song, silence, time and space are far more powerful in revealing and communicating God's gracious presence to us in Christ. They invite us into a realm of mystery where words, no matter how well crafted, fail us. And best of all, pastoral adaptation of these non-verbal languages to the spiritual needs of the particular assembly gathered here and now can happen much more readily and unobtrusively. If only we liturgists can learn to put more trust in them.[4]

Another principle dear to Michael Mathis was his firm commitment to promoting fruitful participation in the liturgy by fostering an understanding of it. Mathis was known for his efforts to help people prepare for the celebration through reflection and prayer. Witness his vigil service, his mimeographed reflections in preparation for the Mass, the study weeks and summer program. He was also a firm believer that such understanding is gained best in the context of liturgy celebrated and lived. "We learn by doing," he said.[5] For that reason, he insisted that the Notre Dame summer program combine the academic study of liturgy with the celebration of the rites themselves.

Here I simply wish to echo Bishop Trautman's call that we undertake a new catechesis of the liturgy as part of our efforts to revitalize the reform.[6] Ministers and people alike are ready for a true mystagogy. Three decades of good celebration have provided us with a wealth of experience on which to reflect. Again and again I find that people already know in their bones what the liturgy means. We only need a way to name what we know and to reflect on it. For a model of how to do this, we have only to look to master catechists such as Thomas Groome or to the growing experience and reflection of those who do mystagogical catechesis in RCIA programs.[7]

Another principle by which Michael Mathis lived was his firm conviction that the liturgy is an art to be practiced as well as a science to be studied. Consequently, practice and theory must be integrated. This he applied most assiduously to his design of the Notre Dame summer program, where so many of the pastoral liturgists now at work among us have received their preparation.

The logic of what Michael Mathis was about was given voice in the *Constitution on the Sacred Liturgy*. The faithful will not derive the true Christian spirit from the liturgy, the *Constitution* reasoned, if pastors do not zealously promote their participation. But to hope for this is futile unless "the pastors themselves become thoroughly imbued with the spirit and power of the liturgy and make themselves its teachers. A prime need, therefore, is that attention be directed, first of all, to the liturgical formation of the clergy" (#14). This holds, *a pari,* for all who have joined the burgeoning ranks of liturgical ministers since then. Much has already been done to prepare ministers imbued with the spirit and power of the liturgy. It is incumbent on us to deepen and enrich our preparation programs. The introduction to the *Lectionary for Mass for Use in the Dioceses of the United States of America* wisely urges us to look beyond technical preparation to a spiritual-liturgical formation (#55). Those of us who teach pastoral liturgy, whether in schools of theology or in ministry preparation programs, can never be content to carry out our study of the liturgy in splendid isolation from God's people who celebrate it. We need to be in dialogue with worshipers and pastoral practitioners; we owe them no less than this. Liturgical practice and theoretical reflection must constantly circle each other in the dance.

A final principle that guided Michael Mathis was his belief that his work was an apostolate, a service meant to build up the Body of Christ. This belief anchored his "single-minded drive and unflagging energy in the cause of liturgy."[8]

Rather than speaking of our work as an "apostolate," today we more commonly name it a ministry, and I want to reflect on it more at length under that rubric. So many of the issues we have been discussing these days are not about liturgy directly. Rather, they have to do with theology, with ecclesiology, and especially with ministry. Michael Mathis was also a scripture scholar, so as we close this conference, allow me to offer a paradigm for ministry that is based on scripture and that fits wonderfully with our conference theme of the Lord's manifold presence in the eucharist and in the midst of God's people. The story is one we cherish deeply, that of the two disciples on the way to Emmaus (Luke 24:13–35). This first eucharist celebrated in the Christian community reveals what every eucharist should be: a time for us to know Christ in the breaking of the bread. It also presents us with a vision of ministry we need to take to heart today, lest the pressures and problems we face cause us to lose sight of what our ministries are all about. I invite you to savor the story of these journeyers once again and to focus on the figure of the stranger who walks the road with them.

The story opens with the two on their way from Jerusalem. What they were leaving was not just a place, but the experience of that Passover week when the fate of the one in whom they had placed their hopes[9] went from a triumphant entry amid shouts of "Hosanna" to abandonment and death on a cross. With Jesus dead and buried, the two were leaving behind their hopes and their fellow disciples.

As they walked along, one whom they did not recognize joined them. The questions the stranger put to them were simple and direct: "What are you discussing . . . what things?" With these gentle questions he was able to draw out of them their story. What a sad ending it had. "We were hoping that he would be the one who would set Israel free." As one commentator remarks, their story is told in the past tense, in terms of failure and hurt bewilderment. What they are saying is that they are "ex-followers of a prophet, with left-over lives, and nowhere to go but away."[10] When our lives feel left-over, what else is there to do? This is the first moment of the stranger's ministry to them. He is the model of the effective pastoral care giver: wayfaring companion, perfect listener.

Once they had exhausted their story, the stranger became the storyteller in turn. He retold that same story, but with a very different ending. "Did not the Messiah have to undergo all this so as to enter into his glory?" Glory—what a marvelous reversal, this new ending! In this stranger we see a master catechist-homilist at work. Beginning with Moses and all the prophets, he used the words and stories already familiar to them to retell the story of their experience, infusing it with a newness of meaning that could not but warm their hearts. This is the second moment of his ministry, a ministry of the word.

The third scene follows quickly. "Stay with us," they said. They had received a double gift from him, the gift of having someone listen to their story with respect until they had told the all of it and then of receiving from him a new story to tell in its stead. Such hospitality demands hospitality in return. "Stay with us."

And so he went in to table with them. But then he turned the tables on them, so to speak. He became their host and led them in the familiar Jewish table prayer sealed in the breaking of the bread. At that, their eyes were opened and they recognized him. As Raymond Brown notes, in the accounts of the resurrection the language of "seeing" refers not to physical sight, but to what might be called faith-insight.[11] When the disciples recognized him, their response as voiced in John's gospel (21:7) was not "Jesus is back," but "It is the Lord!" And in recognizing him as the living Lord, they again recognized themselves as his disciples. Through the table ministry of the stranger now revealed to their unmasked eyes, the two disciples' inner journey has reached completion. They have traveled the road from loss of all hope to full Easter faith. And in a moment of mystagogy, they are now able to name that experience: "Were not our hearts burning inside us while he talked to us on the road and explained the Scriptures to us?" Truly an "arsonist of the heart," as John Shea says.[12]

Their journey did not end in Emmaus. Caught up in the power of that journey to faith on which the risen Lord had companioned them, they rose up and returned to Jerusalem renewed in a disciple's mission. They had a story to tell the others, the story of "what had happened on the road and how they had come to know him in the breaking of the bread." And so his final act of ministry to them was to leave them with a mission.

A first lesson for us is that liturgical ministry alone cannot bring others to recognize the Lord who is present. That is clear if we read the Emmaus story backwards.[13] The two disciples would never have been renewed in mission if they had not recognized the Lord in the breaking of the bread. They would never have recognized him if their hearts had not been set on fire by a new story. And they would never have been able to hear the new story if they had not first been able to tell and let go of their old one. Each moment of ministry depends on the others for all of them to be successful in revealing the presence of the Lord and what it demands of us. Today, as then, the table is simply the place where disciples come to recognize that he has always been with them. But his presence to them does not begin or end there.

A second lesson for us is that liturgical ministry, like all ministry, is something we do in Christ's name. He is our only *leitourgos*, the one "minister of the sanctuary" (Hebrews 8:2). We are the stranger's face he wears; we only stand in for him. Ministry, then, is not our possession, but a gift that we hold in trust. As Michael Mathis well understood, ministry is both gift and a call to service. This has been true from the very beginning. We are told in Matthew's gospel that when Jesus first sent the Twelve out on mission, he instructed them: "The gift you have received, give as a gift" (Matthew 10:8). Every such gift, Saint Paul reminds us, is given to God's holy ones not for their own sake, but "to equip them for the work of ministry, for building up the Body of Christ" (Ephesians 4:12). What we have received as a gift must be freely given to others; we are the assembly's servants.

In these decades of renewal we have been graced with the gift of ministering to God's people who gather in prayer. For this gift, I invite all of you to join me in saying a final *Deo gratias!* on this day. May that giving of thanks to God always find an echo in our eucharist and in our hearts.

1. Robert Kennedy, *Michael Mathis: American Liturgical Pioneer* American Essays in Liturgy 5 (Washington, DC: The Pastoral Press, 1987), 21–2.

2. Consilium, *Instruction on the Translation of Liturgical Texts for Celebrations with a Congregation,* in International Commission on English in the Liturgy, *Documents on the Liturgy 1963–1979: Conciliar, Papal, and Curial Texts* [DOL] (Collegeville, MN: The Liturgical Press, 1982), 284–91 (DOL, 123).

3. Kennedy, 19.

4. Our "low context" culture relies predominantly on words to communicate. Paradoxically, we have become adept at ignoring the barrage of words around us and instinctively mistrust their empty hype. We listen selectively in liturgy as well.

5. Quoted in George Schidel, "Never Too Much: In Memoriam: Rev. Michael Ambrose Mathis, csc (1885–1960)," *Yearbook of Liturgical Studies* 3 (1962), 24.

6. See Donald W. Trautman, "On Receiving the Michael Mathis Award," in Timothy Fitzgerald and Martin F. Connell, eds., *The Changing Face of the Church* (Chicago: Liturgy Training Publications, 1998), 4–10.

7. Thomas Groome, *Christian Religious Education: Sharing our Story and Vision* (San Francisco: Harper & Row, 1980). An earlier brief introduction to his thought may be found in his "Christian Education: A Task of Present Dialectical Hermeneutics," *The Living Light* 14/3 (1997), 408–23. See also James Dunning, *Echoing God's Word: Formation for Catechists and Homilists in a Catechumenal Church* (Arlington, VA: The North American Forum on the Catechumenate, 1993); Philip J. McBrien, *How to Teach with the Lectionary* (Mystic, CT: Twenty-Third Publications, 1992).

8. Kennedy, 22.

9. See Luke 19:11.

10. See Denis McBride, *The Gospel of Luke: A Reflective Commentary* (Northport, NY: Costello, 1982), 317–18.

11. Raymond Brown, *The Virginal Conception and Bodily Resurrection of Jesus* (New York: Paulist Press, 1973), 89–92, 111–12.

12. John Shea, *Stories of God: An Unauthorized Biography* (Chicago: The Thomas More Press, 1978), 8.

13. This idea was first developed in an essay drawing out the relationship between catechesis, liturgy and mission. See my "What We Have Seen and Heard and Touched," in *Sent Forth by God's Blessing: The 1987 Institute of Liturgical Studies* (Institute of Liturgical Studies Occasional Papers 3) (Valparaiso, IN: The Liturgical Institute, 1988), 87–103.

John F. Baldovin, sj

The Church in Christ, Christ in the Church

A number of years ago the great Protestant theologian Karl Barth reacted to the suggestion of Otto Dibelius that the 20th century would be the century of the church. Barth thought the accent was misplaced from the far more important question of God.[1] I am beginning to think that he was right. As a result, while this article addresses the topic of the church in Christ and Christ in the church, I would first like to deal with a number of questions pertaining more to God than to the church.

We can no longer forego the question of God and God's presence in the liturgy — as though it were obvious, and all we had to do was take an orthodox understanding of God and apply it to the liturgy, as many contemporary liturgists and theologians insist, simply derive our fundamental understanding of God from the liturgy itself.[2] There is a way in which this latter approach is very valuable (as I hope to show) but it cannot substitute for the painful search for our understanding of the revealed God of the Christian tradition. Part of the reason that I am insisting on putting ecclesiology on the back burner — at least for the moment — is that we seem to have reached such a dead end with regard to issues that divide the church.

Let me give two examples. The distinguished American Roman Catholic theologian Avery Dulles recently published an article that focuses on the 1997 meeting of the Catholic Theological Society of America (CTSA). The article was entitled, "How Catholic is the CTSA?"[3] His answer in a nutshell is "not very." According to Dulles, the CTSA has drifted in accommodation with the times and away from the church's tradition and magisterium. The theme of the CTSA meeting was "Eucharist for a New Millennium" and I think it safe to say that every crucial issue that Dulles raises with regard to it deals either with the church or sacraments.

Similarly, Francis Mannion has outlined the numerous agendas that are currently operative with regard to reform of the liturgy in the United States. He discerns five of them: advancing the official reform, restoring the preconciliar, reforming the reform, inculturating the reform, and recatholicizing the reform.[4] Some of these agendas overlap, but others, like inculturating the reform (which Mannion identifies with the North American Academy of Liturgy) and restoring the preconciliar (the agenda of the traditionalists) are clearly opposed to one another.

In the cases outlined by Dulles and Mannion, disagreement is such that one must come to the conclusion that various parties in the church have reached an impasse. Little wonder that Cardinal Bernardin's call for "common ground" was greeted with such appreciation, not to mention relief. But if we are to reach any significant kind of common ground in the church, it seems to me that it will be necessary to ask the fundamental questions about God, for I suspect that behind every debate about the liturgy and the church lies the question of who God is and how God relates to us. Those who are committed to the renewal of the church's liturgy can no longer afford to avoid these issues.

I am reminded of the liturgy student some years ago who prepared the intercessions for the Liturgy of the Hours one day. When asked, "Why did you pray 'In thanksgiving to the Holy Trinity, for all that they have done for us,' when it is clearly heretical to refer to the Trinity in the plural?" the student responded, "Oh, I'm studying liturgy, not theology." One hopes that in the course of studies this person was treated to any number of significant works on liturgical theology and was disabused of the notion that one can divorce the study of liturgy from theology as such. In that case the student would have learned that one cannot divorce questions of liturgical aesthetic or history or anthropology from questions about God, Christ, the Holy Spirit, grace and eschatology. That the liturgy is the primary source for these questions, both in its form and content, I have no doubt, and I shall attempt to demonstrate this in the second section of this article.

I want to make a similar point with regard to liturgical music as well. All too often today in liturgies of all sorts one finds but a single theme that can be distilled from the music that is sung, namely "We are church." I am not suggesting that this is not a worthy theme or that it does not need to be prayed, preached and sung. But I am suggesting that if this is the *sum total* of what we can sing, the liturgy is offering us rather thin soup. It certainly can be easier to sing about how we manifest the church: Songs about God can and do run aground on the language we use to address God. But to avoid lyrics that address God is to ignore the One who grasps us and brings us to worship in the first place.

So, I want to talk about God; that is, about theology, and the liturgy. It might seem more palatable or fashionable were I to use the term "spirituality" instead of "theology." I think it would be unfortunate to separate the two. Too often, as Peter Fink demonstrated a number of years ago, liturgy and spirituality are separated, as though they belong to two different worlds.[5] And like Fink, I sometimes fear that my theology students are determined never to let deeper theological questions interfere with their spiritual lives. But one cannot separate the two. Spirituality without theology (by which I mean sustained reflection) is superficial just as theology without spirituality is empty. Liturgy can and ought unite the two.

I should make it clear that I am not suggesting that the theology of the church is unimportant or that the theology of the church does not have profound connections to the theology of sacraments and liturgy. It does. We should recognize that in the past hundred years the church has witnessed a resurgence in sacramental theology because it recovered a lost connection between church and sacrament. But now that this connection has been restored, it is necessary in my opinion to attempt a theology that presents a coherent theology of God, the church and sacraments.

So, I am changing the parameters of the title somewhat to "the liturgy in God and God in the liturgy." Only if we start with God can we come to some fruitful conclusions about the church in Christ and Christ in the church. I propose to approach our topic in three sections. First, I will describe several sets of distinctions in the hopes that they might provide some deeper understanding of the variety in people's experience of God and therefore in the liturgy. Second, I will suggest a way forward based on a trinitarian theology of the cross that stems from the liturgical celebration of the paschal mystery. Third, I will deal with a test case that exemplifies the contemporary struggle over the church's liturgy: the placement of the tabernacle in Catholic churches. I submit that to argue this issue, as is often done, without recourse to the theological premises behind one choice or another leads to a dead end. Therefore we must look for a different direction to take if we are not simply to be resigned to fruitless ecclesiastical warfare.

Images of God: Some Distinctions

I suppose it is completely obvious to everyone that individuals, not to mention cultural groups, have different experiences and images of God. It may be obvious, but in our preparation and performance of liturgy we seem strangely unaware of the fact, perhaps because the issue is so complex and demands such insight. After all, even within the same individual or the same culture there may be differing experiences of God depending on one's stage in life, the culture's historical and social experience and so forth. Is God distant or near? Loving or vengeful? Male, female, neither, both? Does God have a specific will for each individual in each and every choice they make or does God basically set us free to find our own destiny? Has God chosen a people (usually, of course, my people) or are all human beings alike to God? Is God omnipotent or rather powerless in this world? My list is not exhaustive. It could go on and on, but the point is simple: Our basic images of God differ — individually, culturally, historically.

A number of thinkers have attempted to analyze this phenomenon. I will refer to three who may be helpful in our pursuit of "God in the liturgy." The first is Peter Berger, who in his well-known sociology of religion, *The Sacred Canopy*,[6] draws the distinction between priestly and prophetic religion. Berger suggests that the basic function of religion is to create and maintain a *cosmos*, that is, a meaningful universe. The priestly side of religion, therefore, is concerned with maintaining that meaningful world against all other kinds of evidence. On the other hand, religion can have (and often has had) a side that criticizes the world, sees its flaws and works for change. This is represented by the prophetic side of religion.

The same distinction obtains in liturgy. (And here it obtains with a vengeance since liturgical symbols are where the theological rubber meets the religious road.) On the one hand, the liturgy creates or images a world that is meaningful, a world that reflects "heaven"—the way things really are. "This is God!" the liturgy says in its own ritual and symbolic way: "This is the way God's world looks. Take comfort!" On the other hand, the prophetic dimension of liturgy challenges the comfort created by the priestly: "You don't really live up to this imaged reality of God and God's reign." Or: "Your ordinary, everyday social world looks nothing like this. You must change!"

So the one God can be both comforting and demanding. Christians concerned with social justice often view the liturgy as a one-sided affair, a priestly exercise (in Berger's terms) with very little challenge to offer. Often they can be correct. But they can also fail to perceive in the very same liturgy the subversive principles they seek, as Robert Hovda argued time and time again.[7] In other words, the liturgy itself, and not merely preaching, can offer a profound challenge to my world view and my practice, as for example when I find myself unavoidably near someone whom I despise for one reason or another at the time of the exchange of peace.

A second distinction in the way we view God has recently been offered by the essayist Bruce Bawer in his book, *Stealing Jesus: How Fundamentalism Betrays Christianity*.[8] Bawer distinguishes between what he calls the "Church of Law" and the "Church of Love." Admittedly the book is a defense of mainline Protestantism; it is rather dismissive of Roman Catholicism, and is a polemic against evangelical Christianity in the contemporary United States. To be sure, Bawer draws too sharp a distinction. No church exists purely as a church of law or a church of love. But at the same time, I think he points to two very strong tendencies in contemporary American Christianity. They have to do ultimately with how one conceives God. Is God a vengeful and demanding figure who wills to save only very few human beings, the elect, persons who obey every command and have explicit faith in Jesus Christ as well as lives that witness to that faith? Or perhaps is God the attractive and loving lure to holiness and fulness of life, who wills all persons to have true life (a rather more user-friendly God)? Each view has its place in contemporary American Christianity and each, frankly, has biblical warrant.[9] Each view also has correlates in one's approach to what a church ought to look like (both in the physical sense of the building and the wider sense of community) and therefore what liturgy is and ought to be. Moreover, the church of love and the church of law are dividing up American Christianity along lines that no longer look like traditional ecclesial organizations but rather can be described as mainline, evangelical, progressive or conservative. Part of Bawer's difficulty lies in finding an adequate terminology for the divide in Christianity, but surely he is onto something significant. We are naive, I believe, if we ignore the significance of these widely divergent understandings of God. They have serious impact upon what people expect when they come to worship and how they understand Christ to be operative in that worship.

A final distinction has been drawn by Bernhard Lang in his book, *Sacred Games*.[10] Although Lang subtitles his book, "A History of Christian Worship," the work is more a phenomenology of liturgical experience, based on what he calls six games: praise, prayer, sermon, sacrifice, sacrament and spiritual ecstasy. For Lang, each of these games describes a specific approach to God. In the end, however, he attempts to summarize his findings by making a fundamental distinction between the awesome and the familiar deity to whom human beings relate. He employs the familiar vocabulary suggested by Rudolf Otto in his classic, *The Idea of the Holy*. People relate to God as the *Mysterium Tremendum*, or as the *Mysterium Fascinans*: the awe-inspiring, fearful, transcendent God, wholly other and completely beyond us; or the attractive God, in the phrase of Augustine

John F. Baldovin, SJ

intimior intimo meo—closer to me than I am to myself—the God who is a felt presence in community with others. For Lang, these different approaches to God represent "two theological temperaments and, indeed, world views."[11] People can go back and forth between the two. Cultures and historical periods may emphasize one or the other. Men and women may have different preferences in their approach to God along the lines of transcendence and immanence. Social classes within the same culture may tend toward one form of worship or the other. The elites and socially well-off, for example, are not likely to participate in ecstatic spirit-filled worship like that of the Pentecostals.

Certainly a liturgical tradition may emphasize one view at the expense of the other, at least outwardly. For example, one might view the Byzantine Divine Liturgy as wholly transcendent and God-centered, and certainly that form of worship tends in this direction. On the other hand, the Byzantine Divine Liturgy may be an experience of intense intimacy for its participants either individually or corporately. One could express the same caution with regard to the other end of the liturgical spectrum—the Quaker meeting. Among the Quakers, God is extremely familiar and intimate, but at the same time the Spirit of God can powerfully transcend the meeting and make it much less anthropocentric than at first sight.

It is difficult, if not impossible, to discern where the majority of American Roman Catholics stand with regard to the transcendence and immanence of God in worship. My suspicion, based on very informal surveying, is that the majority look for an immanent God in the liturgy and the transcendent God elsewhere. When I have asked what seem like typical middle-class people to describe where they find the awesome God and where they find the immanent God, they tend to say that they find the awesome God only in nature, in the wonder of the expanse of creation. I suspect this says as much about what people are being given in their liturgies by their ministers as much as it does about their theological and spiritual predilections. At the same time there are a good number of American Roman Catholics who decry the loss of transcendence, usually called "the sacred" in their worship. I suggest that although it may be my or our visceral reaction to dismiss them with "old-fashioned" or "pre–Vatican II" or some other pejorative label, it might be better and more productive to listen to what they are trying to say.[12]

So, we have surveyed three sets of basic distinctions that human beings take in their approach to God and therefore to worship: priestly and prophetic; the church of law versus the church of love; transcendence and immanence (or the awesome versus the familiar God). The terms *priestly, church of law* and *transcendence* naturally go together just as *prophetic, church of love* and *immanence* seem to fit.[13] These distinctions, I submit, characterize the basic trends in American religious experience today and are, therefore, what people bring to worship. The temptation to caricature either group (the "transcendence group" or the "immanence group") is great but I will try to avoid it.

Now I want to ask: Can a theology of the presence of Christ in the church and its liturgy somehow move us beyond the impasse that we face when the two sets of approaches to God collide? And can such a reflection help in dealing with very specific of practice? It is to these questions that I will now wish turn.

A Trinitarian Theology of the Cross as Liturgical Theology

Let me start with a simple proposition: The liturgy of the church is Christ-centered from beginning to end. The genius of Christian worship is this: Simple things like the praise of God, the employment of ritual symbols and actions, repentance, witnessing of vows, bathing, rubbing with oil—all very human actions that can be done just as well in another religious tradition altogether—among Christians are done in the name of Christ and the power of his Holy Spirit.

But which Christ? The Christ of transcendent majesty and glory so evident in the Byzantine dome or apse mosaics, or the simple teacher of timeless wisdom from Nazareth, or the radical Galilean peasant revolutionary? Nineteenth- and twentieth-century theology has foundered on the distinction. Neither picture, I submit, is complete or even accurate. Contemporary Jesus research, as exemplified by writers like E. P. Sanders and N. T. Wright (as opposed to the members of the "Jesus Seminar" like Dominic Crossan and Robert Funk), is attempting to provide a fuller picture of the historical Jesus as a man, very much a first-century Jew, who proclaims the immanence of the reign of the transcendent God of Israel. Further, such research draws a portrait of a figure who understands himself to be not only the herald but the very personification of that reign. This is the picture of a demanding prophet, a picture that the writers of the New Testament basically get right, especially in proclaiming the significance of his passion, death and resurrection. Let me suggest that this is a much more productive enterprise than New Testament research that leads us to believe that whatever we hear in the gospels, it is not the voice of Jesus. Rather, these authors are emphasizing the continuity between the so-called Jesus of history and the post-resurrection Christ.

The hinge, of course, must be found in the event of the cross. One finds in the cross the true center of Christian faith, for from the cross issues a theology of the Trinity, a theology not based on abstract philosophical categories but on the experience of the disciples who come to an Easter faith despite the utter scandal of the cross. Naturally I am talking about what liturgists like to call "the paschal mystery." Now "paschal mystery" has become a pretty phrase, but I wonder how often people appreciate its seriousness, or prefer to leap beyond the cross to Easter joy, or too easily adopt a one-sided view of the Johannine perspective of the glory of the cross. How easy it is to miss the fact that the cross renders a very strange God, one who is completely revealed in the experience of Jesus, both in utter abandonment and in vindication. From my perspective, Paul (rather than historians like Crossan and Funk) gets it exactly right when he adopts this famous hymn in Philippians 2:5–11:

> Let the same mind be in you that was in Christ Jesus,
> who, though he was in the form of God,
> did not regard equality with God as something to be exploited,
> but emptied himself, taking the form of a slave,
> being born in human likeness.
> And being found in human form,
> he humbled himself and became obedient to the point of death
> even death on a cross.
> Therefore, God also highly exalted him

> and gave him the name that is above every name,
> so that at the name of Jesus every knee should bend,
> in heaven and on earth and under the earth,
> and every tongue should confess that Jesus Christ is Lord,
> to the glory of the Father.

So much of the interpretation of this passage depends on how one understands "who, though he was in the form of God, did not regard equality with God as something to be exploited." If one reads this as an affirmation of a pre-existent Logos being incarnated one gets a very different picture than if one sees being "in the form of God" as a reference to Adam, who precisely did consider equality with God something to be exploited or (I think a better translation) "grasped at." In the latter case, Jesus' divinity and lordship are predicated on his full acceptance of his humanity, and it is through the event of the cross that we are able to make that confession of faith. In other words, it is through a life so completely lived in trust and in acceptance of his humanity that Jesus undoes the Adamic Fall and becomes the life-giving source of divinization of us all.

To put all of this another way: Our tendency is to have an idea of God, one that emphasizes one or another aspect or dimension depending on a number of factors, as I have already outlined. We then bring this understanding to Christian revelation both in the scriptures and the liturgy and interpret accordingly. A trinitarian theology of the cross does not work that way. It starts from the cross and the experience of the disciples' faith that ultimately finds there both death and life, and it forms our understanding and experience of God on the basis of that event. In other words, if you want to know the Christian belief in God, you start from the cross.

A trinitarian theology of the cross, therefore, takes the utter abandonment of Jesus on the cross with the same seriousness as it does his vindication. The true understanding of God comes not from our human philosophical categories, but rather from the paradoxical event of God in our history — absolutely beyond and absent and at the same time indescribably near. I am making a claim here: The birth of true Christian faith can be found in the cross of Jesus of Nazareth, a cross that reveals that God is to be found in the relationship with the one Jesus calls *Abba* and to whom he gives himself in total and utter faith, a faith that is exemplified by his entire life and the urgency of his preaching of the reign of God. Moreover, this relationship in total faith (the abandonment that Jesus experiences) witnesses to the existence of the Holy Spirit poured out upon Jesus and bestowed back by him to the Father. It is in the act of that bestowal that the church and the sacraments find their lifeblood. This is not a God who can be "grasped at," but rather one who can be found only in self-emptying love. So, the revelation of Jesus' humanity is at the same time the revelation of his divinity.

Therefore, I am suggesting that at least in principle the theology of the paschal mystery I have outlined here can bring together the transcendence and the immanence of God. But it does so in a way that is very strange and ironic because the God who is revealed in the paschal mystery defies our normal expectations by being hidden even in presence.

What has this to do with liturgy? The liturgy is the ritual expression of the mystery of God; or better, it is the ritual experience of this God. As Aidan Kavanagh pointed out so well in *On Liturgical Theology*, it is an error to think that the liturgy is *about* God when it is *of* God.[14] But how precisely is this God of irony and paradox manifested in the liturgy? A very useful way of analyzing how God works in liturgical experience has been offered by Gordon Lathrop in his liturgical theology, *Holy Things*. The category that governs Lathrop's work is juxtaposition.

Lathrop begins by affirming the thoroughly scriptural nature of the spirit and content of liturgy and then by showing that scripture itself is a juxtaposition, for it joins a new situation — that of the writer and the community — with a memory of what God has done in the past, to create a third, new thing. Even the use of scripture in the Mass is a juxtaposition. As far as we know, traditional liturgies of the eucharist have never contained just one reading. They contain two or more readings, juxtaposed to one another. Thus in our Masses no one passage from scripture is ever read "plain." It is always juxtaposed in the liturgy of the word with at least one other passage. (Note that this practice of the liturgy is a convenient antidote to all kinds of fundamentalism that want to extract only one meaning from a biblical text and impose it.)

Further, scripture is not the only content of the liturgy. It is juxtaposed with action—the eucharist—so that word and action are always held in tension. Lathrop goes on to explain the same kind of juxtaposition for the bath of baptism and catechesis, the Sunday and the Pascha, and so on. The work that the liturgy does, therefore, is in the juxtapositions themselves. From this I draw the conclusion that God is to be found in the interstices. In other words, the presence of God in liturgy, though real and active, is also elusive. One cannot speak of presence without also speaking of absence.[15] So too of the trinitarian God revealed in the event of the cross. God cannot be found except only through paradox. It seems to me this is why we speak of Trinity rather than only of Jesus being the incarnate Son of God. If we had only a "bi-nity," as it were, then we could easily say that Jesus is the incarnation of God, without realizing that the matter is far more complex and requires a third personal relationship we call Holy Spirit for us to affirm the essentially relational nature of God. And it is in the relationality of liturgy itself that we find God.[16]

It may seem that I have gotten quite far afield in abstract theology from our topic. But I insist that only a theology of the Trinity can provide an adequate basis for our reflection on the church in Christ and Christ in the church. Edward Kilmartin saw this with great clarity in his liturgical theology.[17] My reasoning goes thus: If we as Christians are convinced that the privileged revelation of God is through the cross of Christ—or through the paschal mystery— then God is revealed to us as trinitarian, in the outpouring of the Spirit through this paradoxical event. Since the liturgy is *of* God and not merely *about* God, as Kavanagh insists (correctly), then only a trinitarian theology of the liturgy will do.

I would like to draw four conclusions from this consideration before going on to analyze the practical questions of the reservation of the consecrated elements and the posture of the assembly. First, the central prayer of the Mass—the anaphora or eucharistic prayer—contains elements indicating that Christian liturgy is the work of the triune God. Praise and thanks are made to the Father as source of all. What is done in the liturgy is done *in and with Christ* as the revelation of the Father *(anamnesis).* And finally nothing is done without invoking the enlivening power of the Spirit *(epiclesis).*[18] This

John F. Baldovin, SJ

last element is, of course, a great recovery of the liturgical movement, not merely because the early anaphoras contained an *epiclesis* (that would be mere archeology) but because we need to acknowledge the grace or gift element of all liturgical prayer and action: We do nothing on our own, as if lifting ourselves by our own spiritual bootstraps, but only in the power of the Spirit.

Second, the element of memorial or *anamnesis* needs to be clarified. Lathrop's theory of juxtaposition is most helpful here. The liturgy is not about the repetition of a past event. It is about the new offer of grace made when the old (the historical event of the paschal mystery) is encountered by our current situation. This is why Robert Taft can claim that liturgy celebrates a living person as the end or goal of history.[19] Using colloquial language we could say Christ is "the Living End." I refer to the work of René Girard who sees Christ as the end of the human project of envy and violence (mimetic desire) by Christ's own free self-sacrifice. Thus the paradox or irony involved in Christian theological language about the "unbloody sacrifice" of the eucharist, which is really a kind of anti-sacrifice.[20]

So the encounter with Christ in worship is pre-eminently personal, and is an encounter with Christ here and now. It is in the Spirit that the church is made to cooperate with Christ, such that the point of the exercise is our identification with Christ. Thus, Saint Augustine makes those familiar remarks about the identification of the members of the assembly with the mystery they see on the holy table.[21] This is not an easy identification or a matter for self-satisfied congratulation, but rather the engagement in a process of self-giving that allows God to be active and powerful in the world. Hence the challenge or prophetic aspect of liturgy, an aspect that always contains an ethical imperative: "You are in Christ and Christ is in you. Now, act like it." To put it another way, a false approach to the presence of Christ in the church and the church's worship would be to make the identification with Christ and not to realize the demand that such an identification makes on us.

Third, the celebration of the liturgy as paschal mystery requires us to affirm a certain centrality or core to liturgical celebration. But the liturgy does not consist merely in such core concerns.[22] There are three perspectives that are necessary when attempting to understand liturgy: core, code and culture. By *core* I mean the essential elements that underlie a specific liturgical act—for example, the meal with prayer for the eucharist, or the bath with instruction for baptism. Most scholars of liturgy postulate such a core, often called essential elements.[23] So far, so good; but these elements never exist outside of a context that is constituted by *code* and *culture,* as I will explain.

The problem is analogous to the question in theology of nature and grace. Theologians who argue for a world of grace (Karl Rahner) realize that there is no such thing as nature in its pure form, that is, without the grace of creation and redemption.[24] So pure "nature" does not exist. However, given the existence of sin and evil, it must be postulated. Similarly, a pure core of Christian liturgy does not exist. If it did, then every celebration of the eucharist would need to be an exact replica of the Last Supper, which has never been the case. Yet, it seems to me that we are compelled to look for some bottom line that must always be present: Without this, or lacking that, there can be no eucharist, or baptism, or whatever the sacrament.

By *code* I mean the specific form that a particular tradition has employed to express the *core.* Thus *code* would include the nature and genius of each particular rite—Roman, Byzantine, Presbyterian, Coptic and so on. Above all, it would be expressed in the liturgical calendar with all of its considerable variations.

By *culture* I mean those aspects of local variation that are peculiar to particular situations that affect both the unfolding of various rituals and the meaning that the rituals have for this group of people. In other words, the same Roman funeral rite will look and mean something very different in a culture where the spirits of the dead are very active than in a secularized society where the dead are little more than corpses.

My point here is that all three elements — core, code and culture — need to be considered carefully when attempting to understand liturgy. At the same time, it is necessary to recognize that the core concerns of liturgy form the foundation that makes a liturgy Christian. (In my opinion, the core concern of the theology of the paschal mystery is sufficient to make a liturgy Christian. Clearly this is a rather minimalist understanding of the essential or core requirements of liturgy. It does not answer questions concerning what constitutes a particular code, and others may well want to put more substance into what I am calling the core than I am willing to do.)

Fourth, our analysis of the paschal mystery through the lens of juxtaposition yields the conclusion that while there are several legitimate approaches to God, and therefore to worship — for example, the priestly and the prophetic, law and love, transcendence and immanence — none of them can do without the corrective of the other. The God who is utterly intimate while transcendent is also utterly transcendent even in intimate nearness. To make this plain, liturgies that exhibit a strong sense of transcendence need to be corrected by a deep sense of the immanence of God and liturgies that strongly celebrate immanence need to be corrected by a similarly profound sense of the transcendence of God. There is a tension or dialectic that is inherent to authentic Christian worship, and our constant task is to strike a balance between valid approaches.

Test Case: Placement of the Tabernacle

Every year when I teach a basic introductory course on Christian liturgy, I try to show my students that the conclusions they reach with regard to practical questions — like the posture of the assembly during the eucharistic prayer or the frequency of eucharistic celebration — should be founded on a theology of liturgy rather than on personal predilections. Every year I encounter the same struggle for consistency when principles need to be applied. Naturally the issue of the placement of the tabernacle is one of the more consternating questions.

First, let me outline a few facts. The "traditional" Roman Catholic practice of placing the tabernacle on an eastward-facing altar in the main body of the church (an altar at which the priest faces in the same direction as the people during prayer) is a relatively late development. It was established only during the fifteenth and sixteenth centuries.[25] (I should add that this does not disqualify the development. It merely demonstrates that it has not been a practice from time immemorial, or one that is essential to the Catholic faith.) Moreover, it is often claimed that the suggestion of reserving the blessed sacrament in an auxiliary chapel of a church was an innovation of the 1978 document of the U.S. Bishops' Committee on the Liturgy, *Environment and Art in Catholic Worship*.[26] This is simply not true. Although the *Constitution on the Sacred Liturgy* says nothing specific with regard to the placement of the tabernacle, subsequent documents from the Holy See make it clear that the preference is always to have the blessed sacrament reserved in a separate chapel suited to the faithful's private adoration and prayer.[27] This is a preference and not a law, and therefore open to interpretation. All the same, the official Roman documents argue for a distinct chapel of reservation in order to foster private adoration of the blessed sacrament (in itself a commendable Catholic practice) and to facilitate the communion of the sick, which is the primary rationale for reservation.

So, there are the facts. But the placement of the tabernacle for reservation is a hotly contested issue that goes well beyond the facts. I suspect that opinions on the matter divide along the distinctions with which we began: priestly, church of law and transcendence on one side; prophetic, church of love and immanence on the other. I have been attempting to take a middle path between these extremes via a theology of the paschal mystery. But it is obvious that one cannot take a middle position on a practical issue such as the placement of the tabernacle. Either it is placed in the main body of a church or it is not. Can the question be resolved based upon the theology we have reviewed?

Let me begin by admitting that there was great comfort for many in having the tabernacle located on the main altar of the church. It represented assurance of the enduring presence of Christ in the blessed sacrament according to authentic Catholic belief. "God is here for you," it said. Now, since our theology of the paschal mystery suggests that to treat the presence of God in liturgy so simply is probably a mistake—for our understanding of God must hold the tension of absence and presence—it would be better for the tabernacle to be situated in a place where it did not draw away the focus of our Sunday worship. Moreover, it is important today to appreciate the manifold presence of Christ in the eucharist, that is, in the elements, the minister, the assembly and the proclamation of the

Word.[28] Clearly affirming Christ's presence within the eucharistic action as well as in the consecrated elements suggests a more elusive presence. It can also help to provide the balance we have been seeking between the transcendence and immanence of God. On this basis I would have to argue, all things being equal, in favor of the placement of the tabernacle in an auxiliary chapel, albeit one that genuinely invites adoration of the reserved sacrament.

I am certainly aware that some might take my argument in a different direction and claim that since the focus of the Sunday eucharist has been placed on the God who is immanent, a reminder of the transcendent God, represented by a central tabernacle, would be a better solution to our question about placement. I would still argue that transcendence can be experienced within the celebration of the eucharist and in encouraging prayer before the sacrament reserved in a distinct chapel.

Conclusion

I began this essay by arguing that only attentiveness to our talk about God and to our experience of God can serve as an adequate basis for our appreciation of the Church and its worship in Christ. I proceeded to outline a theology of the paschal mystery based upon a trinitarian reading of the theology of the cross and to draw some implications for the complex nature of Christian liturgy. I then applied the foregoing to a practical issue facing Catholic worship.

I am not so foolish as to think that my argument will convince all readers. It is predicated upon a theology that is difficult to accept, not so much for its complexity as for its stark implications. To be frank, my suspicion is that neither of the extremes I have noted will be satisfied, but that a middle path through the distinctions we have plotted will be the path of the future of the church in Christ and Christ in the church.

1. Unfortunately I am unable to find the precise citation. Barth's comment was made with reference to Otto Dibelius, *Das Jahrhundert der Kirche*, 1927.

2. For example, Alexander Schmemann, *Introduction to Liturgical Theology* (Crestwood, NY: St. Vladimir's Seminary Press), 1966; Aidan Kavanagh, *On Liturgical Theology* (New York: Pueblo Publishing Co.), 1984; David Fagerberg, *What is Liturgical Theology?* (Collegeville, MN: The Liturgical Press, 1992); Robert Taft, *The Liturgy of the Hours in East and West,* 2nd ed. (Collegeville, MN: The Liturgical Press, 1993), 331–65. On the question of eucharist and ecclesiology, see Paul McPartlan, *Sacrament of Salvation: An Introduction to Eucharistic Ecclesiology* (Edinburgh: T&T Clark, 1995); *The Eucharist Makes the Church: Henri de Lubac and John Zizioulas in Dialogue* (Edinburgh: T&T Clark, 1993).

3. Avery Dulles, "How Catholic is the CTSA?" *Commonweal* (March 27, 1998): 13–4. The same issue contains responses from Mary Ann Donovan and Peter Steinfels. Subsequent issues (April 24, May 8, May 22) contain a vigorous correspondence with regard to the debate. A much more serene, but no less trenchant, reflection on the liturgy by Dulles can be found in his "The Ways We Worship," *First Things* 81 (1998): 28–34.

4. M. Francis Mannion, "Agendas for Liturgical Reform," *America* (November 30, 1996): 9–16.

5. Peter Fink, "Liturgy and Spirituality: A Timely Intersection," in Eleanor Bernstein, ed., *Liturgy and Spirituality in Context* (Collegeville, MN: The Liturgical Press, 1990), 47–61.

6. Peter Berger, *The Sacred Canopy: Elements of a Sociological Theory of Religion* (New York: Doubleday, 1967).

7. See Robert Hovda, "Where Have You Been? Peace Liturgies are the Only Kind We Have," in J. Baldovin, ed., *The Amen Corner* (Collegeville, MN: The Liturgical Press, 1994), 170–6.

8. Bruce Bawer, *Stealing Jesus: How Fundamentalism Betrays Christianity* (New York: Crown Publishers, 1997).

9. I am not even attempting to broaden the question to inter-religious dialogue and understandings of God. Suffice it to say ultimately the encounter of religions will also have a significant impact upon our understanding of God.

10. Bernhard Lang, *Sacred Games: A History of Christian Worship* (New Haven: Yale University Press, 1997).

11. Lang, 419.

12. On this subject, see Patrick Malloy, "The Re-Emergence of Popular Religion among Non-Hispanic American Catholics," *Worship* 72 (1998): 2–25.

13. Though one has to qualify considerably with the notion of prophetic, since prophetic religion can easily fit both transcendence and immanence.

John F. Baldovin, sj

14. Aidan Kavanagh, *On Liturgical Theology* (New York: Pueblo Publishing Co., 1984).

15. The same point is made in a different way by David Power, *Unsearchable Riches: The Symbolic Nature of Liturgy* (New York: Pueblo Publishing Co., 1984), 70–2.

16. On the relational nature of God as Trinity, see Catherine LaCugna, *God for Us: The Trinity and Christian Life* (San Francisco: HarperSanFrancisco, 1991).

17. Edward Kilmartin, *Christian Liturgy: Vol. I Theology* (Kansas City: Sheed and Ward, 1988), 100–11; see also a much more poetic expression of the same trinitarian vision of the liturgy in Jean Corbon, *The Wellspring of Worship* (New York: Paulist Press, 1988).

18. See the ecumenical convergence statement, "Eucharist" #3 – 18, in *Baptism, Eucharist and Ministry,* Faith and Order Paper 111 (Geneva: World Council of Churches, 1982).

19. Taft, 344–45.

20. René Girard, *Violence and the Sacred* (Baltimore: Johns Hopkins University Press, 1977); *Things Hidden Since the Foundation of the World* (Stanford: Stanford University Press, 1987); see also L. M. Chauvet, *Symbol and Sacrament: A Sacramental Re-Reading of the Christian Life* (Collegeville, MN: The Liturgical Press, 1995), 492–537. Lathrop introduces a similar approach to sacrifice by calling it the "wrong word." I prefer the terms "irony" and "paradox."

21. Augustine, *Sermon 272*, in D. J. Sheerin, ed., *Eucharist* (Message of the Fathers of the Church) (Wilmington, DE: Michael Glazier, 1986), 94–6.

22. This is where I would have some criticism of Lathrop's approach in *Holy Things,* which treats very well of core concerns but fails to recognize that these are not adequate for a critique of Christian worship.

23. This is what I take the *Constitution on the Sacred Liturgy* (#21) to mean by immutable elements.

24. See Karl Rahner, *Foundations of Christian Faith* (New York: Seabury Press, 1978), 126–33.

25. See Nathan Mitchell, *Cult and Controversy* (New York: Pueblo Publishing Co., 1982), 168.

26. U.S. Bishops' Committee on the Liturgy, *Environment and Art in Catholic Worship,* #78.

27. See *General Instruction of the Roman Missal #276,* in International Commission on English in the Liturgy, *Documents on the Liturgy 1963–1979* [=DOL] (Collegeville, MN: The Liturgical Press, 1982), #1666. See also DOL #1281–1284, 2201–2202; *Ceremonial of Bishops* #49, 71, 914.

28. See Kilmartin, 303–51, for the complex development of this notion.

Michael J. Begolly

Anointed with the Spirit on the Way to the Table: Celebrating Confirmation prior to First Eucharist — A Case Study

In 1991, the Diocese of Greensburg, Pennsylvania, announced a change in policy for the age of celebration of confirmation, and published a set of guidelines for the sacrament of confirmation. In restoring the original sequence of the sacraments of initiation, the diocese affirmed that all three sacraments are part of the one process of Christian initiation, which begins in baptism, is sealed in confirmation and culminates in eucharist. This threefold celebration marks the beginning of a journey of faith and a process of lifelong faith formation.[1]

How We Arrived at This Point

In 1989, a task force was established to study the diocesan policy of confirming eighth-grade students, with the hope of recommending consistent guidelines to be followed throughout the diocese. The work of the task force led instead to a new diocesan policy for celebrating the sacrament of confirmation at the age of discretion, prior to and in conjunction with the celebration of first eucharist. There were several important factors that led the task force to make this recommendation:

Insights from the RCIA

A study of the theology and practice of the Rite of Christian Initiation of Adults (RCIA) helped to bring about a renewed understanding of confirmation as a sacrament of initiation. The RCIA clearly defines the time for confirming unbaptized adults and children of catechetical age. It notes that they are to be confirmed immediately after the celebration of baptism and then led to the table of the eucharist. In a similar way, those who are received into full communion with the church are to be confirmed immediately after they make their profession of faith. With this as the norm, it seemed to follow that those who are baptized in infancy should be confirmed prior to their first celebration of eucharist.

Inconsistent Practice and Theology

It became evident that the diocesan practice of confirming students in the eighth grade was not consistent with the insights gleaned from studying the RCIA. It was confusing to some that the church requires adults and children of catechetical age who are entering the church to celebrate confirmation as a sacrament of initiation, while those who were baptized as infants celebrate confirmation as a sacrament of maturity. As a sacrament of initiation, confirmation leads to eucharist. As a sacrament of maturity, confirmation is linked to a theology of witness and service that flows from the eucharist. This inconsistency seemed to suggest the need for a new policy.

Concerns with Religious Formation

There was an attitude among many that confirmation was a kind of "graduation" from any process of ongoing formation or education in the faith. The attitude seemed to be that once a person was confirmed, the process was complete. This led to a dramatic drop in attendance at programs of religious instruction after the celebration of confirmation. This also led some to view preparation for the sacrament of confirmation as a *de facto* youth ministry program. This, in turn, led to a very anemic view of youth ministry.

There was also a perception that the celebration of the sacrament of confirmation required greater knowledge and maturity than the celebration of the eucharist. Seeing confirmation as a sacrament of maturity that marked a passage to adult faith led to the development of academic and service requirements that had to be fulfilled prior to the reception of the sacrament. But if the eucharist is at the center of our faith, it seemed inconsistent to require more preparation and more maturity for confirmation than for eucharist. With these factors in mind, the task force recommended that a new policy be established that presented confirmation as an integral part of the initiation process that concludes baptism and leads to eucharist.

Guidelines for the Celebration of the Sacrament of Confirmation

New diocesan guidelines for confirmation were issued in 1991. These guidelines affirmed that baptism, confirmation and eucharist form a threefold process of initiation into Christ's life and the church community formed by Christ. Each of these sacraments relates to the others in drawing out the meaning and purpose for a person's life of faith. No one sacrament is an isolated action, independent of the other movements of one's Christian initiation. Each contributes uniquely to that initiation and reaffirms its mystery and life. Christian initiation is an integrated process, welcoming the individual into the life of grace and the church community formed by that life. The sacraments of initiation are best understood in this context of total immersion into Christ's paschal mystery through the church.

The new guidelines set the basis for the catechesis, understanding and celebration of the sacrament of confirmation in the diocese. Although they presume and must be seen within a total vision and program of religious formation in a parish, they do not present a full philosophy or theology of faith development, but focus on a particular aspect of this issue. Furthermore, these guidelines set foundations and directions for the sacrament of confirmation but do not intend to address every possible specific situation or question arising from a particular parish's circumstances. As situations warrant, pastoral judgements and decisions that arise are to be made by the legitimate local pastoral authorities.

Michael J. Begolly

The Twelve Guidelines

1. For those persons baptized in infancy, the sacrament of confirmation will ordinarily be received at about the age of discretion (seven years old).

2. Catechesis for confirmation should emphasize the theology of Christian initiation, which links the celebration of baptism, confirmation and eucharist into one continual process, into a lifelong journey of conversion in faith.

3. The primary focus in preparing children for the sacraments of initiation should be spiritual formation. A mature understanding of the sacraments of initiation is not possible or expected at this early age. Such a developed grasp of these sacraments should follow their reception, as the child gains the capacity for such knowledge.

4. Three elements are required in the preparation of children for confirmation:

    a. a parents' program aimed at helping them to understand the meaning of this sacrament as part of Christian initiation and offering them support and resources for communicating this meaning to their children;

    b. a substantial program of spiritual formation for the confirmation candidates that is suited to their level of maturity; and

    c. a scheduled rehearsal for candidates and sponsors to coordinate the ritual actions involved in the celebration of the sacrament.

5. Since Christian initiation presumes a church community as both a context and object of initiation, the sacraments of confirmation and first eucharist are preferably prepared for and celebrated with members of a candidate's parish.

6. First penance, confirmation and first eucharist will be celebrated within a relatively short time-frame. First penance is to precede first eucharist. A parish is strongly encouraged to celebrate this

sacrament during the Advent season that precedes the celebration of first eucharist. Confirmation will precede first eucharist according to a schedule suitable to both the diocesan and local parish calendars.[2]

7. A primary emphasis must be placed on the parents' commitment to the religious formation and education of their children. A religious education program should supplement this involvement and provide resources and support for parental efforts at faith formation. When parents are unable or unwilling to take responsibility for their child's religious development, the local parish faith community should make every effort possible to provide an environment and opportunities for growth in faith.

8. The entire parish community is an agent of Christian initiation. Consistent efforts must be undertaken to renew the communal journey of faith through prayer and worship, total education and spiritual formation, social and charitable programs, and evangelization efforts to reach out to those who less regularly participate in church activities.

9. Parishes should address the needs of adolescent members through a total youth ministry program that incorporates some ritual moments for young persons to celebrate their continuing growth in faith.

10. Persons with developmental disabilities have a right to the fullest appropriate preparation for the sacrament of confirmation. They are to be included in the regular parish program of preparation to the extent possible. In celebrating the sacrament, sensitivity to the person's mental, emotional and physical capacities should be shown in the response of the local church community.

11. As the situations arise, baptized children beyond the age of discretion who have not been confirmed should be integrated into the parish preparation and celebration of confirmation in a way that respects their varying ages and levels of development.

Appropriate pastoral judgments should be exercised in these cases according to the particular situations of a parish.

12. Baptized Catholic adults who have not been confirmed should celebrate the sacrament in their local parish on an occasion deemed appropriate by the pastor. In these particular cases, the pastor can obtain delegation by the bishop to confer the sacrament.

Time of Transition

The restoration of the original sequence of the sacraments of initiation was fully implemented throughout the diocese during the Easter season of 1995. The years between 1991 and 1995 were a time of transition; each year the age for confirmation was lowered. This was accompanied by instruction and education programs throughout the diocese to help clergy and laity understand the nature of the sacraments of initiation and the reasons for this change. This process returned confirmation to its traditional place within the sequence of the sacraments of initiation and set the framework for a renewed understanding that a life of faith in the church is a lifelong process of formation through worship, study and daily living according to gospel values.

The process of preparing children for confirmation and eucharist involves an integrated approach to faith formation for the children and their families. The children are led to an understanding of confirmation compatible with their age, as is the case with eucharist. Parents have the opportunity to learn more about their faith from an adult perspective. Intergenerational workshops involve children, parents and other family members in discovering that all are initiated into a belief, an attitude, a perspective, a way of seeing reality through the paschal mystery. All are called to constant conversion and are sustained by the eucharist on the journey of a lifetime that begins at baptism.

Timeline of the Process of Restoration

The following log reflects the time given to the development of the diocesan plan that restored the original sequence of the sacraments of initiation in the diocese.

November 1989: Task Force began study of eighth-grade confirmation toward recommendation of consistent guidelines.

September 1990: RCIA Committee raised question of inconsistent practice regarding initiation of children of catechetical age.

December 1990: Diocesan bishop consulted with clergy on issue of confirmation at age of discretion.

February 1991: Bishop announced that the sacrament of confirmation would be conferred prior to first eucharist.

April 1991: Restoration to Renewal: a day-long workshop that explained new policy to clergy, parish DREs, CREs and Catholic school principals.

July 1991: New policy presented across diocese for professional and general audiences.

October 1991: General guidelines for confirmation issued by bishop.

July 1992: New Department of Education and Spiritual Formation formed.

January 1993: Bishop accepts proposal that confirmation be celebrated at the same liturgy as first eucharist during the Easter season.

May 1993: Confirmation/first eucharist pilot project involving 35 parishes began.

June 1993 – June 1994:   Clergy and staff from pilot parishes met on six occasions for training and evaluation.

September 1994:   Handbook presented to all parishes.

October 1994 – June 1995:   Parish clergy and staff met for training and evaluation.

Easter Season 1995:   All parishes celebrated confirmation and first eucharist at a Sunday liturgy. Parish priests were given delegation to confirm. Bishop confirms and presides at first eucharist in parishes on a rotating basis.

June 1995:   Evaluation and ongoing assistance to parishes.

Confirmation / First Eucharist Pilot Project

The pilot project was intended to provide catechetical materials, liturgical training and models for the celebration of confirmation at the same liturgy as first eucharist. Parishes that participated in the pilot project celebrated confirmation and first eucharist at the same liturgy during the 1994 Easter season. Participants later evaluated their catechetical and liturgical experiences. Necessary modifications were made and the results were printed in a handbook that was distributed to all parishes in September 1994. The timeline for the pilot project follows.

May 1993:   Initial orientation/information meeting. Agenda included:

- overview of pilot process
- consultation on proposed meeting dates and sites
- role of bishop/delegation/ecclesiology issues

August 1993:   Preparation process for first penance. Agenda included:

- liturgical issues

- catechetical models for children, families, parents, parish

November 1993:   Confirmation and first eucharist preparation processes. Agenda included:

- catechetical models for children, families, parents, parish

- liturgical issues

January 1994:   Preparation for Lent/Easter. Agenda included:

- Lent as a means of focusing parish on initiation

February 1994:   Liturgical issues. Agenda included:

- combined ceremony for confirmation/first eucharist

- use of symbols, nature/attention span of young children

- suggestions for music, readings

June 1994:   Evaluation of pilot project. Agenda included:

- effectiveness of catechetical processes

- evaluation of liturgical experiences

- effect of pilot experience on the parish

September 1994:   Handbook distributed to all parishes

Timeline for Year of Immediate Preparation

The decision to celebrate confirmation prior to first eucharist and the experience of those in the pilot project led to the development of the following timeline for the year immediately preceding the celebration of the sacraments.

September–October: Parent meeting on sacrament of penance

October – November: Family/intergenerational workshop on sacrament of penance

Advent: First celebration of sacrament of penance

January – February: Parent meeting on sacraments of initiation and need for ongoing catechesis

February – March: Family / intergenerational workshop on confirmation

March – April: Family/intergenerational workshop on eucharist

Lent: Parish journey toward Easter

Easter Season: Celebration of confirmation and first eucharist

April – May: Family/intergenerational gathering for reflection on the experience of the celebration of confirmation and first eucharist

Catechesis for Confirmation

One of the immediate challenges in implementing this policy was the issue of preparing the children for the celebration of confirmation. In the past, preparing children for the sacraments was a primary focus of the parish religious education program. This program often focused on transmitting information about the sacraments, rather than on formation in the sacramental life of the church. The primary educators of children in their faith became religion teachers in a classroom setting, rather than parents in the context of the domestic church. The shift in the age of confirmation provided an opportunity to develop a new model for sacramental preparation. This model is based on several general principles articulated by the diocese for the sacramental preparation of children of catechetical age:

1. Parental and family involvement in initiation is crucial;

2. Preparation takes place in the home parish of the family;

3. Preparation takes place outside the religion classroom;

4. The sources for catechesis are the rites and symbols; and

5. The role of Catholic schools and parish religious education programs is to support candidates and families through prayer and encouragement, to provide children with ongoing systematic instruction, and to integrate sacramental preparation through an ongoing process of formation.

In addition, this model was developed to assist both parents and children in the ongoing process of conversion. It provides parents with the opportunity to learn more about their faith. In turn, parents are better equipped to assume a greater share of the faith formation of their children.

For too long we had strayed from the biblical model of catechesis in which Jesus taught adults and blessed children. With so much of the church's attention devoted to the teaching of children, many adults never had the opportunity to grow in their knowledge of the faith. However, formation and transformation in faith is a lifelong process, and greater energy and more resources need to be focused on adult catechesis and intergenerational workshops that help children and adults learn together.

Liturgy and Catechesis

In addition to developing new models of formation for children and the use of adult-oriented models of learning for parents, it was hoped that this shift would help to recover the relationship between liturgy and the formation process. *Sharing the Light of Faith: The National Catechetical Directory* suggests a close relationship between liturgy and catechesis.[3] Gil Ostdiek notes this interrelationship by stating that "catechesis first prepares people for full, conscious, and active participation in the liturgy and helps them reflect back on the worship experience to relate it to daily life, so that catechesis and liturgy are caught up in a recurring cycle in which each reinforces the other."[4] Based on the norm of the RCIA that calls for catechesis both before and after the celebration of initiation, the norm for the celebration of every sacrament is pre- and post-celebration catechesis. Pre-celebration catechesis prepares candidates for a sacramental rite, takes place within a specific period of time and is of a more general, elementary kind. Post-celebration catechesis is lifelong and leads people to reflect on their experiences of the sacraments and their meaning for their lives.[5] At present, the Office of Worship and the Office of Initiation and Spiritual Formation are in the process of developing a plan for liturgical catechesis that will further enhance the ongoing formation and transformation of both adults and children throughout the diocese.

Sunday Eucharist as the Heart of Parish Life

A necessary prelude to rediscovering the link between liturgy and catechesis is a renewed emphasis on the priority of liturgy in the life of the community. However, it was apparent that in many places in the diocese, liturgies were poorly prepared and celebrated. There was a sense of minimalism in the celebration of the sacraments and an overemphasis on the verbal aspects of liturgy. John Leonard notes that "liturgies are frequently wall-to-wall explanations, exhortations, commentaries, words; silence is abhorred, fragrance is forgotten, real bread is rarely broken, gestures are half-hearted, movements are unrehearsed, everything is hurried."[6] Parish leaders must invest in quality celebrations so that all who gather to worship are given the opportunity to experience the transformative power of the eucharist.

In 1995, the diocese published a document entitled *Sunday Eucharist: The Source and Summit of Parish Life—Guidelines for Evaluating the Quality and Number of Sunday Masses*. This document outlines the theology of Sunday eucharist and provides the following eight points for use when evaluating the quality of Sunday worship.

1. Planning and Preparation of the Liturgy

Good liturgical celebration does not just happen. It demands both planning and preparation by those involved in the celebration of the liturgy. Presiders, parish directors of liturgy and musicians should meet regularly to plan the Sunday celebrations. Long-range planning should focus on the upcoming liturgical seasons. Short-term preparation should coordinate the diverse elements (for example, ministries, music, environment) for a particular Sunday.

2. Participation of the Members of the Assembly

The liturgy is the prayer of the people who assemble for worship. All in the assembly have a right and duty to take an active part in the celebration. There should be no spectators at liturgy, only participants. All in the assembly are invited to participate in the fourfold movement of the liturgy: gathering, listening to the Word, sharing the meal and going forth on mission. Members of the assembly take an active part in the liturgy by their presence, by taking part in the prayers and song, and by sharing in the eucharist.

3. Liturgical Ministers

At each celebration of the eucharist, liturgical ministers should exercise their rightful place in leading the community in prayer: The presider should lead the assembly in worship; servers should assist the presider; ministers of hospitality (ushers and greeters) should welcome members of the assembly and take up the collection; musicians should lead the community in song; lectors should proclaim the Word of God; special ministers of the eucharist should assist in the distribution of communion. All who serve in the liturgical ministries should receive proper formation in the theology and celebration of Sunday eucharist, and in the procedures for exercising a particular ministry within the Sunday celebration.

4. Music for the Celebration

Music is integral to the celebration of every liturgy. One of the primary ways to involve the assembly in the celebration is through the use of song. A high priority should be placed on acclamations that can be readily sung by the assembly: responsorial psalm; Alleluia; Holy, Holy, Holy; memorial acclamation; Great Amen. Hymns should be appropriate to the season and to their place within the liturgy. When there are many visitors or when large crowds are present (for example, at Christmas and Easter), the acclamations should be very familiar and capable of being sung by the entire congregation.

5. The Primary Symbols of the Liturgy

Of all the symbols in the liturgy, the assembly transformed into the Body of Christ is primary. For this reason the assembly needs to be greeted with hospitality and treated with respect throughout the celebration. Words and gestures should be gracious and unhurried. Times for silence should also be observed. Since Christ is present in both the Word and in the eucharistic elements, there should be a sense of reverence for the lectionary and the ambo, as well as for the altar, the bread and wine, and the liturgical vessels.

6. Simplicity

The liturgy is the ritual prayer of the church, and ritual, by its very nature, is repetitive. For this reason, the liturgy should be as simple and unencumbered as possible. Those responsible for planning the liturgy should avoid the temptation to add all kinds of "extras" to the celebration. Those who prepare the parish's liturgy should focus on the presence of Christ in the assembly, in the Word and in the eucharist.

7. Worship Space

The space used for worship should reflect a sense of the holy. Gathering spaces should be accessible, uncluttered and hospitable. Aisles and pathways should be clear to facilitate the movements of the ministers and of the members of the assembly. The seating arrangements within the worship space should provide everyone with a clear line of sight to the principal focal points of the liturgy: the ambo, the altar, the presidential chair. The acoustics of the space need attention so that both spoken and sung words are audible. When decorations are used, they should enhance the dignity and beauty of the worship space.

8. The Homily

The preacher's job is to help the community that has assembled to understand the good news of God's Word as proclaimed in the liturgy. The homily should reflect the preacher's pastoral concern for the local community that has assembled. The homily should lead the assembly to voice its praise in the liturgy of the eucharist that follows.

Liturgy in the Domestic Church

Sunday liturgy — no matter how well prepared and celebrated — cannot be one's only experience of prayer. Regular family prayer has to play an important role in faith formation. Balthasar Fischer notes that "the most important characteristic of common prayer in the ancient Christian family seems to me to lie in the extension, into the home, of public worship."[7] Louis Weil suggests that "the great texts of the liturgical tradition should appropriately flow over into the family and private devotions of Christians as they live their daily lives during the week, and thus form a bridge leading back to the common assembly the next Sunday."[8] In other words, in order for the liturgical prayer of the assembly to make sense, it has to be rooted in the lived experience of the community.

In the process of preparing their children for the celebration of the sacraments, parents are encouraged to help children explore the meaning of the liturgy's prayers and gestures by using some of them in the home: Family members may bless one another with holy water, pray over one another when they are sick, and create table fellowship around their family meals. Similarly, children and parents are invited to discover how water is a symbol of life and cleansing; how daily meals mirror the eucharist; and how words of sorrow and hugs of reassurance set the stage for the sacrament of penance. Parents are challenged to help prepare their children to hear and understand the Sunday readings by telling the stories of the scriptures during the week. Rituals, prayer and reflection on the scriptures in the home can help to prepare for a more effective celebration of the liturgy.

Michael J. Begolly

The Celebration of Confirmation

At the conclusion of a year of preparation, children celebrate confirmation and first eucharist according to the following norms:

1. The celebration takes place at a Sunday Mass during the Easter season. It is recommended that this Mass be one of the regularly scheduled Sunday Masses. In this way, members of the parish are able to witness and celebrate this aspect of Christian initiation.

2. Children are seated in the assembly with their families.

3. The Mass of the day (one of the Sundays of the Easter season) is celebrated.

4. The readings of the day are used. It is recommended that only two readings be chosen and that they be proclaimed from the *Lectionary for Masses with Children.*

5. The homily should be based on the readings and make a connection with the celebration of the sacraments of initiation.

6. The rite of confirmation follows the homily and consists of the renewal of baptismal promises, an invitation to prayer, the laying on of hands, and the anointing with chrism.

7. The children are to come forward with their sponsors and families for the celebration of confirmation and the reception of eucharist.

8. The primary role of the children is to participate as members of the assembly and to celebrate the sacraments. They should not assume other liturgical roles in this liturgy that would distract from their primary role.

9. Nothing is to be added to the celebration of the liturgy that would unduly lengthen it. Pastors and liturgy planners must keep in mind the age and attention span of the children.

Implications of the Restored Order

After several years of celebrating confirmation with children prior to and in conjunction with the celebration of first eucharist, there are several implications for the ongoing work of the diocese that have become increasingly clear.

1. Celebrating confirmation before eucharist has helped to recover the central role of the eucharist on the journey of a lifetime. Ongoing efforts are needed, however, to help people fully understand the nature of confirmation as a sacrament of initiation, rather than a sacrament of maturity.

2. Existing models of faith formation need to be adapted and new models need to be developed. Parishes and families need to evaluate what works and to adapt models of catechesis to meet the needs of different people. Classroom instruction, home-based study and the Catechesis of the Good Shepherd all have a place in the formation of children. Good models of catechesis suitable for adults need to be developed to assist parents grow in the their faith. Parents need assistance in learning how to share their faith with children.

3. Parishes need to renew their focus on total youth ministry. As children mature into adolescence, parishes need to implement an integrated formation plan for youth that includes the following components: word, worship, community, service, evangelization, pastoral care, advocacy and enablement.

4. The relationship between liturgy and life must be authentic and unambiguous. Quality celebrations of Sunday eucharist are needed to nourish and enhance the life of faith. From the Sunday assembly, the community needs to reach out to meet the needs of the community and work to promote justice and gospel values.

5. Parishes must evaluate their priorities. Members of a parish must place a high priority on the celebration of Sunday eucharist and on their faith formation. The parish budget needs to reflect these priorities.

6. The role of the church in the life of the contemporary family needs to be more fully developed.

Some Concerns with the Restored Order

Since the implementation of the restored order of the sacraments of initiation for children of catchechetical age, a number of issues continue to be a source of concern for some parents and clergy:

1. Some parents feel that they are not qualified to teach the Catholic faith to their children. Most of the parents are young adults (20 – 40 years old) and represent the post – Vatican II cohort. Many do not understand their Catholic faith at an adult level.

2. There is a concern among some parents and clergy that children are not learning the *content* of their faith. These parents and clergy would like to see a return to the former CCD model of religious education. In addition, they would like children to experience the celebration of the sacraments as they did when they were young. It seems ironic that many parents who themselves are ignorant of the faith want to enroll their children in the same types of programs that failed them.

3. There is some concern that too much happens in second grade, and too little afterward. For this reason, parish leaders are encouraged to evaluate the total process of religious formation and to develop models of mystagogical catechesis for faith formation at all levels.

4. With the restored order, there seems to be a myth that religious formation programs "lose" children in grades three through six. Initial surveys across the diocese seem to indicate that that there is a negligible attrition rate (no more than before). The issue of children leaving seems to be a problem in less than ten percent of the parishes. Where there is a problem, it seems to be due to the lack of a unified vision among parish staff members, parents and diocesan workers.

5. Some people object to the fact that the bishop delegates local pastors and parochial vicars to confirm. They fear a loss of connection to the diocesan church. This does not really seem to be a problem for the Diocese of Greensburg since the bishop began a four-year cycle of parish visitations at the same time that he began delegating others to confirm.

6. Since people often move across diocesan lines, there is some concern that policies concerning the celebration of the sacraments are not consistent from diocese to diocese. While this may cause some confusion, it is reflective of the fact that life itself can be messy, and that no single plan, program or process can be expected to provide for all contingencies. As a result, programs need to be flexible so that they are able to accommodate people at different ages and at different stages on the journey of a lifetime.

Conclusion

The restoration of the original order of the sacraments of initiation has been an important step in the life of the Diocese of Greensburg. As the diocese continues to move ahead and build on what has been learned, there is a challenge for all. Adults need to set a good example for children by a commitment to and participation in the sacramental life of the church. Parents and children need to seek out and take part in programs that will help to form them in the Catholic faith. Clergy and other ministers need to provide for quality celebrations of the liturgy so that parents and children can experience the transforming power of the sacraments. All need to pray that God's Spirit will guide and bless this journey of a lifetime.

1. This change in policy was situated within the framework of a larger renewal process in the diocese called *Journey of a Lifetime*. This process involved the establishment of a diocesan Department of Education and Spiritual Formation, which includes offices of worship, initiation and spiritual formation, Catholic schools, parish life and ministry, and clergy formation. Bringing these offices together

into one department helped to emphasize the belief that spiritual formation is the work of a lifetime for all (clergy, religious and laity) on our common journey of faith.

2. At the time when these guidelines were written (1991), it was presumed that confirmation would be celebrated in each parish by the bishop before the celebration of first eucharist. In 1993, the proposal was accepted that confirmation be celebrated at the same liturgy as first eucharist, and that the bishop delegate pastors and parochial vicars to confirm.

3. See also the articles on this topic in "Liturgy & Catechesis," *Liturgical Ministry* 7 (Spring, 1998).

4. Gil Ostdiek, "Liturgical Catechesis," in Peter E. Fink, ed., *The New Dictionary of Sacramental Worship* (Collegeville, MN: The Liturgical Press, 1990), 169.

5. Ostdiek also describes four qualities for liturgical catechesis: It should be Christ centered, formative-transformative, communal, and experientially based. The first concern is that people develop both an individual and communal relationship to the risen Christ by an encounter with Christ in Word, sacrament and community. Second, transformation is a journey of faith and conversion that takes a lifetime, and so is needed by disciples of every age according to their level of development. Third, liturgical formation can only take place within the context of a faith community. Finally, liturgical catechesis should be concerned with making people more attentive to their experiences. It is also important that the process of liturgical catechesis be rooted in human experience. Thus, it is important to evoke the meaning beneath the liturgical symbols and gestures, such as bathing with water and anointing with oil. It is also important to examine multivalent images associated with the symbols: for example, water can give life, but it can also destroy. Making this connection with human experience and liturgy will help people to see their faith as an integral part of life, rather than merely one aspect of life.

6. John Brooks-Leonard, "Introduction: Children of the Promise," in Eleanor Bernstein and John Brooks-Leonard, eds., *Children in the Assembly of the Church* (Chicago: Liturgy Training Publications, 1992), 5.

7. Balthasar Fischer, "The Common Prayer of Congregation and Family in the Ancient Church," *Studia Liturgica* 10 (1974): 118.

8. Louis Weil, "Liturgical Prayer," in Peter E. Fink, ed., *The New Dictionary of Sacramental Worship* (Collegeville, MN: The Liturgical Press, 1990), 954.

Michael S. Driscoll

The Many Modes of Christ's Presence in the Revised Sacramentary

Eucharist and real presence—in Roman Catholic circles these terms have traditionally been correlative. Especially in the period from Trent to Vatican II, Roman Catholicism found its identity in the question of the real presence. Treatment of the theology of the real presence occupied a large part of seminary training, and the art and architecture of the church were aimed at reinforcing this central dogma. The bulk of the treatment on the eucharist, however, dealt with doctrinal defenses of correct "matter and form" in the sacrament, the doctrine of transubstantiation, the effects and kinds of communion, the dispositions required in the communicant and the Mass as a sacrifice.[1] Rather than being a celebration of Christ's presence through the liturgical action, the eucharist was an object of theological speculation and something that needed to be defended from theological error. The doctrine of real presence represented for many Catholics one of the central tenets of their faith.

The theme of our conference, "Church and Eucharist: The Many Presences of Christ," challenges us to explore the doctrine of the real presence of Christ in light of the *Constitution on the Sacred Liturgy* (CSL) and our experience of the eucharist. A serious examination of this subject needs to be undertaken in relationship to the revised sacramentary currently being prepared by the various English-speaking episcopal conferences in conjunction with the International Commission for English in the Liturgy (ICEL) to verify how the multiple presences of Christ are lived out concretely and practically in the official liturgy of the church. How does the current project of the revision of the sacramentary give expression to the manifold presences of Christ? The questions that need addressing are as follows: Where do we find the idea of the multiple modes of Christ's presence in the revised sacramentary? How is this concretely expressed in the church's worship life? If the *lex orandi* becomes the *lex credendi,* how has the past thirty years of experience with the reformed liturgy informed our understanding of real presence in the eucharist and the many forms of Christ's presence in the church?

Introduction

The theme of "the many modes of Christ's presence" is first voiced at the beginning of the Second Vatican Council in the *Constitution on the Sacred Liturgy.*

> To accomplish so great a work Christ is always present in his church, especially in liturgical celebrations. He is present in the sacrifice of the Mass both in the person of his minister, "the same now offering through the ministry of priests, who formerly offered himself on the cross," and most of all in the eucharistic species. By his power he is present in the sacraments so that when anybody baptizes it is really Christ himself who baptizes. He is present in his word since it is he himself who speaks when the holy scriptures are read in church. Lastly, he is present when the church prays and sings, for he has promised "where two or three are gathered together in my name there am I in the midst of them." (#7)[2]

This paragraph functioned as a piece of the blueprint to be used for the immediate renovation and renewal of the liturgy as mandated by the council. But it is also part of a trajectory for subsequent thought about the question of real presence. If the church is sent by

Christ to continue the work of salvation, just as Christ was sent by God to do so, it does not follow that the church can accomplish this mission apart from Christ, any more than Christ can be separated from God. This paragraph underscores that the presence of Christ is affected through the action of the liturgy. It reiterates what Saint Augustine had already written about Christ acting through the sacraments, as well as repeating the doctrine of the Council of Trent and the teaching of the encyclicals *Mystici Corporis* and *Mediator Dei* concerning the eucharist.

What seems to be radically new about this formulation is the insistence that Christ works through the actions of the church to make his presence a dynamic event. If real presence is spoken of in terms of the sacrifice of the Mass, it is first spoken of in regards to the person of the minister before it is linked to the sacred species. The encyclical *Mediator Dei* had already modified the doctrine of Trent on this count. Furthermore, if Christ is present in the sacraments through his power (*virtus* in Latin; *dynamis* in Greek), this marks a degree of presence, somewhat less than the eucharist, but which is much more than a virtual presence. By this statement, we can conclude that sacramental presence must be an active, dynamic presence, rather than a static, localized presence. We have no argument with Augustine: The sacraments are the acts of Christ. CSL paragraph seven is a carefully crafted statement, beginning with the assertion that Christ is present through the liturgical action and ending with the logical conclusion that he is present in the assembly, the locus of the liturgical actions. The church at prayer must be regarded as the *sine qua non* of all liturgical actions and a necessary prerequisite of real presence: Christ is present to and for the church.

Where Vatican II moves the discussion beyond *Mediator Dei* (and in a way that corresponded with the biblical renewal of the time) is in the affirmation that Christ is present when the sacred scriptures are read (it is Christ who speaks) and when two or more are gathered in Christ's name (see Matthew 18:20). Rather than speaking about real presence in purely static terms, the Council speaks about it as an action. Pope Paul VI was especially fond of this more dynamic sense of presence, probably because it had long been noted that when "presence" was used as a noun it lent itself to a very static understanding. Many theologians and historians of eucharistic theology had also commented about the difficulties with speaking of the eucharist not as a dynamic action of the church but as an object of speculation and adoration. The problem of the reification of the sacraments, especially the eucharist (with its attendant questions of matter and form), had long been recognized. With the *Constitution on the Sacred Liturgy,* the church sought to recover the more dynamic sense of presence.

Barely had the *Constitution on the Sacred Liturgy* been promulgated when Paul VI authored his encyclical *Mysterium fidei* (1965) delineating further the consequences of this more dynamic understanding of real presence. Since the notion of the real presence of Christ had been extended to include the various modes, how was one to understand that presence in relationship to the eucharist? Paul VI wrote: "This presence is called real presence not to exclude the other kinds as though they were not real, but because it is real *par excellence,* since it is substantial, in the sense that Christ whole and entire, God and man, becomes present." (#39)

Paul VI was clear in upholding traditional Catholic dogma about the real presence but he was anxious to expand upon a rigidly narrow view. The question that remained concerned the term *"par excellence."* This phrase could be misconstrued to mean that Christ was more present in the eucharist in a *quantitative* sense. But what Paul VI was trying to get at is more of a *qualitative* sense: The eucharist is a privileged mode of Christ's presence. In *Mysterium fidei* (#35 – 37), he delineated several kinds of presence that move the discussion beyond that begun by the *Constitution on the Sacred Liturgy.* Paul VI insists on using verbs to describe the presence of Christ in the church. Taking into consideration what had already been defined by the Council, he expands upon the idea of dynamic presence. Christ is present:

> when the church *prays* (and sings);
> when the church *gathers*;
> when the church *performs works of mercy*;
> when the church *journeys* as a pilgrim toward the heavenly
>   kingdom;

when the church *preaches;* and
when the church *celebrates* the sacraments.

We recognize many of the items on this list from the *Constitution on the Sacred Liturgy.* A new point of consideration is introduced when the presence of Christ extends to the church's social action. In addition, the inclusion of the church when she journeys as a pilgrim offers an eschatological perspective. The real presence is never fully exhausted in this life and it groans for fulfillment in the second coming of Christ. This eschatological perspective also has the advantage of overcoming an overly static understanding of presence because it allows for varying degrees of presence.

The question of presence is never black or white, yes or no. It admits to varying degrees. For example, a person may be physically present but mentally absent. Inversely, often a person's presence can be more intensely felt in times of absence, say, for example, through a letter or a telephone call, each of which mediates the person's presence in spite of the absence. Paul VI has difficulty delineating these various modes of presence because there are some forms that are more privileged than others. In speaking of the eucharist, he declares: "In a manner even more sublime, Christ is also present in the church when it offers the sacrifice of the Mass in his name and administers the sacraments." (*Mysterium fidei,* #38) At the same time that he reaffirms traditional Catholic teaching on eucharistic presence, he challenges us to a more dynamic understanding.

Latin and English Versions of the Sacramentary

When reviewing the work of Vatican II it is important to recall the questions surrounding language. Even before the Council began, tensions developed concerning the consideration and use of Latin as the official language of the Roman church.[3] Already in 1959, shortly after John XXIII announced the Council, pre-emptive strikes appeared in the *Osservatore Romano* insisting upon the use of Latin within the general sessions of the council.[4] Many bishops themselves had practical difficulties speaking and reading Latin. To respond to this difficulty during the Council, special assistance had to be furnished.[5] Among the documents prepared and circulated prior to the opening of the Council, documents that were supposed to be drafted in Latin, we find some in vernacular languages. This led to a decision: Latin would be used at the general sessions of the Council, but there would also be a system of simultaneous translation for those bishops whose Latin skills were lacking. The decision to use Latin as the official language for the public sessions and general congregations is significant for several reasons. Those who favored Latin as the official language were concerned about the questions of visible unity of the church and the formulation of doctrinal statements by the Council. But already the question about the use of Latin during the liturgy was looming on the horizon, and would become one of the most controversial topics in the time immediately preceding the Council's opening.

In 1955, the Holy Office had published a decree limiting the exceptions to the general law about the use of Latin in the liturgy.[6] In the same year, the encyclical *Musicae Sacrae* confirmed the principle of Latin as the official language of the liturgy. In spite of these strong statements in favor of Latin, the debate continued for ostensibly pastoral reasons: If the liturgy was to work its saving effect to the fullest degree, it was necessary that people understand and pray in a language that suited them. At the Congress of Liturgical Pastoral[7] held in Assisi in 1956, the two camps prepared to debate the question once again. Cardinal Cicognani, in an attempt to limit the debate, recalled to the participants the encyclical of Pius XII, *Mediator Dei,* which affirmed Latin as the official language both as a sign of unity and a safeguard against the corruption of true doctrine.[8] Nevertheless, in spite of the various interventions from Rome, the problem of language remained.

In April, 1961, the Commission for Oriental Churches approved a text entitled *De usu linguarum vernacularum in liturgiis,* authorizing the vernacular in the liturgy. This decision had special importance for many of the Eastern churches within the United States that had adopted English for use at their liturgies. Prior to Vatican II, the concern was raised that the use of English in some Eastern churches, such as the Melkite, would cause confusion for American Roman

Catholics. Some of the American Catholic bishops petitioned Rome to intervene and stop the practice of using the vernacular in the liturgy. Patriarch Maximos IV succumbed to the request of Rome that went against the time-honored custom whereby the Eastern churches could take into consideration the pastoral care of their faithful and determine for themselves the language of the liturgy.[9] Despite this action, the problem would not go away.

At the time of the Council the question was again raised by the Commission for Missions in the schema *De sacramentis ac de sacra liturgia,* discussed by the Central Commission at the end of March, 1962. The general principle was put forward that every language is suitable for the praise of Christ and that this praise is best realized in the liturgy where intelligibility must be of primary concern. In stating the "law of intelligibility," the commission affirmed the principle of legitimate diversity as a rich and desirable attribute. Some of the Council Fathers reacted immediately, stating that the unity of the church is made manifest especially in the visible uniformity of worship. One of the primary opponents to the use of the vernacular at liturgy was H. Anglés, a zealous defender of Gregorian chant and director of the Pontifical Institute of Sacred Music. In a circular letter[10] he attempted to raise fears in several Roman circles claiming that the Commission for Liturgy was hostile to Latin and was willing to do anything in order to encourage radical innovations concerning the use of the vernacular. In response, A. Bugnini drafted a memorandum denying the accusation, but stating that the Commission had not yet come to a decision.[11] As a consequence of this debate we read in the first draft of the *Constitution on the Sacred Liturgy* that Latin is reserved for use in the liturgies of the Latin West,[12] with limited exceptions the rule. Only G. Montini, the future Paul VI, argued before the Central Commission in favor of the use of ancient languages other than Latin.

The multifaceted debate about Latin is interesting for many reasons. On one level, it illustrates the complex relationships of the different preparatory commissions among themselves and with the Roman Curia. The question about language raised a deeper ecclesiological concern about uniformity being the guarantee of unity for the universal church. On another level, it raised a question about the unchanging aspect of classical latinity and its relationship to a liturgy that is bound by culture.

The final outcome of the debate took an interesting turn. Without going into the details of the discussions in the general sessions of the Council or the work done behind the scenes by the Council Fathers with the various *periti,* one can simply turn to the approved text of the *Constitution on the Sacred Liturgy,* paragraph 36. While approving the principle that Latin is the official language of the liturgy, special cases were foreseen where the vernacular might be used with appropriate approval of ecclesiastical authorities. In the case of use of the vernacular, however, translations would be made from the *editio typica* of the Roman liturgical books and the translations would need approval from the competent territorial authorities, namely the episcopal conferences.[13] Herein lies the current question.

Vatican II's program for liturgical renewal was officially set in motion with the promulgation of the *Constitution on the Sacred Liturgy* on December 4, 1963. With his *motu proprio* of January 25, 1964, *Sacram Liturgiam,* Paul VI established an ad hoc committee known as the Consilium for the Implementation of the Constitution on the Liturgy. Its purpose was to translate the conciliar principles into concrete changes in the church's rites. The work of the Consilium progressed rapidly. Changes in the liturgy, particularly changes affecting the celebration of the Mass, were made as the Council Fathers continued their discussions, enabling them to experience together the implementation of the changes that were a direct result of their deliberations. This experience of the reformed liturgy undoubtedly affected their future discussions and decisions.

In an address to the Consilium on October 13, 1966, Paul VI stated several guidelines relating to the participation of the faithful in the eucharist: The task of the reform "is to make the liturgical rites plain and clear to the majority of the faithful in their intelligibility, in their form of expression, in the way they are carried out."[14] On May 4, 1967, the document *Tres abhinc annos* appeared. It was the second instruction for the implementation of the principles set forth in the *Constitution on the Sacred Liturgy.* The instruction is particularly interesting from two perspectives. According to suggestions set forth in this document, the Roman Canon was to be greatly simplified, while excessive genuflections and multiple signs of the cross were to be eliminated. Provision was also made for the Canon to be recited in the vernacular.[15]

In the years that followed the Council, the postconciliar documents remained faithful to the directives of the Council Fathers regarding the reform of the liturgy. During the same period, the *Ordo Missae* underwent constant revision, progressively giving a more active role to the faithful. In the Apostolic Constitution *Missale Romanum*, Paul VI indicated the major changes in the new Missal. He referred to the General Instruction of the Roman Missal, which provided both regulations and explanations for the various ministers participating in the celebration, including the role of the assembly. In particular, he was especially clear in addressing the new possibilities for the active participation of the faithful in the liturgy of the word.[16] However, the new order of Mass was greeted in certain circles[17] with some rather severe criticism. As a result of protracted discussion, both the General Instruction and the Order of Mass underwent revision. The final redaction was promulgated in the 1970 *Missale Romanum.*

As a result of negative criticisms of the 1969 edition of the General Instruction, and in an effort to calm the fears of traditionalists who judged that the new Mass was calculated to undermine the theology of eucharist, a revised General Instruction attempted to provide the historical context for the changes. The *editio typica* thus appeared and was ready for translation into the various vernacular languages throughout the world. Although we say that the *editio* was *typica* it was a long way from being *perfecta.* To help in the work of preparing vernacular translations, the Consilium prepared a document entitled *Comme le prévoit* that enunciated a host of principles to assist the scholars in their task.

For the English speakers of the world a joint commission was established in 1963 known as the International Commission on English in the Liturgy, or ICEL. It came into being when bishops of the English-speaking countries decided that it was desirable to have one set of liturgical texts in English. Eleven bishops' conferences (Australia, Canada, England and Wales, India, Ireland, New Zealand, Pakistan, the Philippines, Scotland, South Africa and the United

Michael S. Driscoll

States) are members of ICEL, while 15 other conferences from countries where English is common but not the principal language are associate members. Each of the 11 member conferences elects a bishop to ICEL's governing body, the episcopal board. Thus ICEL is a creation of the 11 episcopal conferences and works in conjunction with the English-speaking countries of the world.

The initial task of ICEL was monumental. Faced with the task of translating all the liturgical books and pressure from the bishops to produce the revised liturgical books as quickly as possible, the translators worked feverishly first to produce the Roman Missal. The Latin church, not having prayed in the vernacular since the fourth century (and it may be argued that the Latin adopted at that time was far from the common tongue of people), was faced with new challenges. The episcopal board of ICEL appointed scholars to work on the translations that would replace the back-room, bootleg translations that had become common around the English-speaking world. In time, the episcopal board selected scholars from many disciplines, such as liturgy, scripture, sacramental theology, classics, English literature and church music, to serve as members of an advisory committee to coordinate the various projects undertaken by ICEL. An editorial committee supervises four subcommittees that work on Translations and Revisions, Presentation of Texts, Original Texts, and Music.

Every project that ICEL undertakes is reviewed by many, sometimes hundreds, of scholars, bishops, pastoral ministers and other interested parties. Each project is approved by the advisory committee before sent to the episcopal board for approval. At any point, a project may be returned for more work. Only after the episcopal board has approved a project is it sent to all the member conferences of bishops. Each conference may accept or reject a particular ICEL work for use in its own country; a conference also may add materials for use in its own country. Before any text may be used it must be approved by a bishops' conference and confirmed by Rome.

One of the primary responsibilities of bishops is to oversee the worship life of the church. ICEL was created by the bishops to assist with one part of this responsibility: the provision of texts for use at worship. In the end, it is the bishops who have final authority over the liturgy. In recent years, ICEL has come under some criticism, notably from a part of the right wing alleging that ICEL has misrepresented or mistranslated the *editio typica*. In one sharp attack from a group called Credo, a lengthy critique was made of *Comme le prévoit,* the Consilium's *Instruction on the Translation of Liturgical Texts,* under which ICEL has been working since 1969.[18] Another article appeared that uses a sampling of a dozen collect prayers supposedly to demonstrate ICEL's ineptitude at translation.[19] The author rejects the principle of "dynamic equivalency" enunciated in *Comme le prévoit,* and produces literal translations of a small, select sampling of prayers. Although these translations have merit, this kind of Monday morning quarterbacking is dismissive of ICEL's original contribution and its ongoing attempt to provide solid translations. Considering the initial task of ICEL, one must admit the value of its work. On the other hand, after thirty years of use, now is the time to develop revised translations based upon our experience of the liturgy over these past three decades.

To translate a text destined for use at liturgy is an art. Nathan Mitchell, in his "Amen Corner," eloquently writes:

> Only art can translate art — and ironically, an artist's duty is, often, to betray the literal for the sake of true fidelity in translation. Faced with poetry, the translator's responsibility is to create song, not to provide an interlinear "pony," "crib," or "trot" (whose job is to return the reader to the source language). . . . Paradoxically, those who demand literal imitation in translation ("The Latin has ten words, while the English has only five"; "The Hebrew has *melek* so you must translate *king*") get a trot, not a translation. Worse still, a trot that pretends to "translate" is not literature; it is a fraud.[20]

The Current Revision of the Sacramentary

The first task in implementing the *Constitution on the Sacred Liturgy* was to provide an *editio typica* for the Mass, as well as for all the sacraments and rites of the church. Working from an *editio typica* has had the advantage of offering a consistent model to the entire

Michael S. Driscoll

church for the style of the rite and the shape of the liturgy. Comparing the various vernacular translations, however, has proven the value of the principle of dynamic equivalency. One example will serve to make the point.

In comparing the *Oratre fratres* in the English and French versions, one is immediately stunned by how slavishly the English translation follows the Latin original, while the French takes liberties that better serve the original intention of the text. In the English version, the assembly is asked to pray ("Pray, my brothers and sisters . . ."). In turn, the people do not truly pray, but rather return a wish to the priest that his sacrifice and theirs might be found worthy by God ("May the Lord accept the sacrifice . . ."). In recent years, as more people become attuned to questions of language, both inclusive language on the horizontal level and vertical language for addressing God, unprompted modifications have become widespread throughout the English-speaking world. It is common to hear: "May the Lord accept the sacrifice at your hands for the praise and glory of God's name, for our good, and the good of all the church." Albeit slight, the modifications recognize that God is beyond gender and reflect this understanding in the proclaimed text.

One simple solution in revising this text would take seriously the command *"Oratre fratres* — Pray, my brothers and sisters . . ." If this were to be taken at face value, one would convert the text into a real prayer: "Lord, accept our offering for the praise of your name and for the good of all your church." This would overcome the difficulties with the gender question concerning God and would be a true prayer. In comparing this to the French version there seems to be a precedent: *"Pour la gloire de Dieu et le salut du monde* — For the glory of God and the salvation of the world." How beautiful in its brevity and intention! In the liturgy should not we say what we mean and mean what we say?

One of the great challenges that faces people who pray in the vernacular, regardless of their culture, is that language is a living and ever-changing reality. For the English-speaking world, which covers different parts of the globe, this means that words that have one particular meaning in one part of the world can have radically different overtones elsewhere. Or, as Oscar Wilde supposedly remarked: "Ah, the Americans and the British! Two cultures separated by a common language." One of the tasks of ICEL in staffing its various working groups is to select individuals from a diverse array of nations in order to provide for the cultural component of the prayer translations. In addition, it is important that there be certain literary quality to the prayer texts. Words that serve for ordinary usage may not be appropriate for use in the liturgy. Because English in the main has a double source for its vocabulary, namely Latin and Anglo-Saxon, there is a wealth of words from which to choose. Decisions must be made to select words that pray well, and for this reason ICEL has been cognizant of inviting poets and writers onto the working committees.

The current revision of the sacramentary has had three areas of focus: (1) pastoral introductions, (2) rubrics, and (3) prayers. Each episcopal conference may compose its own pastoral introduction as an addendum to the general instruction of the sacramentary. This pastoral introduction contains information concerning the celebration of the liturgy within the particular conference. Questions dealing with accommodation and adaptation are likewise addressed. It is within the context of drafting the pastoral introductions that the larger question of the legitimate inculturation of the liturgy has surfaced. Canon law provides that ordinary accommodations for the celebration of the liturgy may be made on a local level, and that adaptations of the liturgy may be made by duly constituted episcopal conferences. Actions involving liturgical inculturation, however, must be referred to the appropriate congregations in Rome for approval. Many of the issues that are dealt with in the pastoral introduction are then addressed in more detail in the rubrics.

Revision Process

A process was developed whereby ICEL would consult with the various episcopal conferences it serves. Additionally, ICEL would enter a dialogue with the English Language Liturgical Consultation (ELLC), a similar kind of organization that deals with ecumenical translations for commonly used texts (for example, the Kyrie, Gloria, Nicene and

Apostles' Creeds, preface dialogues, Sanctus, Lord's Prayer and Agnus Dei). The first task in ICEL's consultation process is the production of "green books" that are distributed to the bishops for general comment. In the case of the revision of the sacramentary, the 1970 edition served as the green book. After comments are submitted and amendments are voted upon, "white books" are produced reflecting the decisions of the episcopal conferences. Regular progress reports drafted by ICEL are mailed to the episcopal conferences to keep them abreast of the work.

A timetable was adopted that would see the initial revision completed by 1996, with final adoption and approval in the Jubilee Year 2000. In the United States, the sacramentary was presented in segments for a vote at the regular meetings of the U.S. bishops' conference (see box below). A decision had to be made to accept, reject or amend the proposed texts presented in each segment. Texts that were amended by the bishops' conference were to be remanded to ICEL, the copyright owner of the proposed materials.

Sacramentary Segments
Presented to Bishops' Conference

I. Ordinary Time, with 18-page Introduction	September 1993
II. Proper of Seasons	April 1994
III. Nine Eucharistic Prayers	August 1994
IV. Order of Mass	February 1995
V. Proper of Saints	May 1995
VI. Common of Saints, Ritual and Votive Masses	February 1996
VII. Masses for Various Needs and Occasions	May 1996

To assist in the task of revision and to learn of the wishes of the bishops of all the participating countries, ICEL devised two consultations. The first took place in 1982 and had as its subject the presidential prayers of the Mass. Over 1400 texts were presented to the bishops and their advisors for study and feedback. The decision was made to ask ICEL to review the general style of the prayers (euchology) and to use a wider vocabulary and shorter sentences in order to facilitate proclamation of the prayer texts.

The second consultation took place in 1986 and dealt with the Order of Mass. ICEL's governing episcopal board made the decision to be very cautious in the revision of the assembly's responses: They should not be changed except in dire cases.[21] It was felt that any unnecessary change would only thwart the renewal of the liturgy if the changes had the result of causing confusion regarding the practices that had been in place for the past thirty years. On the other hand, it was decided that legitimate options need to be better indicated in the revised sacramentary in the hope that they might be implemented more fully.

If the result of the first consultation can be seen as a bold demand for better translations of the texts used at the liturgy, the result of the second consultation seemed to be a retrenchment in favor of a more cautious approach to the revision. The change in attitude reflected in the two ICEL consultations was revealing a wider change in sentiment among many of the bishops of the English-speaking world concerning ongoing liturgical reform.

For proposed texts to pass on to the next phase in the process, namely inclusion in the white book, approval was needed by two-thirds of the *de iure* Latin-rite members of an episcopal conference. Each episcopal conference had the option to vote on the sacramentary in segments or as a whole. Once the texts and the entire book had been approved by all the participating episcopal conferences, it must then be sent to Rome for confirmation by the Congregation of Divine Worship. The goal is to have the book in use by the First Sunday of Advent, 2000.

The sacramentary is detailed and multi-faceted. For the purpose of this article, let us now look at three areas, namely the pastoral introduction, the rubrics, and the revised and newly composed prayers, to see how the multiple modes of Christ's presence are recognized and lived out in the church's celebrations of the eucharist.

Pastoral Introduction

The pastoral introduction is an important companion piece to the General Instruction of the Roman Missal (GIRM) and serves as a preface to the sacramentary. While the General Instruction is intended for the universal church, the pastoral introduction is meant to speak more to the local concerns of the countries for which it was written. The pastoral introduction includes rubrics, some of which are reprinted within the body of the sacramentary itself for easy reference. The pastoral introduction is also a very helpful source of a theology of the liturgy, and of instruction concerning the multiple modes of Christ's presence.

The pastoral instruction begins by speaking of the place of liturgy in the life of the church. The eucharist exists in and for the church, and cannot exist apart from the church. The worshiping assembly is the *sine qua non* of the eucharist. The Second Vatican Council, in its *Constitution on the Sacred Liturgy,* was clear on this matter: "Liturgical services are not private functions but are celebrations of the church which is 'the sacrament of unity,' namely, the holy people united and organized under their bishops." (#26)[22] The assembly is more than a random group of individuals. It is the gathering of God's people to exercise its royal priesthood in the sacrifice of praise. Canon law goes so far as to call the assembly the *leitourgos.*[23] Several elements of the rite for Mass underscore this reality:

1. dialogues between the assembly and the ministers (acclamations are "signs of communal action and means of effective communication");

2. singing ("one of the most potent of all expressions of communal awareness and common purpose");

3. uniformity of posture and gesture ("expresses and fosters unity of spirit and purpose"); and

4. accommodation to facilitate the participation of persons with special needs (for example, children).

A simple survey of the pastoral introduction to the GIRM reveals the many ways in which the word "present" is employed:

Christ is present in the priest: "Christ is really *present* in the person of the priest who presides at the liturgy. The chair stands as a symbol of the priest celebrant's office. It serves to symbolize unity, leadership, and service to the gathered assembly." (#54)

Christ is present in the proclamation of the gospel reading: "Because the proclamation of the gospel reading is the high point of the liturgy of the word, it is distinguished from the other readings . . . . The people stand to hear the gospel reading and acclaim Christ *present* and speaking to them." (#91)

Christ is present in the eucharistic prayer: "The eucharistic prayer, the center and summit of the entire celebration, sums up what it means of the church to celebrate the eucharist. It is a memorial proclamation of praise and thanksgiving for God's work of creation and salvation, a proclamation in which the body and blood of Christ are made present by the power of the Holy Spirit and the people are joined to Christ is offering his sacrifice to the Father." (#111) "At the heart of the eucharistic prayer the account of the Last Supper is recited. Everything for which God has been thanked and praised, all that was accomplished in the history of salvation, is summed up and made present in the person of the crucified and risen Lord." (#119)

Christ is present in the doxology: "Through Christ, with him and in him, all is turned to the Father's glory by the action of the Holy Spirit. At this climax of the prayer the consecrated elements are raised high in a gesture that vividly expresses the true nature of the eucharistic sacrifice as the offering of the church through Christ the high priest, with Christ, who is really present in the church, in Christ who has incorporated his people into himself by the action of the Holy Spirit." (#124)

Rubrics

If the fundamental understanding of liturgy is that it is an action, then the rubrics that govern the action help the praying assembly experience the presence of Christ. The rubrics are not negligible factors, but must be attended to so that the actions reveal the presence of Christ. With this in mind, the revised sacramentary attended to the opening rites of the Mass. The general feeling was that these rites had become too burdensome and complicated. If their function is simply to open the liturgy and prepare the assembly to hear the word of God, then they should be simpler and more to the point. Also, the various options needed to be spelled out in a clearer way so that they might be better utilized.

A second area where legitimate diversity exists is the kiss of peace. Research demonstrated how this element had been introduced, relocated and even removed from the liturgy in the past. The U.S. bishops had reviewed the placement of the kiss of peace within the eucharistic prayer and decided that a better position for the kiss would be after the homily, before the presentation of the gifts. In this way, the fourfold action of the eucharistic prayer (taking, blessing, breaking and giving) would not be obscured by the action of exchanging a sign of peace.[24] Here is a good example of the deeper understanding of the power of the liturgical action to reveal or conceal the presence of Christ. Some bishops favored leaving the kiss of peace within the eucharistic prayer, arguing that many people had come to appreciate that this action also mediates the presence of Christ. Others argued that this element be considered a moveable piece, so that it could move within the liturgy according to the feast or season. For example, during penitential seasons it could be attached to the penitential rite, while at other times it might come at the end of the liturgy. In general, however, it was agreed that positioning the kiss before the presentation of the gifts would be ideal, and the gospel of Matthew was cited for the justification: "So then, if you are bringing your offering to the altar and there remember that your brother has something against you, leave your offering there before the altar, go and be reconciled with your brother first, and then come back and present your offering" (5:24).

In general, there is a greater appreciation for the quality of the liturgical action. Extraneous gestures should be avoided and the posture of ministers and the assembly should contribute to the understanding that Christ manifests himself in and through the celebration of the liturgy. An area of ongoing attention concerns the transitions that exist within the rite itself. The concern about rubrics is ultimately an attention given to the seamless quality of the liturgy. Liturgies that start and stop needlessly throughout do not do justice to their overall shape. An example of one improvement along these lines involves the memorial acclamation. In the current sacramentary there exists but one invitation: "Let us proclaim the mystery of faith." Yet there are four possible responses. But the invitation does not cue the assembly as to which response to make, so the assembly must wait for the presider to initiate the first words. Or in the case of a sung version, the musicians must introduce the response. In the revised sacramentary, there will be four invitations (see box), one for each of the four responses currently in use.

---

1. Great is the mystery of faith. R. *Christ has died . . .*

2. Praise to you, Lord Jesus. R. *Dying you destroyed our death . . .*

3. Christ is the bread of life. R. *When we eat this bread and drink this cup . . .*

4. Jesus Christ is Lord. R. *Lord, by your cross and resurrection . . .*

Ideally these invitations will be set to music so that when the invitation is intoned the assembly will be cued as to which response will follow, and in which key it will be sung. The need to interrupt the liturgy to let the assembly learn of its response will be eliminated. This is but one example where the revised sacramentary is taking steps to preserve the seamless quality of the liturgy.

Prayers

The work of ICEL is divided between the revision of texts translated from the *editio typica* and the composition of new texts to complement the translated texts. Thirty years of experience have proven invaluable for the procurement of better translations. Once example is in Eucharistic Prayer III. In the *editio typica* we find the expression *"a solis ortu usque ad occasum*—from the rising of the sun unto its setting." This is taken directly from Psalm 113:3, the first of the six

Hallel psalms used for the great Jewish feasts, including the conclusion of Passover. In the current sacramentary this is rendered as "from east to west," which arguably captures the sense of the sun's rising and setting. On the other hand, the rising and setting of the sun are temporal metaphors marking the limits of the day, while east and west are spatial metaphors. In both cases we insist that the name of God be praised, but in the case of the temporal metaphor we are praying that God's name may be on our lips all the day long, while the spatial metaphor prays that wherever we go, God's name may be praised. It is little wonder that the geographical understanding has had prevalence over the temporal and frequently one hears interpolated in the eucharistic prayer, "from east to west and from north to south." Most recently I have even heard this expression rendered as "from coast to coast." One can almost hear the strains of "This land is your land, This land is my land, From California to the Gulf Stream islands . . . ." The revised version will recapture the temporal sense of the Hallel psalm, which the synoptic gospels mention Jesus prayed at the Passover.[25]

In addition to the revised translations, newly composed texts will be found in the sacramentary that reflect the ongoing presence of God throughout history. Prayers have been composed for situations that until recent times were unheard of or ignored: in time of industrial conflict; for victims of abuse; for the addicted.

Conclusions

If the major attempt of the current reform aims at revising the sacramentary in light of the past thirty years of experience, and with the view of facilitating the fuller participation of the entire assembly, then we will not be disappointed with the outcome. On the other hand, questions concerning a theology of priesthood in relationship to the assembly's participation need further development. Several years ago Mary Alice Piil sounded the clarion call for ongoing theological reflection when she wrote: "Any conflict of theology of ministry, specifically the ministry of the presiding priest, present in the conciliar and postconciliar documents, emerges as a result of the primary emphasis of the reform on the full, active participation of the faithful in the eucharistic act."[26] In the discussion of Christ's presence in the eucharistic action, we have focused on the dynamic aspects of presence, preferring to speak with verbs rather than nouns. Instead of speaking about the presence of Christ as a result of human agency, we repeat what Saint Augustine said long ago: "In the sacraments it is Christ who acts."[27] On the other hand, we see God acting through human agency in the assembly, the ministers and the priest. All are important and essential elements for the liturgical actions. However, the argument is vain to try to decide who and what are most essential. All are essential, as the revised sacramentary underscores in many different ways. What matters is that Christ's presence is made manifest in the praying community that gathers in his name.

The challenges that still face us concern the quality of the ritual action. Vigilance must be taken to insure that the various parts of the liturgy are effected in such a way so that the many modes of Christ's presence may be experienced to the fullest. In the U.S. bishops' document on sacred music, *Music in Catholic Worship,* the statement was made that "good celebrations foster and nourish faith. Poor celebrations may weaken and destroy it."[28] Hopefully in the Jubilee Year 2000 the revised sacramentary will appear for the English-speaking world. Efforts have been made by the bishops of the English-speaking world, by liturgists and especially by ICEL that this revised book be a tool of divine grace. It still remains for those receiving this book put it to good use.

1. Symptomatic of this kind of treatment is the *Catechismus Romanus,* dating from the period of the Counter-Reformation. This approach is certainly reflected in the Theological Manual tradition that was a central part of seminary education even into the 20th century.

2. The list of modes of presence in this paragraph should not be interpreted as though they are arranged in descending order of importance. Latin semantics often favors the final element in a long list as the most important.

3. G. Alberigo, ed., *Histoire du Concile Vatican II (1959–1965): vol. I. Le catholicisme vers une nouvelle époque: L'annonce et la préparation* (Paris: Cerf, 1997), 235–52.

4. E. Bacci, *"In quale lingua si parlerà nel futuro Concilio ecumenico?" Osservatore Romano* (February 11, 1959).

5. A French Redemptorist who was serving as bishop in a French-speaking country in Africa kept a daybook of the Council in which he never failed to comment that he could not make out what a certain high-ranking American churchman was saying whenever he took the floor. The American speaks Latin, he wrote, *"comme une vâche espagnole* [like a Spanish cow]." This story serves to illustrate that even some of the Council Fathers had their difficulties in expressing themselves in Latin, some of whom were staunch defenders of maintaining Latin as the official language of the church.

6. See A.-G. Martimort, *"Le problème des langues liturgiques de 1946 à 1957," Maison Dieu* 53 (1958): 23–55.

7. The European pioneers of the liturgical movement had been insistent in calling their centers and their work under the title "liturgical pastoral" rather than what we might be inclined to say today as "pastoral liturgy." Although the difference is highly nuanced, it was their concern that the emphasis fall upon the pastoral dimension, which the liturgy must serve, and not vice versa.

8. See *The Assisi Papers: Proceedings of the First International Congress of Pastoral Liturgy, Assisi-Rome, September, 18–22, 1956* (Collegeville, MN, 1957). The title in English (Pastoral Liturgy) did not maintain the nuance sought by the European participants.

9. See F. McManus, "Comments on a Recent Decision of the Holy Office," typed text (Cairo, May 1960).

10. H. Anglés, *"Il prossimo Concilio Ecumenico e la Musica Sacra," Bollettino degli Amici del Pont. Istituto de Musica Sacra* 11 (1959): 6.

11. See A. Bugnini, *La riforma liturgica* (Rome, 1983), 34–6.

12. *"Latinae linguae usus in liturgia occidentali servetur," Acta Synodalia Sacrosancti Concili Oecumenici Vaticani II* (Vatican City, 1970), 272.

13. *"Conversio textus latini in linguam vernaculam in liturgia adhibenda a competenti auctoritate ecclesiastica territoriali, de quo supra, approbari debet."* Vatican II, *Constitution on the Sacred Liturgy* (Sacrosanctum Concilium), 36.

14. Paul VI, *Address to the members and periti of the Consilium* (October 13, 1966).

15. See Congregation of Rites (Consilium), *Instruction (second)* Tres abhinc annos, *on the orderly carrying out of the Constitution on the Liturgy* (May 4, 1967).

16. See Paul VI, Apostolic Constitution, *Missale Romanum.*

17. One such reaction: A group of anonymous Roman theologians, "A Critical Study of the *Novus Ordo Missae," Triumph* (1969): 22–4.

18 "Proposed Liturgical Translation Standards," *The Catholic World Report* (July, 1994): 25–41.

19. E. Leiva-Merikakis, "The catechetical role of the liturgy and the quality of liturgical texts: The current ICEL translation," *Communio* 20 (Spring, 1993): 63–83.

20. N. Mitchell, "Amen Corner," *Worship* 69 (1995): 454.

21. The following four principles were adopted as guidelines: (1) Ritual responses and other short prayers memorized by the people should be left unchanged if possible. Revisions required for serious reasons should be made in such a way that they not create undue pastoral problems for the assembly; (2) Short texts that are publicly proclaimed by the presider or other ministers and that invite a congregational response (for example, greetings and invitations) should not be changed unless the current translation is inaccurate; (3) Longer occasional prayers (for example, the blessing of water) that are often not memorized may be more readily changed for style and accuracy of translation; (4) Inaudible prayers of the priest should be examined for difficulties and may be changed.

22. *"Actiones liturgicae non sunt actiones privatae, sed celebrationes ecclesia, quae est 'unitatis sacramentum,' scilicet plebs sancta sub episcopis adunata et ordinata."*

23. "In the celebration of the sacraments, it is thus the whole assembly that is the *leitourgos,* each according to his function, but in the 'unity of the Spirit' who acts in all." *Code of Canon Law,* can. 1144.

24. Thomas Reese, "In the Catholic church, a kiss is never just a kiss." *America* 172 (April 15, 1995): 12–19.

25. See Matthew 26:30 and parallels.

26. M. A. Piil, *Shaping the English Liturgy,* P. Flink and J. Schellman, eds. (Washington, DC: Pastoral Press, 1990), 174.

27. Augustine, *Tract. in Joh. 5, 18* (PL 35, 1424).

28. See Bishops' Committee on the Liturgy, *Music in Catholic Worship* (Washington, DC: USCC Publications, 1972), 6.

Dorothy Dwight, BVM

The Cantor and the Presence of Christ in the Singing Assembly

The Song of God

The universe with all its inhabitants is the music of a God radiantly alive in everything at its depths. All of creation is God's song, a chorus of jubilation awakened by God's singing of the Word out of love. Each of us is a song of God sung into existence out of the love of our God who is Song. And together we make a grand chorus of praise with sun and moon, mountains and rivers, creatures on the land and in the seas and skies; with all peoples of the earth and those who have gone before us.

And the creative Spirit of God who moved over the waters in the beginning moves deep within and among us even now. The Spirit plays upon our hearts, drawing us into the song of the universe, joining us with the Living Song of God, the Singer of God's Song *par excellence,* the Song of God's fidelity to humankind, the One in whom all the music of eternity was expressed: Jesus the Christ.[1]

Eugene LaVerdiere once suggested that we consider the image of Jesus as the Song of God. He suggested that, given what we know about the proclamation or cantillation of the scriptures in the synagogue in Jesus' time and what know of other sung forms, instruments and dancing in Temple worship, we can well think of Jesus as singing (and dancing) — as communicating God's creative life and Spirit through song. Drawing on this image, LaVerdiere proceeded to share a wonderful paraphrase of the prologue of John's gospel:

> In the beginning was the Song, and the Song was with God, and the Song was God. That Song was life, and everything that came to be came alive with the life of that Song. The Song came into the world and was made flesh. The noise of the world tried to destroy the Song but the noise could not drown it out. The Song of God would always be there.[2]

LaVerdiere then extended the image by proposing that we Christians are meant to reflect Jesus' identity as God's Song. We are meant to sing and to move, to express and communicate the Song in our hearts, who is Jesus Christ, so that others might say of us, "They are starting to sound like the Song of God."[3] We are invited to sing in our world today Jesus' song of mercy and compassion, his melody of graciousness and generosity.

It is our Singer-God who, in the person of the Spirit given us by Jesus, sings us into being as an assembly, into the Body of Christ, into a new, fresh church where all are welcome to join the song. It is that life-giving Spirit of the risen Lord, the bond between creator Mother-Father and redeemer Son, bursting all bounds and burning with energy and love, who forms and strengthens the bonds among us as a people and at the same time bonds us with our God and all the people of the earth.

There is a deep, implicit music, a living sacrifice of praise that we make in our lives. But when we gather and join our voices to make one song together as an assembly, we participate in an explicit way in the song of Christ himself. And our song, as an integral part of the actions of our rites, reveals God's active, transforming presence in our midst.

The Presence of Christ in the (Singing) Assembly

Christ is clearly present in and to the assembled people of God by reason of our baptism: "Where two or three are gathered together in my name, there am I in the midst of them" (Matthew 18:20). As stated so clearly in the *Constitution on the Sacred Liturgy,* Christ is *really present* at Mass in the presiding minister, the word, the bread and wine, and "when the church prays and sings" (#7). By our presence to one another at liturgy, our contribution of our energy to the ritual and through our actions, we ourselves become recognizable presence of Christ. When we gather, listen and respond, when we bless and praise, when we remember, offer, break and receive, and when we disperse in mission, we are doing so as the Body of Christ. Christ is present with us, transforming us into his Body.

The early Christians assembled in order *to house God's presence* — to realize (that is, to make real, to actualize) Jesus' promise to be present where two or three would gather. They expected and knew the risen Christ somehow to be in their midst when together they heard the word, gave thanks, broke bread, and sang "psalms and hymns and spiritual songs" together (see Ephesians 5:19; Colosians 3:16).

Today, we gather as a people of faith as did our ancestors in the faith, expecting to know the presence of the same risen Lord among us. We come together to stand in awe of a God who loves us intimately beyond our wildest imaginings. As we begin to attend to one another in the act of gathering, welcoming each and hearing each one's stories, and as we enter into the song being "rehearsed," we allow Christ's life-giving presence to be released in our midst. It is not that he is not present in the rest of our lives. Rather, here in table fellowship we remember and meet the risen Christ who is present in the whole of our lives.

However, we realize and recognize Christ's real presence to us and with us and in our midst only when we act, and when we allow the word, the bread and the wine, the presiding minister, and ourselves to *act upon us:*

- when we *gather and are welcomed* by the presiding minister;

- when we *listen* to the word proclaimed *and respond* with a commitment to proclaim the message of healing and reconciliation that Christ has entrusted to us;

- when we *remember* the story of our salvation in him *and join in offering* our lives with his self-offering;

- when we *reverence* bread and wine radically transformed by the Holy Spirit and *eat and drink* together *and allow our lives to be transformed* by his very personal presence.

Our song, a symbolic reality in its own right, is integrally linked to each of these actions and assists us in entering more fully into them.

The Power of Music as Symbol

As symbolic language, music carries the power to connect us with our deepest selves, with our God, with others, and with the whole of creation. It draws us down into our center to touch there the Holy One, the mystery that is God, evoking in us a sense of wonder and beauty, moving us to contemplation. At the same time, music expands us outward into another experience of the Holy as we resonate with the song of the universe. As a human creation, music is a symbol of human presence. But when wedded to word, music shares the power of God's creative word (in Hebrew: *dabar*) to reveal and effect divine presence as epitomized in the Word-made-flesh.

Because music is a temporal art, intangible and transitory, it serves as a way to communicate with a God who is mystery, both present and hidden, distant and yet closer to us than we are to ourselves. When melody clothes a text, dimensions of meaning, feeling and intuition are unveiled that go beyond the text. Concepts and deep emotions can be expressed in especially powerful and profound ways. Felice Rainoldi, speaking to the *Universa Laus* meeting in 1990, aptly expresses the reality this way:

> The word is already, in itself and of its essence, a musical event: the ancient orators called it *cantus obscurior*. The word manifests the interior life of a person, and when it is exteriorized, modulated by the fascinating vibrations of the vocal apparatus through the agency of timbres and rhythms, then the process of communication takes a real leap in quality. . . . Singing can link the sender and the receiver in a way that makes them "vibrate at the same frequency." . . . Singing is a language that gives off high-voltage symbolic energy, energy that makes spoken language

penetrating and persuasive, crisscrossing it with increasing and diminishing rhythmic movements, and rendering it articulate. Singing is a language through which the word throbs with a greater emotion, becoming more suggestive and evocative through fluctuations in the sound curve.[4]

Christian Ritual Music

The common song of Christians assembled in worship schools us in prayer; it shapes and forms us in faith, in a certain way of living and looking at life. We are brought to life as an assembly, molded into one voice, one action as we express a common faith and unity of purpose rooted in our baptism. Our song draws us into the ritual, sets a tone, invites us to experience God's presence in our midst as mystery and as shared presence. It calls us to see the needs of those around us, evokes tenderness and compassion in us, and challenges us to commit ourselves to Gospel living.

Just as every act of music sets up sympathetic vibrations, thereby changing the sound environment, so too music has the power to change, to transform, to unite in communion those of us who sing and listen. Music, communicating as it does to the whole of our being — body, mind, heart, spirit — becomes an agent of our conversion, providing us new vision through hearing, moving us to transcendence and union.

Christian ritual music is music at the service of the structure of the rites and their authentic communal celebration. We sing in liturgy because music is intimately bound up with the rite, because, as Gabe Huck has noted, *our liturgy as ritual needs song:* "The sung word is at the heart of liturgy."[5] Huck reminds us that our singing is not optional but rather is something we do as part of the total liturgical act.

Because we are members of a royal priesthood by our baptism, *our singing* with one voice *is worship.* The song we make is a vital part of our worship. We sing to accompany ritual actions and movement and words. We sing that we might be brought deeper into communion with our God and each other. And we ultimately sing to be compelled to service beyond this particular assembly. Rite and music do carry the power to draw us into both communion and service.

In our rituals we have:

- processions that need music;

- psalms which by their nature as poetry are most properly sung;

- words of scripture, and prayers of praise and thanksgiving, that beg for proclamation or cantillation;

- acclamations that cry out to be sung (Alleluia; Amen; Hosanna; memorial acclamation);

- litanies of intercession that overflow from minds and hearts moved by the deep alienation and need for reconciliation that pervades our world and in solidarity with the world's pain; litanies that gain in intensity of expression through repetition of a refrain or ostinato; and

- statements of belief and faith affirmed and expressed in sturdy hymns that call us to yet deeper faith.

Musical Forms and the Gathering of the People

Our worship begins with the gathering. Already in our coming together we become the Body of Christ. The gathering music — be it hymn or ostinato, litany or otherwise responsorial in form — functions to foster an awareness of ourselves as the People of God. The choice of music for the gathering rite will vary with the season or occasion, the worship space, and the nature of any procession. Whatever the form, the music functions to draw us disparate individuals into a unity of song and spirit, into a single voice of praise and thanksgiving.

Even as it forms us into a praying body, uniting us in action with a common voice, our gathering music discloses in our midst a Christ who is present already as we gather and before we do anything else. Our awareness of Christ's presence at this time will enable us later to experience and receive Christ as we listen to the scripture

proclaimed and as we respond with an offering of our lives as a sacrifice of praise in union with Jesus the Christ.

Various musical forms shape us differently and tell us different
things about ourselves and our relationships to one another. Together
they tell us something about who we are as church: a discipleship of
equals within a hierarchical church with a diversity of ministries.
Both "unity forms" and "responsorial forms" have their role to play
in our rites, some forms better serving certain ritual moments than
others.

The *hymn,* with its fusing of voices into a single melody, has the
power to forge a group of diverse individuals into an assembly united
in faith and worship. The use of a hymn form says that we are an
assembly of equals. Employed at the beginning of liturgy, a hymn can
set the mood of an event or season. With its rhythm, cadences and
isosyllabic structure, a hymn is sturdy enough with its multiple stan-
zas set to the same tune (sometimes with a refrain) to accompany a
procession. In addition to serving the gathering rite, the hymn also
finds a suitable position at the thanksgiving and praise after communion or as a closing song.

In some cases a song or psalm in *responsorial* form, consisting
of verses for a cantor or choir in alternation with a refrain for the
assembly, better serves the assembly's needs. Responsorial forms are
dialogic in nature. Because the refrains are generally short and easy to
memorize, the assembly can readily become engaged in the dialogue
without a participation aid in hand even as they watch a procession
or move in one themselves. However, the refrain must be substantial
enough and repeated often enough to really gather us together.
Requiring the presence of a cantor or choir, responsorial forms speak
to a differentiation of roles within the singing assembly. They speak
of interdependence and of the necessity of multiple ministers — at
least one cantor or choir, and an assembly — if dialogue is to occur.

A specific responsorial form with a low-keyed and repetitive
structure — namely, the *litany* — is able to establish a contemplative
mood and engage the assembly in a dialogue. In the litany, there is a
quick alternation between cantor and assembly, in call-and- response
fashion. The invocation by the cantor and the short response by the
assembly are linked together in a strict rhythm and meter so that the

assembly finds itself immediately caught up in an energizing action. Sometimes we are in direct dialogue with God in a litany. At other times we are in a conversation with each other that mirrors God's dialogue with us and the shape of our whole ritual: God calls and we respond. The resources needed for a litany are few: an unaccompanied cantor and an assembly. In addition to its use for the penitential rite and the litany of saints, the litany is well suited to accompany such ritual actions as processions and the breaking of bread.

In recent years the *ostinato* has found its way into Western liturgies and might serve well to gather us during some seasons and on certain feasts. Its simple, repetitive, mantra-like nature slows us down, clears the mind of distractions and opens us to contemplation. The form allows for recurring use over a period of time within a rite. The ostinato speaks of interdependence with a simple unison line for the assembly and simultaneous complementary parts for choir, cantor and instrumentalists.

Although not used in the gathering rites, the *acclamation* rounds out our cursory discussion of musical forms. A stylized, intense shout of affirmation sung by the assembly at key ritual moments, the acclamation expresses solidarity in faith.

At this point in time, our assemblies have a stable, memorized repertoire of eucharistic prayer acclamations and gospel acclamations in various styles that people are singing with some assurance and conviction. Likewise, our people have a substantial body of psalm refrains that they can call their own, and they regularly enter into dialogue with the cantor or choir for the responsorial psalm and the communion song or psalm. In many places our people know and regularly sing various settings of the Gloria (both as a hymn and often in responsorial form) and join in the singing of litanies and ostinato forms.

Perhaps we would be wise now to give attention to encouraging the singing of strong hymns that will help to gather us as a body in Christ, strengthen our faith and send us forth on mission. Already we have wonderfully crafted texts by such poets as Dolores Dufner and Brian Wren. New tunes and texts from other cultures are coming to us through the music of John Bell and the Iona community. And we are beginning to rediscover early American hymnody.

We need to get beyond stodgy stereotypes and let individual tunes sing themselves.

The Cantor and God's Presence

Of the musical forms we have mentioned, the responsorial form, the litany and likely the ostinato are dependent upon the prayer leadership of the cantor. Let us consider now that leader of prayer.

The Cantor as a Mediator of God's Presence

The cantor stands within the assembly as a mediator who lets God's presence shine through. The cantor is as a reed through whom God plays a song of salvation in Jesus Christ, the living Song of God. Through the cantor, the Song of God is spoken to the assembly. When God's life, God's music vibrates in this human reed, sympathetic vibrations are set off in those who hear. The cantor is a connection-maker, a conduit, a bridge-builder between God and the people. Having been transformed by the Word, the cantor works to help the assembly shine with God's presence.

The Cantor as a Leader of Prayer

The cantor's primary ministry is to be a leader of prayer, to bring the assembly to sung prayer. By a gracious, reverent and welcoming presence, the cantor enters into a relationship with the members of the assembly and encourages them to enter a song that becomes their prayer. By gentle invitation and inspiration, the cantor creates an ambience that allows the prayer that is already within the assembly's heart to be released. By musical interpretation and quality performance, the cantor invites the assembly to sing well; and as the quality of singing improves, so does the level of engagement in prayer.

The cantor is to be a discreet minister, one who emerges from within the assembly as a servant leader of its prayer. The cantor's song never substitutes for the people's sung prayer but is to draw the people into the life of the words they are hearing and singing. The cantor serves by singing litanies, by leading the assembly in its singing of unaccompanied hymns and songs and by singing the verses of the responsorial psalm.

The Cantor and the Psalms

When serving as psalmist, the cantor is a minister of the word, a herald of God's living word. The task of the cantor as psalmist is to help the word of God come alive for the people, and this is a task for which the cantor needs preparation. In the words of Abraham Heschel: "A cantor is a person who knows the secret of the resurrection of the words."[6] The cantor first must enter the world of the original singer(s) of the song, live with the text and appropriate its lyrical expression of human emotions. Then the members of the assembly will experience how the word has taken flesh in the cantor, and will be encouraged to listen and respond with their whole bodies and from their own experience as well. Second, the cantor must have a strong conviction that he or she is a bearer of God as he or she interprets a particular psalm. Third, the cantor must be attentive to those elements of diction and musical artistry by which the Word will be communicated to the people. Fourth, the cantor must develop a love for the psalter and "infect others with it."[7]

The cantor must be able to enter into and pray each psalm so that he or she can deliver the psalm text in song in such a way that it touches the spirits of those who join in the psalm. As a psalmist, the cantor is to use his or her song to enable the members of the assembly to name where they are with their God, to stand in naked vulnerability, and to know that our God, having become one of us and prayed these very psalms, understands our every need.

Spirituality and Preparation of the Cantor

How does the cantor prepare to lead the assembly in psalmody and its other sung prayer? In addition to the direct and immediate preparation of voice, music and psalm text, there is a preparation that is more indirect and ongoing—the development of a cantor's spirituality.

First, it would seem beneficial for the cantor to develop a contemplative stance toward life, that is, the capacity to enter into each
moment with a sense of wonder and expectancy knowing that each
experience carries the potential to reveal the action of God's love and
grace. To contemplate is to "be in temple with," and for the cantor
this would mean being in temple with nature in all its beauty and
power; with people near at hand, listening to their stories, binding
up their wounds, experiencing with them their deep joys; with persons about whose pain and victories we read and hear; with the God
who fashioned it all. If the cantor works at being present to the grace
of the moment, he or she will be that much more able to stand in
awe of the holiness that is revealed in the assembly.

Second, the cantor would do well to give time regularly to
prayer, either alone or with others in communal prayer: prayer with
the scriptures, expecially the psalms; prayer attuned to strong arche-
typal symbols that form the heart of Christian sacramental life;
prayer engaging the whole body through posture, gesture, speech,
song, movement, listening; prayer that accompanies the keeping of a
journal or listening to music; making intercession for our world, ourselves, our church, our city and neighbors.

Third, the cantor must give some time to being with fellow
parish members, their families and others who have special needs:
those who are ill or homeless; those who are incarcerated or otherwise removed from society; those who are challenged in mind or
body; and those who grieve. Fourth, the cantor must join with others
to advocate in some manner for the realization of basic human rights
for those persons whose dignity is not respected and whose basic
needs for health of body and spirit are not met.

Conclusion

Some good questions a cantor might ask after a service are: Did I
pray and call my people to prayer? To what extent did I feel myself as
one with the assembly? How might I better assist the people to experience their song as prayer? How might I more effectively facilitate
the assembly's sung prayer? Remember always that the ultimate goal

of the ministry of the cantor (indeed of all ministry) is to built up the assembly of Christ's faithful in prayer and to help the people of God experience the Risen Lord in their midst.

1. For further treatment of the notion of Jesus as the Song of God, see Adrian Van Kaam, *The Music of Eternity* (Notre Dame, IN: Ave Maria Press, 1990), 31–42.

2. "Musician: Model for Church Ministry," *Pastoral Music* 10 (October–November 1985): 13.

3. Ibid.

4. Felice Rainoldi, "Cantillation Begins with Text," *Pastoral Music* 15 (February–March 1991): 25.

5. Gabe Huck, "A Reflection on Music and Ritual: Part One: How Can They Keep from Singing?" *Liturgy 80* (May–June 1987): 2–3.

6. Abraham Heschel, *The Insecurity of Freedom* (New York: Farrar, Straus & Giroux, 1966), 251.

7. Eric Routley, *Musical Leadership in the Church* (Nashville: Abingdon, 1967), 86.

Joseph A. Favazza

The Eucharistic Table, a Reconciling Table? Our Belief, Our Experience, Our Dilemma

The second eucharistic prayer expresses the simple yet eloquent hope that "we might be brought together in unity." Nowhere is it clearer that the table of the eucharist is a table of reconciliation. We believe that in the celebration of the eucharist we remember Jesus the Christ whose death and resurrection has "reconciled to himself all things,"[1] and who effects the unity of believers to himself and one another in lives of peace, justice and reconciliation. In our Catholic tradition, the many presences of Christ in the eucharist stand as the source and summit of the many manifestations of a community reconciled and reconciling.

While this is all right and just as a statement of theology, something appears to have gone terribly wrong on the pastoral level. Large numbers of Roman Catholics in the United States find themselves officially excluded from the table of the eucharist for reasons of canon law or moral theology. This includes those Catholics in non-canonical marriages, as well as unmarried cohabiting Catholics — including gay and lesbian Catholics. A growing number of pastoral ministers name children under age seven as the largest single group canonically excluded from the eucharist. Beyond these, we have Catholics who disagree with the teaching church on matters of belief that, according to a recent letter by the Congregation for the Doctrine of the Faith, require "firm and definitive assent" even if such doctrines "have not been proposed by the magisterium of the church as formally revealed."[2] Examples include feminist Catholics and Catholics who are members of organizations that disagree that only men can be ordained. Finally, we must mention other members of the baptized who find themselves barred from the Catholic table due to divisions caused by events in history, differences in doctrine or impositions of disciplinary measures.

From this partial list of those excluded from the table, one sees the dilemma. In our theology, the eucharist is what binds us together; in our pastoral practice, it is what breaks us apart. Is there any hope for reconciliation? In order to explore the answer to this "tradition-impacting" question, I wish to undertake two tasks: (1) to trace carefully the theology and history that connects eucharist and reconciliation as emerging ritual strategies in the tradition; and (2) in light of a recalibration of the understanding gained through a review of theology and history, to develop new approaches to reconciliation in a pastoral context.

Reconciliation: It's Not Just a Sacrament Anymore

As Catholics, when we hear the word reconciliation we immediately tend to associate it with that particular rite and sacrament that has gone by a variety of different names in our tradition: penance, confession, forgiveness, conversion.[3] However, reconciliation is too grand to be limited to a sacrament; in fact I believe that our tradition supports the view that reconciliation is really the core metaphor or way to describe what Christians believe about the unique activity of Jesus the Christ. Paul himself inspires such a conclusion: "[I]f anyone is in Christ, there is a new creation: everything old has passed away; see, everything has become new! All this is from God, who reconciled us through Christ to God, and has given us the ministry of reconciliation; that is, in Christ God was reconciling the world to God's own self."[4] Paul draws the conclusion that Jesus has established a new relationship between the divine and the human that has implications for relationships between human and human. Paul makes the startling yet overlooked point (especially if we come to understand Paul only through the Letter to the Romans) that every ministry, starting with the ministry of Jesus, is a ministry of reconciliation. This is an insight with enormous implications for theology.

One such implication, which owing to our appreciation of the sacramental comes as no great surprise for us Catholics, is that we should stop worrying about salvation. In other words, while "salvation" is a perfectly good interpretation of what Jesus accomplished, it is one that is antecedent to the more fundamental act of reconciliation. Just as we cannot imagine a relationship being "saved" without reconciliation between the parties, so it is that we cannot speak of salvation without primary reference to the more fundamental event of reconciliation. Salvation is possible only because reconciliation is possible. One might go further to say that since reconciliation is necessarily a mediated experience, making reconciliation the key metaphor for the life-event of Jesus establishes the necessity of the community. One needs others in order to be reconciled.[5]

The 20th-century saint and martyr Dietrich Bonhoeffer wrote about this in his letters, when he said that the point of Christianity is not salvation, or even religion: It is relationship with a weak and powerless God. God reconciles us through Christ who has let "himself be pushed out of the world on to the cross."[6] God helps us to be reconcilers not with power but with weakness; we embrace the ministry of reconciliation in the world *etsi deus not daretur* (as though God were not there).[7] If nothing else, Bonhoeffer's words confirm that concern about salvation has nothing to do with religion and is ultimately tantamount to spiritual self-indulgence. On the other side, concern about reconciliation is all-consuming and active; it engages the "other" and leaves questions about the afterlife to God. So the next time inquirers about the state of your salvation come to your door, you can respond by announcing that such a question is only penultimate in its urgency. The real question has to do with action on behalf of reconciliation.

If reconciliation is the core interpretation of Jesus' ministry, it suddenly makes sense that the dominant activity reported by the gospels is his eating and drinking with others. The meal signified a new reconciled relationship. It is a deep pastoral insight, especially if one reflects on how uncomfortable it is to be present at a meal when one participant has an unresolved claim against another. The kingdom that Jesus preached is the same kingdom Jesus ate and drank. It is a kingdom of plenty and presence: plenty because every hope of every human has been fulfilled in Christ and so the time of fasting is over; presence in that the kingdom is now and not just reserved for some future consummation. Jesus communes with others as a sign of a new communion, a new kingdom of reconciled relationships. All barriers as to with whom you may eat are removed: Welcome the gentiles, the tax collectors, the prostitutes, those with leprosy . . . and so on.

From the Kingdom to the Church: Baptism and Eucharist

The early 20th-century theologian Alfred Loisy reportedly made the observation that Jesus preached the kingdom, but what we got was the church! Even though Loisy was eventually excommunicated, he was essentially right; just as Jesus mediated the kingdom in his preaching and table fellowship, so too his followers developed a number of institutional strategies to keep Jesus' memory alive. Central to this process were two ritual activities, both connected in the historical ministry of Jesus: water baptism and sharing a meal in Jesus' memory. The first admitted one to the second, and the two were the great marks of identity for our early Christian ancestors. From the beginning, water baptism was the *primary* sign of reconciliation with God, while eucharist was the *ordinary* or normative sign of reconciliation, whereby right relationship with the community was a sign of reconciliation with God.

Joseph A. Favazza

Extraordinary Strategies of Reconciliation: A Survey of the History

Just as in our contemporary parishes, a few of the baptized in the early church did not fit the neat ritual categories and ended up betwixt and between. These were the folks that Paul and other early Christian writers tell us about who failed to live up to the faith and morals demanded by their new identity. New strategies of reconciliation—beyond the primary (baptism) and the ordinary (eucharist) strategies—had to be developed as responses to these "pastorally challenged" persons. In the beginning, the most common strategy was to isolate the sinners from the rest of the community lest they contaminate others by their sin. We get a glimpse of this in the threefold admonition found in the Gospel of Matthew.

> If another member of the church sins against you, go and point out the fault when the two of you are alone. If the member listens to you, you have regained that one. But if you are not listened to, take one or two others along with you, so that every word may be confirmed by the evidence of two or three witnesses. If the member refuses to listen to them, tell it to the church; and if the offender refuses to listen even to the church, let such a one be to you as a Gentile and a tax collector.[8]

By the third century, a shift occurred from mere social isolation to pastoral segregation. While some evidence suggests that penitents were present when the community gathered, they were prohibited from gathering at the table of the eucharist. We read the witness of Tertullian.

> Exomologesis, then, is a discipline which . . . bids the sinner to lie in sackcloth and ashes, to cover his body with filthy rags, to plunge his soul into sorrow, to exchange sin for suffering. Moreover, it demands that you know only such food and drink as is plain; this means it is taken for the sake of your soul, not your belly. It requires that you habitually nourish prayer by fasting . . . and weep and groan day and night to the Lord your God, that you prostrate yourself at the feet of the priests and kneel before the beloved of God, making all the brethren commissioned ambassadors of your prayer for pardon.[9]

This was the beginning of the order of penitents that parallelled the order of the catechumens and provided for a "one time only" means of reconciliation with the community. Tertullian called it the *paenitentia secunda,* a second penance that was available after the first penance of baptism.[10] What Tertullian lacked in specificity, his North African successor Cyprian, writing just fifty years after Tertullian, provided. With Cyprian we get the first witness to a rite of reconciliation by which a penitent was readmitted to the eucharist.

> One does penance for an appropriate period; the penitent then must make public confession after his life has been examined; and nobody can be admitted to communion without first having had hands laid on him by the bishop and clergy.[11]

In this critical third century, the process of reconciliation was both a pastoral and an extraordinary strategy. Pastorally, it was to help the sinner repent of his or her wrongdoing and be healed; yet it was always rare. Few actually undertook it; most sins were handled by the usual antidotes: prayer, fasting, almsgiving and most especially eucharist. In fact, this raises two points that bear repeating: Eucharist remained the *ordinary* ritual strategy to effect reconciliation, and reconciliation strategies beyond baptism and eucharist were legion!

By the fourth century, the order of penitents metamorphosed into canonical penance, with its imposition of harsh juridical obligations on the newly reconciled. These obligations ranged from lifelong exclusion from ecclesiastical office to lifelong celibacy. At the same time, we note a shift in the practice of excommunication. Before the fifth century, we see exclusion from communion as an invitation to reflect deeply on the scriptures and to undertake a reform of life. After this time, excommunication is slowly loosed from its sacramental moorings until it becomes a punitive action to control behavior and affirm the authority of the church to protect its goods. Certainly by the late Middle Ages, the practice of excommunication is nearly totally disconnected from the practice of reconciliation, a canonical situation that exists even to this very day.[12]

Other extraordinary strategies emerge in the sixth and seventh centuries with Celtic monastic penance, a practice based on a spiritual direction model of encounter. This was a more privatized form of penance and had the innovative feature of being repeatable. Eventually, its abuse in the form of tariffed penance (when every conceivable sin was matched with every conceivable penance that a penitent could then pay someone else to perform) led to greater definition as to what constituted "sacramental" reconciliation. By the end of the twelfth century, the Fourth Lateran Council defined the now well-known four required actions in sacramental penance: contrition, confession of sin, penance, absolution. It was a solution given popularity by Thomas Aquinas and official sanction by the Council of Trent.

Yet, other strategies of reconciliation still abounded throughout the Middle Ages. Besides canonical penance, which remained a valid liturgical form until the Council of Trent (though rarely used), individual works of mercy, pilgrimage to certain shrines and fighting in the Crusades are but a few examples. Perhaps the plethora of ways for sins to be forgiven can be understood against the backdrop of the extreme drop-off in the reception of communion by the faithful. In practice, the eucharist loses its place as the primary sacrament of reconciliation; as a result, other extraordinary strategies emerge to fill the void.

The Legacy of Trent: Extraordinary Becomes Ordinary

With the Council of Trent's need to reaffirm, reassert and reconform Catholic teaching and practice in the face of the Reformation, private ecclesiastical penance controlled entirely by the ordained was canonized over all other forms of reconciliation.[13] Reading Trent, one cannot find any hint that this ritual practice both began as an extraordinary pastoral response and took a variety of ritual forms throughout its history. Rather, the rhetoric of Trent attempts to convince believers that the sacrament in its present incarnation existed from the earliest days of the church. Trent affirms that reconciliation was individual rather than ecclesial, having to do with the restoration of personal purity. Rather than an end in and of itself, reconciliation was now confirmed as the means to salvation. Trent canonized the trajectory of the sacrament throughout the Middle Ages: Reconciliation became a juridic, clerical and privatized practice that purified you before communion or death, whichever came first.

Such a definition left some obvious casualties. First, it sealed the loss of reconciliation as the core Christian metaphor and made reconciliation subordinate to a privatized notion of salvation. Second, with its truncated view of history and tradition, Trent gutted eucharist as the ordinary sacrament of reconciliation. Third, it replaced eucharist with "confession" as the ordinary sacrament of reconciliation and, by so doing, canonized the already ingrained practice of confession before communion. Fourth, it defined reconciliation only through a juridic, privatized and clerical lens; all sense of reconciliation being an ecclesial act with the community having an integral role to play as reconciler is lost.

The Rite of Penance (1973): A Mixed Bag

When the Second Vatican Council called for the reform of the sacraments noting that "[l]iturgical services are not private functions" and that "rites which are meant to be celebrated in common, with the faithful present and actively participating, should as far as possible be celebrated in that way rather than by an individual and quasi-privately," it probably had no idea how contentious sacramental reconciliation would be.[14] The drafting of the new rite of penance took over six years, involved two different commissions and resulted in the production of more than twelve schemas. It brought into focus the disagreement between those who wished to hold onto Trent's juridic vision and those who wanted the new rite to be informed by the broader tradition.[15] What we get with the 1973 *Rite of Penance* is essentially a compromise between these two visions. For our purposes here, we note the second paragraph of the rite's *praenotanda* that can be seen as an attempt to recover a theology of reconciliation in baptism, eucharist and sacramental penance.

> The victory is first brought to light in baptism where our fallen nature is crucified with Christ so that the body of sin may be destroyed and we may no longer be slaves to sin, but rise with

Christ and live for God. For this reason, the church proclaims its faith in "one baptism for the forgiveness of sins."

In the sacrifice of the Mass, the passion of Christ is again made present; his body given for us and his blood shed for the forgiveness of sins are offered to God again by the church for the salvation of the world. For in the eucharist Christ is present and is offered as "the sacrifice which has made our peace" with God and in order that "we may be brought together in unity" by his Holy Spirit.

Furthermore, our Savior Jesus Christ, when he gave to his apostles and their successors power to forgive sins, instituted in his church the sacrament of penance. Its purpose is that the faithful who fall into sin after baptism may be reconciled with God through the restoration of grace. The church "possesses both water and tears: the water of baptism, the tears of penance."[16]

While neither using the language of primary, ordinary and extraordinary, nor attempting to define the relationship between them, the rite does identify more than one sacrament of reconciliation. The vision of the renewed rite, mixed as it is, has inspired ongoing historical research and pastoral experimentation to recover the broader tradition.[17]

Where Do We Go From Here?

What does all this mean for a Catholic community serious about the renewal of the tradition of sacramental reconciliation? At the risk of sounding pedantic, our history leads to some obvious conclusions. First, the eucharist really is the ordinary sacrament of reconciliation. It is the heart of it all—that to which reconciliation leads and from which reconciliation goes. Pastors and catechists have been saying this since the Second Vatican Council; perhaps one way to interpret the non-practice of the sacrament of penance in our parishes is that we finally got the message.

Second, baptismal (primary) and post-baptismal (extraordinary) reconciliation both lead to the table of the eucharist. They are parallel journeys but without parallel rituals. Is there a problem here? Third, sacramental reconciliation must be multi-strategic. No ritual is a "one size fits all." If the tradition teaches us anything, it is that this, rather than the ritual conformity demanded by Trent, is our authentic history. Simply put, present extraordinary strategies of reconciliation do little more than maintain the essential paradigm proposed by Trent; as such, they have become inadequate as rituals and pastoral practices.

Fourth, it is time to explore what it means to be both a community of judgment and a community of reconciliation. How should we exercise judgment that does not exclude the possibility of reconciliation? In the past, our judgment has been exercised juridically through such strategies as censure and excommunication. Such strategies are medieval accretions that must be excised; otherwise, we will continue to be stuck in our present situation where eucharist is the very thing that breaks us apart.[18] One of the great pastoral challenges we face is how to manage table fellowship that both excludes and embraces. It is to this important issue we must now turn.

The Reciprocity Model of Interpretation

Like it or not, the community of believers must undertake the difficult and daunting task of interpreting the tradition about Jesus the Christ. Based on this interpretive enterprise, the entire church has the authority to teach doctrine, ethical norms and ritual activity. In the Catholic tradition, the authority of the entire church is exercised by the members of the hierarchical magisterium, who have the unique role by virtue of their office of interpreting the tradition and teaching authoritatively.[19] In other words, the teaching church (the magisterium) must make judgments about the living tradition that keeps us connected to the reconciling life-project of Jesus. It is an incredibly difficult job; yet, to abdicate this necessary interpretive task is to petrify the tradition. After all, we ascribe to a living tradition rather than a dead one.

But the very activity of interpreting a living tradition is fraught with possibilities and problems. On the one hand, where the interpretive activity is so hidden by the authority of the interpreter that it is no longer viewed as an interpretive judgment but Truth itself, this leads to dogmaticism, objectivism and a reification of the tradition that makes it less responsive to contemporary issues. As a church, we have been there and done that. We only can hope we are not moving in this direction again.[20] On the other hand, to view the interpretative process without any reference to the authority of the one interpreting leads to subjectivism, situationalism and a bending of the tradition to fit every opinion and lifestyle. In this scenario, the teaching of the church becomes just one more voice among many voices, all equally right, with none but my own having any power to bind or influence thought and behavior.

William E. Paden, in his book *Interpreting the Sacred,* develops another way to approach the dilemma of the interpretative process.[21] He calls it the reciprocity model and it should not sound too startling to those of us with analogically imaginative ears![22] Paden holds that the world gives itself to us to be interpreted. There is a reality out there, but it can never be grasped in and of itself; rather, "reality" is the point of contact between the object of interpretation and the context and experience of the interpreter. To perceive any reality is to perceive it as something. Hence, a reciprocity exists between reality "out there" and how it is interpreted "in here." Such a perspective affirms two principles, both them equally important for a religious person in a pluralistic age.

First, reality is more than we grasp, so we should focus on affirming that which we interpret and to which we commit ourselves rather than denying what others interpret and to which they commit themselves. Second, what we affirm is ultimately an interpretation that cannot be separated from the context (that interrated network of experiences, beliefs, cultural influences, psychological and genetic make-up, timing, place, authority, etc.) of the one engaged in the interpretive process.[23]

Applying this model to our ecclesial situation today, we affirm, indeed, must affirm that the teaching church must make judgments. Sometimes these judgments are hard to swallow or, more radically, put individuals or groups of persons in direct conflict with the hierarchical magisterium. Such conflict can take many shapes but conflict really is not the problem here. Conflict in our community is proof that the tradition is so alive that we need to bring it into dialogue with the most contentious issues of our day. Conflict is a sign that the Catholic community deeply values the tradition that effects continuity with the past and identity in the present. Finally, conflict reminds us that we live in a community of adults who both refuse paternal treatment and desire gentle direction.

Even if the teaching church creates conflict from its interpretative judgments about the tradition, the tradition itself is conflictual. So it is with a church that has a strong tradition of laws yet a stronger tradition of dispensations, a strong tradition of respect for authority yet a stronger tradition of freedom of conscience, a strong tradition of excommunication yet a stronger tradition of reconciliation.[24] As an entire chorus of contemporary theologians have indicated, conflicting traditions are but one more sign of our wonderful Catholic analogical way of imagining the world.[25] It has been speculated that another word for grace in Catholic tradition is schizophrenia. Thank God; otherwise we would be tediously consistent.

The rub, then, is not the conflict but what to do with the conflict, especially when one can find support within the tradition to uphold both the magisterial authority and the authority of the individual. One way, and the way with which we seem to be most familiar and comfortable, is a juridical model that condemns or excommunicates individuals or groups. This model assumes that the best way to handle conflict is not to confront it but to sweep it under the rug, or perhaps better, out the door. Excommunication, however, spends more time denying the position of the "out group" than affirming the position of the interpreter. It also devalues the context of interpretation by canonizing the interpretation of one group while "demonizing" in some way the position of the other. While notorious examples range from our handling of the Protestant Reformation to the recent excommunication (and later rescinding of the excommunication) of the Ski Lankan theologian Tissa Balasuriya, less notable examples exist in every parish. Even if parish ministers attempt to overcome the juridical obstacles in particular cases, it is too late to rescind the implicit message that law is more important than love.

Another model, based on Paden's reciprocity model, might be called a relational model. Here, the teaching church does not abandon its prophetic responsibility to interpret the tradition, but does so with

Joseph A. Favazza

one eye on its own interpretive context. In this model, tradition would not be viewed as a self-contained box of jewels to be opened every time someone disagrees with or doubts some as aspect of doctrine. Rather, tradition is understood as the result of a reciprocity between its expressions throughout history and our contemporary context. The hoped-for result would be the continued commitment of the teaching church to make interpretative judgments about the tradition without feeling threatened by others who have come to different judgments about it. In a relational model, the energy spent is on the articulation of, and commitment to, what is affirmed rather than on the "demonizing" of what is denied. One hallmark of such a model is a willingness to enter a dialogue about points of disagreement rather than issue summary judgments of condemnation or, worse, refuse even to put a matter on the table.

As a church, we must find a way to stay faithful to the necessary interpretive enterprise without doing so in a way that is alienating. Interpretation is always contextual and therefore necessarily open to reform. Adults need not be threatened when other adults disagree; in fact, disagreement may be the opportunity to deepen a friendship, begin a relationship or grow as a person. The church's ability to reform itself and to be reformed, as noted by the Second Vatican Council, is more than just a case of revisiting old instances of exceptional ecclesial hubris; it is an invitation to relationship and to reconciliation, based on the understanding that no one interpretation of the gospel can fully contain the gospel.[26]

If the authority of the teaching church is to survive in a pluralistic world, where even the baptized hold different and diverse views and practices among themselves, it will do so not by being exercised in ways that exclude but in ways that are relational, reconciling and seek to be inclusive. Certainly it might be argued that such an approach by the hierarchical magisterium might blur our ecclesial borders, slacken ecclesial identity and send an "anything goes" message regarding faith, morals and discipline. There is no denying this risk. Yet, the risk of blurring lines — say between saint and sinner, woman and man, Gentile and Jew, clergy and lay — seems to be an important part of our tradition. The point is to move away from a juridic approach with its harsh call to conformity, and toward a relational approach with its gentle yet insistent invitation to reform. What we would be left with is not a message that "anything goes," but a gospel that affirms that no one is irreconcilable.

Models of Extraordinary Reconciliation

If we are serious about creating a reconciling church in a pluralistic age, what implications does this have for the sacramental practice of what we have called extraordinary reconciliation? Based on the ideas, insights and experiences of countless others, I have identified three approaches to ritualized reconciliation that have emerged and are emerging in our sacramental practice. Since this is literally a work in progress, I am not prepared to spend much time giving flesh to each approach. However, I put them here now to evoke reaction and response.

Reconciliation as restitution/satisfaction with emphasis on restoration

This approach assumes that sin is some "karma-like" entity that always must be accounted for. The "stain" on the soul resulting from unacceptable acts of commission or omission can be removed or satisfied only through the acts of confession, contrition and penance by the sinner and the granting of absolution by a bishop or priest. Once the sin is removed, purity is restored, at least until the next act of sin. Based on a medieval understanding that defined the human person solely in terms of act, grace becomes that divine power that restores the sinner back to a previous state.[27] Essentially, as we have emphasized earlier, this is Trent's vision. While some pastoral situations demand restitution before the penitent can return to the table, for the most part this approach to sin no longer fits more complex cases of alienation. Nonetheless, this is the approach modeled by our current rites of extraordinary reconciliation found in the 1973 Rite of Penance.

Reconciliation as mediated resolution with emphasis on compromise

Mediation is the hard task of finding a working compromise between two or more sides in conflict. As a church, we do not have much experience with this, perhaps as a result of a juridic approach to conflict where authority has been exercised in a summary way without benefit of prior dialogue. In a word, neither the teaching church nor individual church members have done a very good job of keeping the dialogue open with those who disagree with them. In the future, I hope we will see more instances of the teaching church and church members being willing to enter a dialogue with others about differences. Bringing a sacramental dimension into it, points of agreement could be ritualized. Again, the point here is to affirm different beliefs rather than to deny the validity of other perspectives. Our rituals here must be hopeful enough to celebrate a shared agreement or covenant, yet honest enough to recognize that such an agreement may or may not get us to the table of the eucharist. The value of this approach is that conflict is not swept out the door, but is recognized by both sides who must create a safe place where different interpretations of the tradition can be discussed and respected. Relationship is more important than difference, love more important than law. In case this all sounds familiar, it is based on an ecumenical model that has unlimited potential as a sacramental rite.[28]

Reconciliation as emancipatory transformation with emphasis on integration

In this approach, an act-centered understanding of the human person gives way to a deep appreciation of human alienation in all of its existential depth. At the pastoral level, the kinds of experiences that have occasioned alienation from the table usually are not act-centered faults in moral perfection, but are complex patterns of behaviors and attitudes. Experiences of addiction, dysfunctional relationships, emotional and physical abuse, changes in life partners and commitments, deep-seated memories of violence, rejection, anger—all these are but examples of the kinds of alienation found in every faith community.

This third approach to sacramental reconciliation is process- and community-centered: A single sacramental encounter gives way to a process that demands the commitment of the community in a variety of ministries celebrating a variety of rituals over time. The support offered must be unconditional; otherwise, the safe place where reconciliation can occur is violated. As every twelve-step group knows, once a person has experienced something, it cannot be unexperienced; the single experience itself must be assimilated into all of the other experiences of a life. In the same way, this approach to sacramental reconciliation attends carefully to this journey of integration, not with the goal of restoring a person back to a pure state but leading one to a new place, a renegotiated place, a place of integration and liberating transformation. This journey toward emancipatory reconciliation leads to the eucharistic table, where we encounter the living memory of Jesus the liberator and healer.[29] In case this all sounds familiar, it is an approach modeled by the "ReMembering Church" workshop of the North American Forum on the Catechumenate and by parishes around the country that are experimenting with new approaches to the ministry of reconciliation.

Conclusion

The tradition of reconciliation in our Catholic tradition is the pearl of great price. It gives us a powerful voice to speak to the instances of alienation found in our contemporary context, including the alienation between some of the baptized and the teaching church. Yet, if we cannot figure out a way to be relational, reconciling and inclusive within the borders of our own community of faith, our witness to the world is seriously diminished. How can we speak words of justice and forgiveness to groups and individuals who have trampled civil and human rights when we refuse even to dialogue with our own family members who disagree with us or who are struggling under the weight of their own alienation? The very tradition of the table of the eucharist as a table of reconciliation must be preserved not just as orthodoxy but as orthopraxis. Perhaps in some small way the episodes and pastoral approaches raised in this article might assist us in "coloring outside the lines" and to move us through our present conundrum.

1. Colossians 1:20.

2. Joseph Cardinal Ratzinger, "Commentary on Profession of Faith's Concluding Paragraphs," *Origins* 28 (July 16, 1998): 116–9.

3. *Catechism of the Catholic Church* (Washington: USCC—Libreria Editrice Vaticana, 1994), 357–8.

4. 2 Corinthians 5:17–19.

5. This is not to say that one does not need others to be saved. However, salvation as a theological category has been so privatized by truncated understandings of role of the community that, at the very least, one can argue that the term reconciliation carries less theological "baggage" as a mediated experience.

6. Dietrich Bonhoeffer, *Letters and Papers from Prison,* edited by Eberhard Bethge (London: SCM Press, 1971), 360–1.

7. Ibid.

8. Matthew 18:15–17. For a discussion of isolation as a penitential strategy during the first two centuries see my *The Order of Penitents* (Collegeville, MN: The Liturgical Press, 1987), 68–120.

9. Tertullian, *De paenitentia* 9.3–4, in William Le Saint, trans., *Tertullian: Treatises on Penance,* Ancient Christian Writers 28 (New York: Newman Press, 1959), 31–2.

10. Tertullian, *De paenitentia* 7.

11. Cyprian of Carthage, Letter 17 2.1, in G. W. Clarke, trans., *The Letters of St. Cyprian of Carthage: Letters 1–27,* Ancient Christian Writers 43 (New York: Newman Press, 1984), 97.

12. For example, see the 1983 *Code of Canon Law,* canons 1354–1363, as to how various penalties, many of which involve excommunication, are remitted.

13. James Dallen, "History and the Reform of Penance," in Robert J. Kennedy, ed., *Reconciling Embrace: Foundations for the Future of Sacramental Reconciliation* (Chicago: Liturgy Training Publications, 1998), 86.

14. Vatican II, Constitution on the Sacred Liturgy (*Sacrosanctum concilium*) 26–7, in W. Abbott, ed., *The Documents of Vatican II,* rev. ed. (Grand Rapids: Eerdmans, 1992), 26–7.

15. See James Dallen, *Reconciling Community* (New York: Pueblo, 1986), 209–27.

16. *Penance and Reconciliation in the Church* (Washington: USCC, 1975), 12.

17. One notes the intervention by Joseph Cardinal Bernadin at the 1983 Synod of Bishops recommending a fourth form of the rite modeled on the Rite of Christian Initiation of Adults and the resulting work by The North American Forum on the Catechumenate to develop such a model in its "ReMembering Church" workshops.

18. John Paul II, in his post-synodal apostolic exhortation, *Reconciliation and Penance* (Washington: USCC, 1984), 135, explains that those who have divorced and have entered into non-canonical marriages cannot celebrate the sacraments "until such time they attain the required dispositions."

19. The debate continues as to whether the hierarchical magisterium only includes the pope and the bishops or also includes those with scholarly competence. See Richard McBrien, *Catholicism,* rev. ed. (San Francisco: HarperSanFrancisco, 1994), 65–6. While my reading of early Christian literature supports McBrien's belief that these sources assign magisterial authority to those with scholarly competence, it would take us too far afield to develop a cogent argument here.

20. However, the recent apostolic letter, issued *moto proprio,* by John Paul II, *Ad Tuendam Fidem,* is not a hopeful sign. See *Origins* 28 (16 July 1998): 114–6.

21. William E. Paden, *Interpreting the Sacred* (Boston: Beacon Press, 1992), 125–35.

22. Paden's reciprocity model touches on what Richard McBrien calls critical realism and what Bernard Lonergan calls Christian realism. See McBrien, 1192–6.

23. Paden, 110–24.

24. McBrien, 1195–6.

25. David Tracy, *The Analogical Imagination* (New York: Crossroad, 1981), 193–229; Andrew Greeley, *The Catholic Myth* (New York: Collier, 1990), 34–64; Richard McBrien, 15, just to name a few.

26. On the teaching of the Second Vatican Council on the ongoing reformability of the church, see the Dogmatic Constitution on the Church *(Lumen gentium)* 8, and the Decree on Ecumenism *(Unitatis redintegratio)* 6.

27. Timothy E. O'Connell, "A Theology of Sin," in Lawrence Cunningham, ed., *A Catholic Reader* (New York: Paulist Press, 1988), 199–202.

28. This approach apparently led to the recent reconciliation of Tissa Balasuriya with the church. See the fascinating description of the "conflict resolution" process in "On File," *Origins* 27 (12 March 1998): 630.

29. For a wonderful reflection on the connection between reconciliation and what she calls "emancipatory anamnesis," see Toinette M. Eugene, "Reconciliation in the Pastoral Context of Today's Church and World," in Robert J. Kennedy, ed., 1–14.

Maxwell E. Johnson

The "Real" and Multiple "Presences" of Christ in Contemporary Lutheran Liturgical and Sacramental Practice

In this article I will reflect briefly from within my own Lutheran ecclesial tradition on what an Evangelical Lutheran Church in America (ELCA) liturgical-sacramental practice and theology that took seriously the multiple presences of Christ underscored by paragraph 7 of Vatican II's *Constitution on the Sacred Liturgy* (hereafter, CSL 7) would look like. In doing so, I simply must state up front that there is a certain artificial quality about this exercise from the very beginning. To take what is a Roman Catholic "recovery" of the multiple presences of Christ in the church and then apply that "recovery" to a Lutheran—or even Anglican or Protestant—liturgical-sacramental context seems to me, at first sight anyway, to move in a backward direction. That is, the emphases of CSL 7 on the multiple "real" presences of Christ in the church within its liturgies—the ministers, the eucharistic species, the sacraments in general, the word, and the community itself at prayer[1]—sound to Lutheran ears, at least, like a Roman Catholic vindication of what the Lutheran Reformers themselves argued within the overall context of the 16th century.

The Lutheran Confessions, for example, could not be clearer in their assertion that what traditionally has been called the "means of grace" includes, rather broadly, the spoken Word, baptism, eucharist, the power of the keys (confession and absolution) and the "mutual conversation and consolation of brethren,"[2] while being unconcerned with the precise enumeration of what may or may not be called specific "sacraments."[3] Similarly, at least Lutherans would want to point out that with regard to the presence of Christ in the "ministers," the Confessions again not only equate the "office" of ministry with word and sacrament as the very means by which the church is called into being by the Holy Spirit in the first place,[4] but have no qualms in asserting that the ordained "do not represent their own persons but the person of Christ" *(repraesentat Christi personam)* and that "when they offer the Word of Christ or the sacraments, they do so in Christ's place and stead" *(Christi vice et loco porrigunt).*[5] As such, ordination itself can appropriately be called a "sacrament" by Lutherans[6] if for no other reason than that the ordained, "representing" the person of Christ in and to the church through the actual doing of the ministry of word and sacrament, become themselves concrete, embodied or "sacramental" signs of Christ's continued presence.

At the same time, a Lutheran reading of CSL 7, especially with regard to the presence of Christ in the community itself, would want to underscore that the ecclesiology of the Lutheran Confessions is precisely an ecclesiology of the liturgical assembly: "The church is the assembly of saints [or believers] in which the gospel is taught purely and the sacraments are administered rightly."[7] And—might I be so bold as to point out—it was Luther himself, who, while limiting the number of sacraments to three, based on the defining criteria he *inherited* from the Western medieval tradition, nevertheless stated, in words that sound downright prophetic vis-à-vis modern Roman Catholic sacramental theology, that "if I were to speak according to the usage of the scriptures, I should have only one *single* sacrament [Christ; see 1 Timothy 3:16], but with three sacramental signs."[8]

Hence, when Lutherans read CSL 7, or read in the 1993 Directory for Ecumenism that baptism "constitutes the sacramental bond of unity existing among all who through it are reborn,"[9] or hear Pope John Paul II say in his 1995 encyclical *Ut Unum Sint* that "in the fellowship of prayer Christ is truly present; he prays 'in us,' 'with us,' and 'for us,' "[10] they recognize a common theological bond, heritage and participation in the "real" presence of Christ. And, they would underscore strongly the following statement by Karl Rahner and Heinrich Fries about the very *sacramentality* of the Word itself:

> *Pulpit fellowship* is already being practiced in many cases; and it no longer presents a disquieting exception, even to Catholic Christians. But one really should think about this more than ever, *since it is precisely a pulpit fellowship which presupposes a community of faith.* Consider the reality of salvation of the Word of God; consider Christ's presence in its various forms, including the form of proclamation; finally consider the theological conformity of Word and Sacrament — sacrament as visible Word *(verbum visibile),* the Word as audible sacrament *(sacramentum audible).*[11]

Because there is so much in common between CSL 7 and the classic Lutheran confession, liturgy and theology, *the* question is *not* really how the *Roman Catholic* recovery of the multiple presences of Christ might shape *Lutheran* liturgical-sacramental practice and theology (even if Lutherans would most grateful for this recovery in Roman Catholic thought and practice). Rather, the question is what does a Lutheran liturgical-sacramental practice and theology look like when, in an ecumenical context, it takes its own classic tradition seriously? With regard to this I will divide my comments into two major sections: (1) What in fact has been and is happening toward a richer liturgical-sacramental life among Lutherans, especially those of the ELCA; and (2) What factors still need serious attention?

Developments toward a Richer Liturgical-Sacramental Life among Lutherans

The general answer to the question of what a Lutheran liturgical-sacramental life looks like that takes the multiple presences of Christ seriously is rather simple. Given the commonality in texts, rites and rubrics in the worship books of Lutherans and Roman Catholics today, it looks very much like what post – Vatican II Roman Catholic worship is also supposed to look like: that is, where the word of God is proclaimed clearly, audibly, intelligibly and with dignity by carefully prepared readers; where ministers, presiding and otherwise, know their particular roles in the assembly and carry them out in a manner befitting the worship of the trinitarian God; where bread that looks, smells, feels and tastes like (and, of course, *is*) real bread is broken and shared and where wine, rich and good wine, is shared in common; where the other sacraments or "sacramental rites" are seen as corporate and communal events with the rich and abundant use of water and oil and the healing and benedictory gestures of handlaying and touch; where the Liturgy of the Hours is the church being itself in its constant, prayerful, eschatological, intercessory and expectant vigil; where the Triduum is seen as the pulsating center and heartbeat not only of the liturgical year but of life in Christ; and where the community itself, both in assembling to do *leitourgia* and in scattering for its missions of *martyria* and *diakonia* knows itself—"fully, actively, and consciously"—as that Body of Christ it receives and celebrates so that it may itself be broken for the life of the world. Indeed, within these general themes, there are several positive developments to note and to celebrate among contemporary Lutherans.

First, as the *Lutheran Book of Worship* makes clear, the place, dignity and celebration of baptism, including infant baptism, within the public liturgical assembly of the church is emphasized. Similar emphasis is given to immersion as the preferred mode of baptism, and to the postbaptismal handlaying and anointing to signify the baptismal gift of the "seal" of the Holy Spirit. In this regard there is a shift toward providing baptismal pools and fonts that facilitate immersion. At the same time, between 1987 and 1996 the ELCA alone, according to the annual reports of 10,196 reporting congregations, celebrated some 32,615 adult baptisms.[12] Not surprisingly, then, the renewing and formative power of the Catholic RCIA has led to new and recent adaptations of the catechumenal process in Lutheran circles—including Missouri Synod and Evangelical Lutheran Church in Canada (ELCiC) cooperation—with the development of several catechumenal and liturgical resources under the general title of *Welcome to Christ*.[13] And along with this, of course, comes the continual need and opportunity for the development and training of parish catechists and sponsors, and the reorganization and renewal of parish life in general centered around sacramental-liturgical formation and catechesis. While still in its infancy among Lutherans, such holds great promise for the future.

With further regard to issues concerning Christian initiation, it should also be noted here that, like the unbroken initiatory tradition of the Eastern Orthodox churches, and like the Episcopal Church USA, the express wishes of the American Catholic Federation of Diocesan Liturgical Commissions,[14] and its Canadian Lutheran (ELCiC) neighbors to the north,[15] the ELCA has also moved decisively toward instituting the communion of all the baptized, including the first communion of newly baptized infants, within the baptismal eucharist. The ELCA's recently approved 1997 statement on sacramental practices, *The Use of the Means of Grace: A Statement on the Practice of Word and Sacrament,* says clearly that "infants and children may be communed for the first time during the service in which they are baptized."[16] Although this statement was not officially adopted until August, 1997, sixty congregations reported in 1995 that communion was, in fact, already being given "in infancy" within their parishes. Such is surely a harbinger of things to come within the ELCA.

Second, in spite of some fears among Lutherans of "becoming too Roman Catholic" in liturgical-sacramental practice, there is no question but that the recovery of the Lutheran confessional norm of the centrality of Sunday and feast day eucharist is gradually happening within the ELCA. Thanks in part to the influence of Gordon Lathrop's recent book, *Holy Things: A Liturgical Theology,*[17] Lutherans are increasingly coming to understand that the very *ordo* of Christian liturgy is constituted by the Sunday assembly of the baptized, who gather, hear the word, share the meal and are sent on mission in the world. Indeed, what some have begun to refer to as "Gordo's Ordo," — based on the resurrection appearances of Jesus in the New Testament (cf. especially the Emmaus account in Luke 24), the mid-second century description of Justin Martyr in his First Apology, and the liturgical ecclesiology of the Lutheran Confessions — is clearly the conceptual framework behind not only the recent Lutheran liturgical resource *With One Voice,* but the recent ELCA statement *The Use of the Means of Grace.* Whereas in 1989 only 1,690 of the 10,196 reporting ELCA congregations listed the celebration of eucharist on every Sunday as their normal practice, that number in 1995 almost doubled to 2,305. If in relationship to Roman Catholic practice that still sounds rather low, one should remember that within the not so distant past the norm for those churches now comprising the ELCA[18] was a celebration of eucharist only on the first Sunday of the month, and within the first half of this century, the norm in those churches was the continuation of the late medieval practice of communion reception only four times a year. To have moved, then, from this to a situation where over 20% of ELCA congregations now celebrate eucharist at least every Sunday is highly significant.

Hand in hand with this recovery of more frequent celebration of the eucharist is a dramatic change in the style of celebration, so dramatic, in fact, that contemporary celebrations of the eucharist among Lutherans, Roman Catholics, Episcopalians and others often look, sound and are essentially the same. This change is due in no small part to the ecumenical nature and influence of the liturgical movement. It is for this reason that I often challenge my Roman Catholic undergraduate students at Notre Dame to experience liturgy at some of the local Lutheran and Episcopalian parishes in the South Bend and Mishawaka area of northern Indiana and tell me what they perceive to be the real differences in relation to the experience of their own parishes (with the general exception of the fact that people might regularly sing better in these other places). And, Professor James White likes to say of his own United Methodist parish, Broadway United Methodist Church in South Bend, that the primary difference, compared with Roman Catholic practice, is that Broadway uses real bread while Roman Catholics use real wine.[19] (Another major difference, of course, is that one might actually encounter an ordained woman presider, vested in alb, stole and chasuble, in some of these churches.)

Lectors, communion ministers and lay assistant ministers who often fulfill roles at the liturgy that are traditionally assigned to deacons in some traditions are frequently employed in contemporary Lutheran practice. Between the minister's (or altar) edition of the *Lutheran Book of Worship* and the recently published supplement,

With One Voice, ELCA Lutherans now have at least 14 complete eucharistic prayers available for their use, a highly significant development when one considers that the use of any eucharistic prayer—beyond preface, Sanctus and institution narrative—has been an issue of some argument and debate within Lutheran circles for the past 30 years or so.

At the same time, the recovery of the centrality of the eucharist has led to a concern for the inclusion of those unable to attend the Sunday assembly due to illness, hospitalization and other factors. Here is to be noted the increasingly frequent practice among Lutherans of using lay ministers who are dismissed from the Sunday assembly in order to bring communion to the sick and homebound from the Sunday liturgy itself, again along the lines of Justin Martyr's own mid-second century description of this practice and some 16th-century Lutheran *Church Order* practices.[20] Using a new-for-Lutherans rite of "Celebration of Holy Communion with Those in Special Circumstances,"[21] in which the already "consecrated" eucharistic gifts are shared in the context of the reading of the word and prayer, has not only fostered some kind of recovery of the propriety of eucharistic reservation for the communion of the sick but has actually led in some places to the practice of ongoing eucharistic reservation itself. In South Bend and Mishawaka, for example, at least three of the seven ELCA parishes regularly reserve the eucharist—both bread and wine—in a visible ambry somewhere within their worship spaces. One of these parishes does so even on the former high altar in the very center of its worship space, and another of them, for good or ill, not only regularly uses this reserved eucharist for distribution to the assembly on Sundays in addition to the newly consecrated bread and wine, but, in clear imitation of current Roman Catholic practice, actually distributes communion to the assembly on Good Friday from what was solemnly reserved in a special place at the conclusion of the Holy Thursday liturgy the evening before.

Third, an ELCA Lutheran focus on the multiple presences of Christ in the liturgy would not limit the signification of that "presence" either to the particular gender of ministers, presiding and otherwise, nor to being in a situation of "full communion" with a specific ecclesial tradition. With regard to the reading and proclamation of the word of God itself, ELCA Lutherans have not only recently adopted and adapted the *Revised Common Lectionary* but now use regularly the *New Revised Standard Version* of the Bible as that translation has come to be offered, finally, in an actual, large and dignified lectionary designed for Lutheran liturgical use.

Given the fact that both male and female together reflect the very "image of God," according to Genesis 1:26–27, and given Saint Paul's radical baptismal reversal of ethnicity, social status and gender in terms of the identity of the church itself in Christ, according to Galatians 3:28 (in Christ Jesus "there is no longer Jew nor Greek . . . slave nor free . . . *male nor female*" [emphasis added]), ELCA Lutherans—as several other ecclesial traditions today—have been able to receive gratefully the gift of women's ordination to the office of ministry in the church and have, albeit with some resistance and difficulty, accepted women pastors among those who "do not represent their own persons but the person of Christ" and who, "when they offer the word of Christ or the sacraments, they do so in Christ's place and stead."

With regard to ecumenism, ELCA Lutherans hold that since "admission to the [eucharist] is by invitation of the Lord presented through the church to those who are baptized,"[22] eucharistic hospitality toward members of other Christian traditions is practiced. To that end, "all baptized persons are welcomed to communion when they are visiting in the congregations of [the ELCA],"[23] and "when a wedding or a funeral occurs during [the eucharist], communion is offered to all baptized persons."[24] Eucharistic hospitality to individuals, however, should not be taken as a substitute for the pursuit of "full" communion between different churches, a goal toward which the ELCA is also oriented and firmly committed.

At the same time, the practice of eucharistic hospitality and the goal of full communion between currently separated churches are related. Viewed as constituting a *source* for and means *toward* full communion, rather than simply the *expression* or *summit* of Christian unity, the ELCA and Episcopal Church USA, recognizing substantial agreement between themselves on various issues of doctrine and practice, have been involved together since the early 1980's in an officially recognized "interim eucharistic sharing" together leading toward the eventual establishment of full communion.

But with regard to the sharing of the eucharist between Lutherans and Roman Catholics — in light of the above-quoted statement of Roman Catholic theologians Karl Rahner and Heinrich Fries that "a pulpit fellowship . . . presupposes a community of faith," that Christ is "present" in "the form of proclamation," and that there is a "theological conformity of word *and* sacrament — sacrament as visible word *(verbum visibile)*, the word as audible sacrament *(sacramentum audible)*," and pointing to CSL 7 as well as to other recent Vatican statements on the sharing of the "real" presence of Christ in word, baptism, assembly and prayer in common, ELCA Lutherans might wonder how seriously such "modes" of Christ's *real* presence are actually taken in and by the Roman Catholic church. Indeed, if Christ is *present* in such multiple ways, then he is *"really"* present. And if his *"real"* presence in the word is acknowledged to exist in other communions to such an extent that the ELCA and the American Roman Catholic bishops could actually produce a (now already out of print) "Lutheran-Catholic Service of the Word" for common use, then what *does* the "theological conformity of word *and* sacrament" actually imply? If divided Christians can already share *some* "modes" of that *"real"* presence *officially,* why not the eucharistic mode as well?

Similarly, with the Lutheran World Federation and Vatican "Joint Declaration on the Doctrine of Justification," signifying, finally, a rather explicit and substantial *unity in faith* between Lutherans and Roman Catholics, one can only wonder what kinds of implications for eucharistic hospitality or "interim eucharistic sharing" might eventually result. But in the meantime, because ELCA Lutherans see a consistency in theology flowing from the conformity of audible word and visible word (sacrament), welcoming all the baptized to Christ's inclusive, egalitarian and community-building table companionship naturally follows. Both word and sacrament, in Lutheran thought at least, function together under the category of the "proclamation" of the gospel, one an audible proclamation, the other visible.

Fourth, and finally for this section, other liturgical-sacramental practices recovered among contemporary ELCA Lutherans in the years since Vatican II should at least be noted as they relate to this question of "multiple presences." In the *Lutheran Book of Worship* and *With One Voice,* ELCA Lutherans have for their use a style of the Liturgy of the Hours clearly rooted in the "cathedral" rather than "monastic" tradition, at least with regard to evening prayer and its *lucernarium* and Psalm 141. Regular provisions for private confession and absolution, as well as corporate confession and absolution, have been made in the current worship books. There has even been a recovery of the practice of the laying on of hands and "anointing of the sick," with forms provided for individual use in ministering to the sick and for public celebrations within a eucharistic liturgy or liturgy of the word,[25] forms that several congregations employ on a fairly regular basis. And of course, at least in principle, the importance of preaching the word of God has remained a constant and abiding emphasis. All in all, with regard then to the multiple presences of Christ in word, meal, assembly, ministers, sacraments and prayer, the practice and theology of the ELCA, at least according to the texts of its rites and its statements, has been one of recovering its classic liturgical-sacramental heritage within a contemporary ecumenical context. As such, an ELCA liturgical-sacramental practice that takes the multiple presences of Christ seriously looks a lot like the vision of Vatican II and the worship books of the Catholic tradition.

Issues Still Needing Serious Attention

All things liturgical and sacramental within the ELCA, however, are not rosy and I certainly do not want to give the deceptive impression that they are. In fact, there are several issues that still need serious attention in the ELCA if renewal of the liturgy is to go forward from this point. Let me simply list here—without too much additional comment—what I see some of those to be.[26]

1. In spite of frequent attempts and some notable examples to the contrary, the eucharist itself remains but an "occasional service" in too many places, celebrated either monthly, bimonthly or "after" others have been dismissed from the principal Sunday assembly. Out of a total of 10,196 parishes, 2,305 celebrating eucharist every Sunday is still only about 20%, and for that matter these statistics do not indicate whether the eucharist is celebrated in these parishes at every Sunday service or not.

2. In spite of a clear preference for the use of authentic and generous sacramental signs in the celebration of the liturgy,[27] minimalistic use of water in baptism (administered in some places even by only a finger dipped in the font and on the head of the candidate), mass-produced communion wafers instead of real bread, and what I refer to as (often even pre-filled) individual "shot glasses" for the reception of the eucharistic wine, has continued in far too many places. Never mind that the concern of the Lutheran Reformers for communion under both elements was the sacramental significance of sharing the *cup*, not merely the reception of wine.

3. In spite of the 14 eucharistic prayers currently available for use, a bare-bones *verba* (institution narrative) alone often constitutes the normative pattern of eucharistic "consecration" — occasionally without even preface and Sanctus — in still far too many places on "Communion" Sundays.

4. In spite of what I can only assume to be solid seminary-level education in liturgy, at gatherings of recently ordained pastors, when asked to list what they consider to be among the "essentials" of Sunday worship, they are quick to list the "children's sermon" but not the meal with its great thanksgiving prayer.

5. The recent ELCA acceptance of "full communion" with various Reformed churches in the United States calls into question, theoretically at least, the credibility of the Lutheran confessional position on the real presence of Christ in the eucharist.

6. The paschal Triduum has yet to be even experienced by the majority of Lutheran clergy, much less instituted as the center of

a parish life around the light of Christ risen from death, the stories of salvation history, the font and the table of the Lord after a Lent that is oriented toward baptismal renewal and affirmation rather than a 40-day "Passion Sunday" or "Good Friday."

7. Occasional proposals to move or do away with the season of Advent altogether in the name of an ambiguous "inculturation" in the modern world find some sympathetic response and reveal a church rather unsure of the theology, meaning and overall purpose of the liturgical year itself.[28]

8. Even the normative priority of Sunday itself as the day of resurrection, day of encounter with the crucified and risen Lord, and the day for the Christian assembly around word and table, as expressed in *The Use of the Means of Grace*,[29] is met with some incredulity and resistance.

9. Often with synodical and national support, "contemporary" and non-sacramental forms of "worship," in the name of an ambiguous "hospitality" for "seekers," based on what some have called "entertainment evangelism," is permitted to substitute for or provide an alternative to "traditional" Sunday worship (i.e., the classic Sunday worship of the one, holy, catholic and apostolic church centered in word *and* table).

10. Contemporary or locally created "Statements of Faith" are permitted to modify or even replace the classic Nicene and Apostles' Creeds themselves and so call into serious question the precise relationship of some local Lutheran congregations to the historic faith of the church.

11. In spite of the Lutheran confessional preference for continuing the historic episcopacy, full communion with the Episcopal Church USA was voted down last summer (albeit by only six votes short of a two-thirds majority), precisely *because* of the requirement that the ELCA adopt that episcopacy.[30]

12. The medieval and Thomistic emphasis on the one office of ordained ministry (that of presbyter or priest) is maintained with a tenacity approaching a *status confessionis* (i.e., a "state of confession" for which there is no compromise permitted), in

spite of the fact that the contemporary Roman Catholic and Anglican emphasis on the "threefold" office and "ordination" of bishops, presbyters and deacons has moved beyond this context and owes more to a recovery of a patristic understanding of "orders" within the church, including the laity as an "order" itself(!), than it does to the priestly ordination theology of Western scholasticism.

13. In spite of the traditional Lutheran emphasis on the importance of the oral proclamation of the word in the assembly, far too often, in my experience, the overall performance and quality of the proclaimation of the Sunday readings, by lectors and presiders alike, pales in comparision with the dignity, care and attention to oral proclamation that I often experience within post–Vatican II Roman Catholic practice.

14. In spite of the classic Lutheran emphasis on preaching the word, it is downright frightening, but significant, to note that according to a list that appeared in *Time* magazine a couple of years ago[31] of the ten top preachers in the United States, Walter Burkhardt, SJ, was included but not one single Lutheran preacher was mentioned.

No, all is not yet rosy within ELCA liturgical-sacramental practice, even if it is moving, generally, in what I consider to be the right direction. Issues of ecclesiology and ministry, and the recovery of a rich and full liturgical-sacramental practice that corresponds to and expresses its theology still loom large for the future, as the ELCA, now only 11 years old itself, seeks to find its ecclesial and ecumenical place at the end of the 20th and beginning of the 21st century.

Conclusion

Lest my reflections seem overly critical or negative, let me underscore the fact that it has been only 35 years since the *Constitution on the Sacred Liturgy* was adopted at Vatican II, only 28 years since the appearance of the approved ICEL version of the Missal of Paul VI, only 20 years since the publication of the *Lutheran Book of Worship,* and only ten years since the final approved version of the RCIA was adopted in the United States. When one considers what *has,* in fact, taken place with regard to the renewal of the liturgy in that relatively short period of time the only response can be one of grateful awe and humble *"eucharistia."*

In spite of the several issues needing attention that remain in all of the major liturgical traditions today, what has been accomplished already from these few years of hard work should also give us both a sense of hope and a renewed call to work for the continued implementation of that common ecumenical liturgical-sacramental vision centered in the multiple and "real" presences of Christ among us. Never can we allow the occasional calls for the "undoing" of the reform of the liturgy, the so-called "reform of the reform" or a "restorationist-revisionistic" reinterpretation of that reform based on an incomplete late medieval ecclesiology and sacramental theology, or for Lutherans a 16th-century fundamentalist repristination, to deter or detract us from that continued implementation.

For at stake in all this is not really the liturgy itself but the very identity and life of the people of God for whom the liturgy exists to serve in the first place. And it serves them in forming them to be what they celebrate, to become what they receive, in lives of *diakonia* and *martyria,* lives broken and shared for the sake of the world that others too may may come to the fullness of life in the "real" presence of the crucified, yet living, Christ, who is known not only in the apostolic teaching and *koinonia,* in the breaking of bread and the prayers (see Acts 2:42), but is known and revealed especially there.

1. A. Flannery, ed., *Vatican Council II,* vol. 1 (Collegeville, MN: The Liturgical Press, 1975), 4–5.

2. See *The Smalcald,* Articles IV–VIII, in T. Tappert, ed., *The Book of Concord* (Philadelphia, 1958), 310–13.

3. See *The Apology of the Augsburg Confession,* Article XIII. 17, in Tappert, 213.

4. See *The Augsburg Confession,* Article V, in Tappert, 31.

5. *The Apology of the Augsburg Confession,* Articles VII and VIII. 28, in Tappert, 173.

6. Ibid., Article XIII. 11–12, 212.

7. *The Augsburg Confession,* Article VII, in Tappert, p.32.

8. M. Luther, *The Babylonian Captivity of the Church,* in *Luther's Works,* vol. 36, 18 [emphasis added].

9. Pontifical Council for Promoting Christian Unity, *Directory for the Application of Principles and Norms on Ecumenism,* 129, in *Origins* 23 (July 29, 1993).

10. John Paul II, Encyclical Letter *Ut Unum Sint,* 22, in *Origins* 25 (June 8, 1995).

11. *Unity of the Churches: An Actual Possibility* (New York/Philadelphia: Paulist Press and Fortress Press, 1985), 125 [emphasis added].

12. I owe these and other ELCA statistics in this essay to the kind assistance of The Rev. Dr. Paul Nelson, Director of Worship, the Division for Congregational Ministries, Evangelical Lutheran Church in America, Chicago, Illinois.

13. Evangelical Lutheran Church in America, *Welcome to Christ: A Lutheran Catechetical Guide* (Minneapolis, 1997); *Welcome to Christ: A Lutheran Introduction to the Catechumenate* (Minneapolis, 1997); and *Welcome to Christ: Lutheran Rites for the Catechumenate* (Minneapolis, 1997).

14. See *FDLC Newsletter* 22 (December 1995): 45.

15. Evangelical Lutheran Church in Canada, *Statement on Sacramental Practices,* (Winnipeg, 1991), 5.8, 6.9.

16. Evangelical Lutheran Church in America, *The Use of the Means of Grace: A Statement on the Practice of Word and Sacrament* (Minneapolis: Augsburg Fortress Press, 1997), 3.37D, 42.

17. Minneapolis, 1993.

18. The major Lutheran bodies forming the ELCA in 1987 were the former Lutheran Church in America (LCA), The American Lutheran Church (ALC) and the Association of Evangelical Lutheran Churches (AELC). With the exception of the AELC, formed by several former Lutheran Church–Missouri Synod congregations, the LCA and ALC were themselves the result of various Lutheran "mergers" of several Lutheran churches in the United States and Canada in the early 1960's.

19. J. F. White, "Roman Catholic and Protestant Worship in Relationship," in *Christian Worship in North America: A Retrospective: 1955–1995* (Collegeville, MN: The Liturgical Press, 1997), 3.

20. On this see F. Senn, *Christian Liturgy: Catholic and Evangelical* (Minneapolis: Fortress Press, 1997), 353.

21. *The Occasional Service Book* (Minneapolis/Philadelphia, 1982), 83–8.

22. *The Use of the Means of Grace,* 49.A., 52.

23. Ibid., 49, p. 52.

24. Ibid., 49B, p. 52.

25. See the *Occasional Service Book,* 89–98; 99–102 .

26. Several of these issues are also cited in my essay, "The 'Joint Declaration on the Doctrine of Justification' and Lutheran-Roman Catholic Unity: Some Unresolved Questions," forthcoming, from *Lutheran Forum.*

27. See *The Use of the Means of Grace,* 25 and 26, pp. 31–32; and 44A, p. 48.

28. See S. K. Wendorf, "Let's Move Advent," in *Lutheran Partners* (November/December 1991), and the numerous favorable letters her plea engendered in *Lutheran Partners* (March/April 1992). For my response to this see my "Let's Keep Advent Right Where It Is," in *Lutheran Forum* 28 (November, 1994): 45–7.

29. *The Use of the Means of Grace,* 6, p. 13.

30. To be fair, however, a new version of the Lutheran-Episcopal *Concordat,* entitled "Called to a Common Mission," will still necessitate the ELCA adoption of the historic episcopacy for the sake of full communion. This new version includes the welcome addition that the ELCA is to receive this episcopacy not only from the Episcopal Church USA, but from those Lutheran Churches (e.g., Sweden, Tanzania, and El Salvador) where that episcopal succession has continued through the present day.

31. I am unable to locate the precise issue of *Time* in which this list appeared.

Theresa F. Koernke, IHM

The Many Presences of Christ: Recovering the Tradition, Renewing the Churches

Taking Apart the "World" in our Imagination

The Scholastic theology of the Trinity, and the associated catechesis (with which most of us grew up), presented us with a notion of God "in-God's-self." We spoke of the Unmoved Mover of Neoplatonic and Aristotelian philosophy, indeed, of God as somehow untouched by the ambiguities and changes of our created world. That theology of the Trinity encourages a view of God as distant from human history, and as only occasionally involved at distinct moments. This is not a view of God as revealed in the Judeo-Christian tradition.[1] Restricted by the categories of Greek philosophy, Scholastic theology spoke of the generation of the Son from the Father and of the spiration of the Holy Spirit as the Love beween the Father and the Son,[2] thus bypassing the data of the life of Jesus.

In his contribution to this collection of articles,[3] John Baldovin, SJ, draws attention to the trinitarian faith of the church, not simply as belief in God "in-God's-Self," but to a doctrine of the Trinity that is rooted in scripture and is unfettered by the rigid categories of Scholastic theology. Such a trinitarian theology based on scripture begins by reflection on the historical Jesus who lived his life and gave himself to God unto death on the cross by the power of the Spirit. In this view, the triune God is revealed precisely where it seems as though God is not — in human flesh and in death — and is so revealed for the sake of teaching that no form of death can separate us from God.[4] Quite a world-shattering statement, indeed.

In keeping with a theology of the Trinity that is based on scripture, the words, "Christ always present in the church" (Vatican II, *Constitution on the Sacred Liturgy (Sacrosanctum concilium)* [CSL], #7), may well be the most world-shattering statement in all of the documents of the Second Vatican Council. I would emphasize world-shattering. To take the statement seriously implies a reevaluation of all the relationships in the body of Christ, the church. As the church increasingly deepens its grasp of this biblically rooted statement, the answers to the following questions make all the difference for the mission of the church in this world. The questions are: What is happening to the churches as we shift our understanding of Christ among us? What are the practical implications for the ministries—of the assembly, of proclaimers of the word, of ministers of bread and cup, and of presidency of the eucharist? What is happening to our understandings of eucharist and christology and liturgy? And lastly, are the implications of the statement, "Christ is always present in the church," so unsettling of the stratified, individualistic and authoritarian relationships we have known in the church that, at some level of consciousness, some of us are afraid to ask: Are the churches avoiding the radical ethical significance of eating and drinking in the context of the celebration of the eucharist? This last question is my constant preoccupation and receives my attention here.

Scholastic Questions about the "Real Presence" of Christ

Most of us grew up asserting and trying to understand and to explain how the risen Christ in heaven would *become present* under the forms of bread and wine.[5] It was our badge of Catholicity, along with unquestioning loyalty to the pontiff. We referred to the "real presence" of Christ in the sacrament with such intensity that we found it difficult to speak of the real, true presence of Christ in the proclamation of the scriptures or anywhere else except, perhaps, in the ordained minister to whom we referred as *alter Christus* (another Christ). Theologians gave themselves to articulating how, by the force of the words attributed to Jesus at the Last Supper—"This is my body" and "This is my blood"—the priest had the power to bring

Christ in heaven down upon our altars. We are familiar with the clericalism that that stratified, pyramidal image of the church gave us until this century.

This was the world view of most of us at the time of Vatican II, even though many of us had growing suspicions about its adequacy. And so, for the Council to have made the statement that Christ is *always* present in the church, in the assembly at prayer, in the scriptures and in the presider was to shed intense new light on the patriarchal social organization of the church as we knew it. In this new light, no one group of persons could any longer claim to be the sole channel of the real presence of Christ among us. Indeed, taking that statement seriously has opened theology to questioning the completeness of our former thinking about the meaning of leadership at the liturgy. Theologians were called to plumb the significance—the sign value—of the entire celebration of the eucharist as an ethical activity itself, and to retrieve the tradition about the meaning of eating and drinking in the context of the eucharist. As research into the scriptures and the history of the liturgy shows, recovering the tradition about the meaning of the entire celebration of the eucharist places former questions in anew light.[7] Is the question, "How can Christ alone become present on our altars?", worthy of the tradition? Indeed, the question that is worthy of the tradition is this: What is the meaning of the entire celebration of the eucharist, of the liturgy of the word, of the eucharistic prayer, and of eating and drinking in that context?[8]

Where is the Risen Christ? Or, The Many Modes of the Real Presence of Christ

To be sure, the questions that we ask and the answers that we hear each reflect our own paradigm of reality or world view—that is, the way in which we make sense of reality, especially the relationships among us, and of all of us to God. Contrary to the contents of the New Testament, that pyramidal and patriarchal view of the world given to us by Plato and Aristotle and absorbed into our image of the church placed the risen Christ up in heaven, outside of so-called profane history. People concluded that the resurrection and ascension of Jesus implied a pervasive distance between the risen Christ and the church in the world. And if we asserted that Christ was truly present in the sacrament at Mass, we then needed to explain that presence in this otherwise messy world. And such was the case for most people at the time of Vatican II.

An illustration might be helpful to demonstrate this point. For example, much of the contents of the *Constitution on the Sacred Liturgy* were the result of advances in the fields of scripture and liturgical history. Research showed that the Neoplatonic Aristotelian image of reality and of the occasional or sole sacramental relationship of the risen Jesus to us was simply not the case. And yet, the debates on the floor of the Council regarding paragraph seven, as well as the discussions since then, indicate that we were and are struggling with a magic transformation of the very way we have been looking at the relation of God to the world in Christ by the power of the Spirit. The issues are world-shattering. For if, in virtue of the Word-become-flesh, we now say that the Christ is present to the whole of creation (as proclaimed by the Letter to the Colossians), how are we now to distinguish that universal presence of Christ to those who are baptized into his death? And if the Christ is always present to the church in virtue of the fact that we are inserted by baptism into his self-offering to God, how are we to distinguish the modes of Christ's presence[9] in the assembly from that in the scriptures, from that in the sacrament that we eat and drink, and so on? I would suggest that our image of the relation of God to the church is crucial to our deliberations.

Images of the Church and the Presence of Christ

It is commonplace, for example, to acknowledge that there are at least two images of the church in the *Dogmatic Constitution on the Church*. Chapter Two, "On the People of God," includes the clergy among the people of God, all members of the church having an ongoing relationship to Christ in the Spirit; on the other hand, Chapter Three, "The Church is Hierarchical," has been read to imply that access to the presence of Christ comes through the clergy. Both chapters are present in that document, leaving it to subsequent reflection to integrate them. A brief illustration of the struggle to integrate these two images of the church, and the notions of the presence of Christ attached to them, might be helpful.

Variant Readings of the Conciliar Documents

In the years since the promulgation of the *Constitution on the Sacred Liturgy,* a variety of practical conclusions have been heard or drawn from the statement that Christ is always present in the church. On the one hand, among some persons the logic followed this path: If Christ is always present in the church, then why bother celebrating the eucharist at all? Or, if Christ is always present in the church, then anyone may preside; indeed, all one need do is go through the actions of the eucharist and it is "real." Or, since we all share in the one priesthood of Christ in virtue of baptism, and since we want to avoid clericalized celebrations and to encourage participation, ordained ministry is a thing of the past. And so on.

On the other hand, members of traditionalist movements immediately recognized the world-shattering consequences of the assertion that Christ is always present in the church. Mother Angelica and others represent the clear response of those who see the world-shattering consequences. Many of us today note a resurgence of requests for the celebration of the liturgy of Trent and for perpetual adoration of the reserved sacrament in which, as we said for centuries, we have "the real presence." For this latter group, the statement that Christ is always present in the church implies "always present in the sacrament confected by the priest." But most of us know that, as alluring as these proposed options might seem, they are not consistent with the call to renewal of the Second Vatican Council.

How can we appreciate these responses, while furthering the call to the deep spiritual, liturgical and ethical renewal—dare I say reform—implied by the conviction of that faith that Christ is always present among us? In order to do this, it seems fitting to reflect briefly on world views or philosophical systems that have had impacts upon our account of the faith regarding the presence of Christ at eucharist.

Shifting Images of the World

A system of philosophy proposes to explain what is. Contemporary studies in the origin and meaning of systems of philosophy assert that a such a system is itself a reflection of the social relationships of the persons who articulate it and that these social systems, in turn, shape the notions of the relation of God to creation, as well as the language considered suitable for imaging God. And, when that system is taught and widely accepted it tends to reinforce and defend the social relationships and view of divine activity that it describes. Consequently, and this is true of every cultural explanation of reality, that culture or social system is then said to be the will of God or the gods.[10] These insights are helpful in understanding how the statement, "Christ is always present in the church," is world-shattering. How is this so, and why would anyone want to preserve the former world view?

The Influence of Greek Philosophy on Ecclesial Practice and Thought

The church was born not only into a centuries-long Judaic culture, but also into Hellenistic culture. Indeed, the convictions of both, but especially of Hellenism, would reinforce patterns of belief about the relationship of the divine to human beings and all creation. Further, Hellenism also provided patterns of social relationships that, in my view, have served to impede the full force of the gospel message and the radically ethical meaning of the full celebration of the eucharist. It is this combination of Neoplatonic Aristotelian philosophy and Judaic culture that would give us not only a deep suspicion of the value of matter and of our very bodies, but also would give us a notion of God as distant and of the spiritual realm as superior to the material world. Access to God would then imply the need for escape from materiality, or the sense that God on occasion needs to be injected into an otherwise profane world.

There was a time in which most of us would have equated philosophy with this Neoplatonic Aristotelian philosophy—the root of Catholic Scholastic theology. That system of thought grounded Roman Catholic and some Protestant theology until this century. Its language of form and matter, substance and accidents, spiritual and material, and so on, is inherently dualistic. That is, form, substance and the spiritual, in this world view, are superior to matter, accidents and material. And the unquestioned assumptions of that world view are alive and among us today.

Implications of Greek Thought on Eucharistic Practice and Thought

How does all this relate to our questions, especially to whether we might be avoiding the radical ethical implications of eating and drinking in the context of the eucharist? Briefly, when Christian theology rather uncritically absorbed the language and culture of Greek philosophy, it absorbed the assumption that the material world is suspect, and that the spiritual world is the really real. The great Augustine, as Neoplatonic philosopher, found it extremely challenging to imagine that the eternal Word of God took on the flesh of humanity. And he likewise found it an affront to Neoplatonic logic to say that, by virtue of the resurrection, the human flesh of the risen Jesus participated in the spiritual realm! Only Augustine the Christian believer could take delight in saying that the risen Christ was intimately and always united to the members of his body, the church.[11]

With the death of Augustine in the mid-fifth century, the dualistic assumptions of Greek philosophy washed over the Christian theological imagination. The resurrection and ascension of Christ came to be understood as the departure of the Christ from this world. Thus, the lone risen Christ was located "in heaven." This "localizing" of Christ in heaven in a rather physicalist sense left Christian theology with the centuries-long problem of answering a very crippled question: How can Christ alone in heaven become present alone under the forms of bread and wine? And from the ninth century on, it would be safe to say that Christian theologians did not reflect upon the entire celebration of the liturgy of the eucharist. Rather, they gave their efforts to explain what happened to bread and wine when the priest spoke those words attributed to Jesus, to whether one received the whole Christ when receiving bread alone, to how long Christ remained present in the communicant after communion, to how Christ could be present on several altars at the same time, and so on.

Eucharistic Practice and Theology: The Challenge Today

Once that we can see that a given system of philosophy—in this case, Neoplatonic Aristotelian philosophy—has shaped our Scholastic theology, pastoral practice, spirituality and catechesis; once we can see that the view of reality at the root of that system is a hierarchical (in the sense of stratified) one that defends and preserves a patriarchal social system; once we can see that that system cripples our ability to genuinely acknowledge that Christ is always present among us, then we are free to ask questions that are far more demanding. If Christ is always present in the church, what is the relationship of the presider to the assembly at liturgy? Whom do we acclaim in the scriptures proclaimed in our midst? Through whom and for what purpose is the eucharistic prayer prayed in the hearing of the assembly? To whom do we say "Amen" in eating the bread of heaven? To what do we give ourselves in agreeing to drink of the cup of eternal salvation? Is the Scholastic question about the real presence of Christ to the sacrament any longer the best one in the light of the tradition? If it was a logical question in the past, is preoccupation with the question of the presence of Christ to the sacrament today an escape from the radically ethical meaning of baptism into the self-offering of Christ and the memorial of it in the celebration of the eucharist? I submit that it has the potential to be.

In conclusion, it is my conviction that ordained liturgical ministry is crucial to the life of the entire people of God. But, the ordained minister is not a sole source of the presence of Christ, but is one who convenes the church, who calls the church to its heart, to consciousness of its relationship to Christ crucified and risen, so that it might do in this world the salvation (the ethics of God) into which it has been baptized. The ordained minister does not act in the person of Christ as an actor playing a role of Christ up on some celestial cloud, and who can command the Christ to come down. Rather, the bishops and presbyters of this church act in the person of Christ who is always present and active in this holy and sinful church. It is an awe-full thing to convene the church, to address the church in the name and voice of the ancestors and to bid the assembly to "Lift up your hearts" in the midst of this world and at this time in the church.

Upon hearing the proclamation of the scriptures, the assembly acclaims, "Thanks be to God," and "Praise to you, Lord Jesus Christ." We do not acclaim, "Praise to you, O Book." Sunday after Sunday, for almost 2000 years, this church has acknowledged the real presence of Christ among us, speaking to us, interpreting our lives to us, telling us whose we are and what we are good for: the peace and salvation of all the world in Christ. In the eucharistic prayer, the ordained minister addresses God in the hearing of the assembly and in its name, proclaiming the great deeds of God among us, through, with and in Christ by the power of the Spirit, precisely because we are knit to the Christ in his saving activity, always and everywhere.

In communion, we say "Amen" to the body of Christ, that is, we say "Amen" to all our ancestors in the faith, to those who inspire us today, and to those in this holy and sinful church who soundly irk us. "Be sure that you know to whom you are saying 'Amen,'" cautioned Augustine, "so that your 'Amen' may be true. Be sure that you are as careful not to drop the sacrament, as you are careful not to drop each other."[12] Dare we now say that we consume the church, and in doing so, admit that we belong to God with each other in the Christ? No less challenging is the image of blood, the image of the one eternal self-offering of Jesus the Christ on the cross. To put the cup of eternal salvation to our lips is a consolation and a judgment: consolation, because we belong to each other and to the Christ in his self-offering; judgment, because we often resist the Spirit that knits us to that saving activity with others. To drink the blood of Christ is to give oneself to God's ethics, to drink of the salvation of God at the cost of our lives.

Recovering the tradition beyond the categories of Scholastic theology leads to a simple realization: We need not worry about the real presence of the Christ. As my teacher Edward Kilmartin, SJ, would say: The real presence of Christ in the church has been taken care of when God raised him from the dead, and when the Christ bestowed his Spirit upon the whole church. We are not related to a pretty Jesus, but to one whose entire life was rewarded by an attempt to silence the truth about us before God, and about the real presence of God in Christ among us. Domesticating this reality, taming it, limiting it to questions about what happens to bread and wine, rather than to what has already happened to us in Christ and what that demands for our worship and our lives, is not something for which we ought to have to make an account before the God of Jesus Christ.

> *Affairs are now soul size.*
> *The enterprise is exploration into God.*
>
> —Christopher Fry

1. For an analysis of the difference between the notion of god in Greek philosophy and the Christian notion of God as revealed in Jesus Christ, see Julian Marias, *History of Philosophy,* Stanley Appelbaum and Clarence C. Stowbridge, trans. (New York: Dover Publications, 1967), *passim.*

2. Thomas Aquinas, *Summa Theologica,* Part I, qq. 27–43.

3. See "The Church in Christ, Christ in the Church," in this volume, page 9.

4. See Catherine Mowry LaCugna, *God For Us: The Trinity and Christian Life* (New York: HarperCollins Publishers, 1991), 217–32.

5. *The New Revised Baltimore Catechism and Mass, No. 3* (New York: Benziger Brothers, Inc., 1949), qq. 343–356.

6. Edward J. Kilmartin, SJ, "The Catholic Tradition of Eucharistic Theology: Towards the Third Millennium," *Theological Studies* 55 (1994): 405–57. Kilmartin begins by saying that "the prevailing official Catholic eucharistic theology that has its roots in the synthesis that began to take on characteristic traits in the 12th and 13th centuries no longer does justice to this central Christian mystery."

7. Gilbert Ostdiek, OFM, "Ritual and Transformation: Reflections on Liturgy and the Social Sciences," *Liturgical Ministry* 2 (Spring 1993): 38–48.

8. Enrico Mazza, *The Origins of the Eucharistic Prayer,* Ronald E. Lane, trans. (Collegeville, MN: The Liturgical Press, 1995), l.

9. For an articulation of the many modes of the presence of Christ, see Edward J. Kilmartin, SJ, *Christian Liturgy: Theology and Practice,* I. Systematic Theology of Liturgy (Kansas City, MO: Sheed & Ward, 1988), 303–50.

10. See John B. Carroll, ed., *Language, Thought, and Reality: Selected Writings of Benjamin Lee Whorf* (Cambridge, MA: The MIT Press, 1995), passim.

11. Gustave Martelet, "The Gap Widens," *The Risen Christ and the Eucharistic World,* (New York: Seabury Press, 1976), 122 ff.

12. Augustine of Hippo, *Serm. 227,* PL 38, 1099–1100; and *Serm. 272,* PL 38, 1246–1247.

"And How Many Will There Be for Dinner?": Inclusion and Exclusion and the Eucharist

Rev. John P. Beal, professor of canon law at the Catholic University of America, describes the following scene in his family:

> Several years ago, when my nephew Jason was five years old, I was visiting his family in New Hampshire. As part of this family gathering we decided to celebrate the eucharist together. As the family's designated presbyter I presided over the celebration. At communion time, Jason's parents, grandparents, aunts and uncles, and a few family friends came forward to receive the Body of Christ and in their wake Jason too came forward and piously extended his hands. Not wanting to create a scene, I gently said to him, "Sorry, Jason, not this time." With that Jason stormed out of the room and out of the house. A half an hour later, when the liturgy had been concluded and we were all sitting in the living room, Jason reappeared, glared at all present and announced, "I just spoke to all the living creatures—the birds in the sky, the trees and the plants in the garden—and I told them you would not let me share in the Body of Christ." With that pronouncement, Jason disappeared again.
>
> A few minutes later, Jason reappeared with a dish towel around his neck like a stole and a bell in his hand to summon us "to church." Soon we all found ourselves gathered around the

table that had only recently been the focus of our eucharistic celebration, but this time it was Jason who presided. A few slices of bread and a cup of grape juice were set atop a white napkin on the table before him. Jason then launched into a reasonably complete and accurate rendition of the Mass, replete with hymns and acclamations, which we were enjoined to sing. When communion time arrived, he reverently broke the bread and shared it along with the cup of grape juice with his younger brother and sister and then beckoned the adults to approach the altar. As each of us came forward and extended our hands, we heard a familiar refrain— "Sorry, not this time." When we had all been duly chastened, Jason returned to his presider's stool and offered a concluding prayer: "Dear God, I hope that the adults now know how it feels to be refused a share in the Body of Christ." The Mass was ended and we went in something less than peace.[1]

John Beal's nephew Jason is by no means alone in his experience. There are many others who also have felt the pain of being refused a share in the Body of Christ. Yet the church proclaims that "the eucharistic sacrifice, in which the sacrifice of the cross is perpetuated over the centuries, is the summit and the source of all Christian worship and life; it signifies and effects the unity of the people of God and achieves the building up of the Body of Christ."[2] Moreover, the church "earnestly desires that Christ's faithful, when present at this mystery of faith, should not be there as strangers or silent spectators."[3] So the question is: If the eucharist is the summit and the source of all Christian worship and life; and if it signifies and effects the unity of the people of God; and if the church desires that people not be at the eucharist as strangers or silent spectators, how is it that some people are excluded from our eucharistic celebrations?

This article will attempt to investigate this question. I will be writing from the perspective of canon law, but this is not to say that I will be writing from a legalistic perspective. Pope John Paul II, in promulgating the Code of Canon Law, spoke of the canons only in the context of sacred scripture and the documents of Vatican II. He stated:

I would like to draw for you, as an illustration and a reminder, an ideal triangle: at the top, there is sacred scripture; on one side, the acts of the Second Vatican Council, and on the other, the new Code of Canon Law. And in order to go back in an orderly coherent fashion from these two books, drawn up by the church of the twentieth century, up to that supreme and undeniable vertex, it is necessary to pass along the sides of that triangle.[4]

Thus, the Code of Canon Law does not negate the insights of theology and scripture, but complements them. This discussion will begin within the context of the reception of sacraments in general, as well as an indication of who can receive the sacraments. It will then deal with those who are prohibited from receiving the eucharist, first by church law and then by church practice. It will be helpful, then, to look at why the church so closely relates the reception of the eucharist with the sacrament of marriage, and what it means to participate in the eucharist. Finally, this article will conclude with some reflections on the meaning the eucharist as the sacrament of unity, and the many sources of disunity in our lives.

The Reception of the Sacraments

There does not appear to be much debate over the fact that, with the exception of baptism itself, the sacraments are for the baptized. This is because baptism is seen as the "gate to the sacraments," in which four things happen: (1) people are freed from sin; (2) they are reborn as children of God; (3) they are configured to Christ by a perpetual bond; and (4) they are incorporated in the church.[5] Once this occurs, then, those who have been baptized are seen as suitable candidates for the other sacraments.[6] In other words, canon 849 is the statement of a right in the church: namely, that those who have been baptized have a right to receive the other sacraments.[7] Other laws that restrict that right must always be read within this context: They represent a restriction of the rights that are given to the Christian faithful simply by virtue of their baptism. The church may legitimately restrict these rights, since it has a caretaker's responsibility for the sacraments.[8] But it always must be kept in mind that since c. 849 states the right of the Christian faithful, any restriction of that right must be seen in light of the church's canonical tradition on the restriction of rights. Thus, c. 18 states that any law that restricts the free exercise of a person's rights or that contains an exception to the general law must be interpreted strictly.[9] That is, a law that restricts the free exercise of rights should not be extended beyond the cases described in that law.[10]

It is for this reason that c. 843.1 states, "The sacred ministers cannot refuse the sacraments to those who ask for them at appropriate times, are properly disposed and are not prohibited by law from receiving them." This canon allows for the greatest exercise of rights in the church, but it also allows the universal church, as well as the local communities, to determine when and with whom it is appropriate to celebrate the sacraments.

Examples of the law itself restricting the reception of sacraments have already been given above.[11] There are also instances where either universal law or local law specifies appropriate times for the reception of the sacraments, or indicates that someone is suitably disposed to receive the sacraments. In many parishes, for example, there are policies that indicate what is considered an appropriate time to celebrate the sacrament of marriage or when the sacrament of penance is normally celebrated. In the universal law of the church, it is recommended that the sacrament of baptism be celebrated on Sunday.[12] There are similar restrictions in liturgical law regarding the celebration of the sacraments during the Triduum, and it is recommended that ordinations take place on a Sunday or on a holy day of obligation.[13]

There are also ways in which universal law as well as local legislation specifies how people might be considered "properly disposed" to celebrate the sacraments. Canons 1063–1072 give guidelines for marriage preparation, with many dioceses and parishes having similar guidelines based upon these laws. Canon 1025 details what is necessary for someone to be ordained to the priesthood or the diaconate, while c. 242.1 requires that each nation should have a program for priestly formation and c. 243 requires that each seminary have its own rule that adapts the national program to local circumstances. Penitents are required by c. 987 to have repudiated sin and have a purpose of amendment; and c. 913 states that children who approach the table of the eucharist for the first time must be prepared by parents, pastors and the whole community so that they "understand the mystery of Christ according to their capacity, and can receive the Body of the Lord with faith and devotion." Moreover, this universal law of the church urges further adaptation on the part of local communities so that the Christian faithful might more properly be prepared for the reception of the sacraments.[14]

Who May Administer and Who May Receive

While the general rule regarding the sacraments is that Christian baptism opens the gate to the other sacraments, the Code of Canon Law further specifies who can administer the sacraments and who can receive them. It does so by first stating a general rule, and then following it with exceptions.

Canon 844.1 states that as a general rule "Catholic ministers may licitly administer the sacraments to Catholic members of the Christian faithful only and, likewise, the latter may licitly receive the sacraments only from Catholic ministers."[15] This is not simply an arbitrary judgement on the part of the church, or a simple desire to "keep it within the family." Nor is it an attempt to portray a triumphalist attitude toward the other Christian communities. Rather, the general rule "Catholics minister to Catholics and Catholics receive from Catholics" is based upon the fact that the sacraments are one of the things that indicate we are in full communion with the Catholic church.

According to canon law, there are three ways that we indicate we are joined with Christ in the visible structure of the church: by the common faith that we profess (including those things that are defined as articles of faith), through the celebration of the sacraments (this would presume all seven sacraments), and through the specific structure of governance that constitutes the church (which is sometimes referred to as a hierarchical communion).[16] Thus the celebration of the sacraments is one of the ways we identify ourselves. It is not a matter of excluding other people, but a way of identifying ourselves. Because the celebration of the sacraments is an identifying mark of those in full communion with the Catholic church, it is only right that they should be celebrated only by those who are in that communion. This does not mean that those who do not receive the sacraments are any less acceptable to God. It just means that they are not in full communion with the body of Christ in its visible form, the church.

It should also be pointed out that this does not mean that the person is not fully joined to Christ. It is by baptism that we have been joined to Christ and made members of God's people. It is through the bonds of profession of faith, the sacraments, and ecclesiastical structure that we are identified with the church. The Second Vatican Council taught that there should be no difference between these two realities,[17] but the fact remains that human sinfulness can prevent those two realities from being joined as the Lord willed them to be joined.

The Exceptions

While the general rule has been that Catholic ministers administer the sacraments to Catholic members of the Christian faithful only, and that Catholic members of the Christian faithful receive the sacraments from Catholic ministers only, the Code of Canon Law does provide for exceptions.

Catholics Receiving Sacraments from Non-Catholic Ministers

The law states that under certain circumstances the sacraments of penance, eucharist and anointing of the sick may be administered to Catholic members of the Christian faithful by non-Catholic ministers.[18] There are four cautions contained in this canon, however: (1) There must be some genuine need for the Catholic party to receive the sacrament or some genuine spiritual advantage that will come from the reception of the sacrament; (2) there should also be avoidance of any danger of error (for example, a mistaken belief that the non-Catholic minister is in fact a Catholic minister or that the non-Catholic church is in fact a Catholic church, thereby not respecting the integrity of our sister churches) or of indifference (for example, leading the person to conclude that all the churches are the same, or that they do not have their own distinct character); (3) it must be either physically or morally impossible for the Catholic member of the Christian faithful to approach a Catholic minister for the sacrament; and (4) the Catholic church must recognize the sacrament as valid in the non-Catholic church.[19]

Non-Catholics Receiving Sacraments from Catholic Ministers

The law also provides that Catholic ministers may administer the sacraments of penance, eucharist and anointing to other members of the Christian faithful under certain circumstances. It deals, first of all, with those churches that are most similar to the Catholic churches with regard to the sacraments. Thus, the sacraments can be administered to members of the Eastern non-Catholic churches, as long as they ask for the sacrament on their own and are properly disposed to receive it. This is also the case for members of other churches that the Catholic church judges to be in the same condition as the Eastern non-Catholic churches as far as these sacraments are concerned.[20] The canon is careful not to specify which churches these might be, since it does not want to provide a definitive list. Discussions continue with many of the churches regarding the meaning of the sacraments, and the law wishes to remain open to all the possibilities that might come out of those dialogs.

Finally, the law provides that Catholic ministers may administer the sacraments of penance, eucharist and anointing of the sick to other members of the Christian faithful, even if they are not in full communion with the Catholic church. As with the members of the Eastern non-Catholic churches, other members of the Christian faithful must ask for the sacraments on their own and be properly disposed. But there are also four other requirements: (1) In danger of death, the sacraments can always be administered; (2) outside the danger of death, the diocesan bishop or the conference of bishops can determine cases of "grave necessity" in which those not in full communion with the Catholic church may receive the sacraments; (3) the non-Catholic member of the Christian faithful must not be able to approach a minister of his or her own community for pastoral ministry; and (4) the person must manifest Catholic faith in the sacrament. If these conditions are fulfilled, then, Catholic ministers can administer the sacraments of penance, eucharist, and anointing of the sick to those who are not in full communion with the Catholic church.

Interecclesial and Ecumenical Considerations in the Law

The *Decree on Ecumenism (Unitatis redintegratio)* of the Second Vatican Council highlights five aspects of the ecumenical movement:

(1) the elimination of those things that make mutual relations difficult; (2) dialogue that deepens the knowledge among all the faithful; (3) cooperation in service for the good of humanity; (4) common prayer; and (5) an examination by each ecclesial community of its own faithfulness to Christ's will for the church, and the undertaking of renewal and reform.[21] In keeping with the spirit of this decree, the Code of Canon Law also actively promotes dialogue among the churches regarding the administration and reception of sacraments. Thus c. 844.5 enjoins the diocesan bishop or the conference of bishops from issuing general norms regarding the interecclesial administration or the reception of the sacraments of penance, eucharist or anointing of the sick without sufficient consultation with those communities who would be affected by these norms.[22]

For example, no norms can be enacted on a diocesan or a national level regarding the reception by Catholic members of the Christian faithful of the sacraments of penance, eucharist or anointing from ministers of non-Catholic churches without consultation *at least* with the local leaders of those non-Catholic churches, although it would seem that the preference is for a wider range of dialogue to take place. Similarly, before a diocese or a national conference could enact norms regarding the administration of the sacraments by Catholic ministers to non-Catholic members of the Christian faithful, a similar dialogue must take place. Finally, a similar dialogue must take place between a diocesan bishop or conference of bishops and the leaders of the affected non-Catholic churches before guidelines could be issued regarding the administration of the sacraments to non-Catholic members of the Christian faithful.[23]

Those Invited and Those Excluded from the Table of the Eucharist

Having examined the canons on sharing of the sacraments in general, as well as the canons on the sharing of the sacraments of penance, eucharist and anointing of the sick, it is now possible to take a closer look at who might be invited to the eucharistic table. However, a distinction must also be made regarding what is meant by participation in the eucharist, for it can be understood both in a wide sense and in a narrow sense. In the wider sense, we can speak of what the Second Vatican Council called the "full, conscious, and active participation in liturgical celebrations,"[24] while in the narrow sense, we can speak of sharing at the table of the eucharist.

Those Invited in the Wider Sense

The Second Vatican Council states that "the full and active participation by all the people is the aim to be considered before all else, for it is the primary and indispensable source from which the faithful are to derive the true Christian spirit."[25] Furthermore, the Code of Canon Law states: "In the eucharistic banquet the people of God are called together, with the bishop or, under his authority, a presbyter presiding and acting in the person of Christ; and all the faithful present, whether clergy or laity, participate together, in their own way, according to the diversity of orders and liturgical roles."[26] The Code urges that "the celebration of the eucharist is to be so arranged that all who take part receive from it the many fruits for which Christ the Lord instituted the eucharistic sacrifice."[27]

In this wider sense, "full, conscious, and active participation" occurs when the people have been gathered together, when someone is presiding over the gathering and when they each take part in the celebration to the extent that they are supposed to. For some, that will mean assuming various liturgical roles, while for others it will mean joining in the prayers and the songs. For some, it will mean proclaiming, while for others it will mean listening. For some, it will mean the reception of the eucharist, while for others such eucharistic sharing will not be possible. In this wider sense, no one is prohibited from participating fully in the eucharist. All are welcome, and all can participate. It is for this reason that the *Constitution on the Sacred Liturgy* states:

> Liturgical services are not private functions but are celebrations of the church which is "the sacrament of unity," namely, "the holy people united and arranged under their bishops." Therefore, liturgical services pertain to the whole body of the church. They manifest it, and have effects upon it. But they also touch individual members of the church in different ways, depending

on their orders, their role in the liturgical services, and their actual participation in them. (#26)

The fact that all are welcome and all can fully participate in the eucharist in this wider sense is evident from various documents that have been issued since the *Constitution on the Sacred Liturgy*. For example, the 1993 Directory on Ecumenism, after defining liturgy as that worship that is "carried out according to books, prescriptions, and customs of a church or ecclesial community presided over by a minister or delegate of that church or community,"[28] goes on to recommend prayer in common for various needs and participation both by Catholics in non-Catholic worship services, and by non-Catholics in various Catholic worship services.[29] Furthermore, in discussing those who have divorced and remarried, Pope John Paul II reminded pastors and the whole community of the faithful

> to help the divorced and with solicitous care to make sure that they do not consider themselves as separated from the church, for as baptized persons they can and indeed must share in her life. They should be encouraged to listen to the word of God, to attend the sacrifice of the Mass, to persevere in prayer, to contribute to works of charity and to community efforts in favor of justice, to bring up their children in the Christian faith, to cultivate the spirit and practice of penance and thus implore, day by day, God's grace. Let the church pray for them, encourage them and show herself a merciful mother and thus sustain them in faith and hope.[30]

Even those who are under the penalty of excommunication, while they cannot assume a ministerial role in liturgical celebrations, can nonetheless take part in such celebrations to the extent they are able.[31]

The extent to which people are allowed to participate is often the subject of local legislation, however. For example, diocesan bishops, conferences of bishops or parish priests establish guidelines regarding who is eligible to celebrate the sacraments of baptism, confirmation or marriage, or to serve as a godparent at a baptism or confirmation,[32] as a witness to a marriage,[33] on diocesan or parish pastoral councils,[34] on diocesan or parish finance councils,[35] or in various liturgical roles. To the extent that these laws do not contradict the universal law of the church, they are valid. However, local laws cannot be enacted that are contrary to universal laws.[36] In enacting such local laws with regard to participation in the eucharist, the prescriptions of c. 899 are to be kept in mind: that all the people of God participate together in their own way so that all may receive from the celebration some spiritual advantage.

Those Invited in the Narrower Sense

Those invited in the narrower sense are those who are invited to receive the body and blood of Christ. As might be expected from the discussion above, church law sets down general rules on the reception of the eucharist, and then qualifies those rules with certain exceptions. The general norm can be found in c. 912: "Any baptized person who is not prohibited by law can and must be admitted to Holy Communion." This canon does not raise any distinctions between persons. It simply states the principle that, since baptism is the gate to the other sacraments, baptism is absolutely necessary in order to be admitted to the table of the eucharist.

We have already seen the distinctions that have been made in c. 844 regarding sacramental sharing. Since these are found in the canons governing all the sacraments, and since they also mention the eucharist in particular, it is clear that they are applicable in the present case. The church also establishes guidelines for eucharistic sharing through general directories, which are documents written by one or more of the Roman congregations, commissions or councils, or through instructions issued by diocesan bishops or conferences of bishops. Examples of these have been seen above.

In addition, although the general law of the church excludes minors from acting or being acted upon apart from their parents,[37] the church allows for the admission of children and those equivalent in law to children[38] to the table of the eucharist, after first reminding parents and pastors of their responsibility in preparing them for this.[39] According to their capacity, children should be able to understand the mystery of Christ that is present in the eucharist, so that they can receive the sacrament with the necessary knowledge and understanding of what they are doing.[40] In danger of death, what is required is reduced even more: The child need only be able to distinguish the eucharist from ordinary food.[41]

Once admitted to the eucharistic table, however, all the faithful are bound to receive the eucharist at least yearly, preferably during the Easter season.[42] While the following of this precept has generally not been overlooked in the Catholic church in the United States, it should nonetheless be noted that the universal law of the church requires *all the faithful* to receive the eucharist on a yearly basis. Once again, the canon makes no distinctions between persons. The obligation is imposed upon all the Christian faithful. However, since the precept is "merely ecclesiastical law," that is, law that is established by church authority for the internal ordering of the church, it only applies to those who have been baptized into the Catholic church or those who have been received into it.[43] Those who are not in full communion with the Catholic church would therefore not be bound by this precept. They would have to follow the norms of c. 844, as well as those issued in an ecumenical directory or established by the diocesan bishop or the conference of bishops regarding the administration or the reception of sacraments.

"Full Participation" vs. "More Perfect" Participation

When speaking of the eucharist, it is clear from church documents that "full participation" is not equated with the reception of the body and blood of Christ. "Full participation" is had when all have been gathered together around the one presiding, and when each is taking part in the celebration according to his or her abilities and roles within the community of the faithful.

A different term, however, is used when speaking of the reception of the eucharistic elements. The *Constitution on the Sacred Liturgy* refers to the reception of communion variously as the "more perfect form of participation" (#55),[44] the means by which the faithful participate "more fully" in the eucharist,[45] or as "a special sign of participation in the mystery celebrated in the Mass."[46] This is something different from "full participation," then. A person may participate fully in the liturgy without participating "more perfectly," or "more fully," or "more completely."

This idea follows from the nature of the eucharistic liturgy. The Second Vatican Council wanted to emphasize the many presences of Christ in the church, as well as the many activities of God's people. To this end, the *Constitution on the Sacred Liturgy* warned against an overemphasis on the eucharistic liturgy as the only presence of Christ, stating at one point: "The spiritual life, however, is not limited solely to the participation in the liturgy" (#12), and at another point, "the sacred liturgy does not exhaust the entire activity of the church" (#9). The Council taught that even within the eucharistic liturgy itself

> Christ is always present in his church, especially in her liturgical celebrations. He is present in the sacrifice of the Mass not only in the person of his minister . . . but especially in the eucharistic species. By his power he is present in the sacraments so that when anybody baptizes it is really Christ himself who baptizes. He is present in his word since it is he himself who speaks when the holy scriptures are read in the church. Lastly, he is present when the church prays and sings. (#7)

It would seem, then, that to equate the reception of communion with full participation in the eucharist can lead to an overemphasis on the eucharistic bread and wine as the only real presence of Christ, to the detriment of the many other presences of Christ which exist within the eucharistic celebration itself and within the entire church. It is certain that Christ is wholly and substantially present in the eucharistic bread and wine. But it is also certain that Christ is just as much present in the other sacraments, in the word, in the song, and in the prayer of the community. If we hold that in order to fully participate in the celebration of the eucharist, a person must receive the body and blood of the Lord, then we have lessened the Council's teaching about the many presences of Christ. We will have given the impression that Christ is only partially present in these other forms, or that the other manifestations of his presence do not really count as much as his presence in the eucharistic species. This seems to be what the Council sought to change when it spoke of the many presences of Christ. In addition, the overemphasis on the individual's reception of the eucharistic bread and wine can also lead to an inappropriate emphasis on the eucharist as individual worship, rather than an understanding of the eucharist as the worship of the church.

Those Excluded from Reception of the Eucharist by Church Law

There are four instances where the Code of Canon Law excludes a Catholic member of the Christian faithful from receiving the eucharist. The first instance is where the person has had an excommunication imposed or declared.[47] An excommunication is considered a "medicinal penalty" by which the church attempts to remedy a situation which has injured the Christian community in some way. Some of these penalties are called "automatic" *(latae sententiae)*, while others are called "inflicted" or "imposed" *(ferendae sententiae)*.[48] But even the automatic penalties do not have automatic effects in the external forum; they bind in the internal forum. For the most part, an automatic penalty has to be declared by a church court in order for it to have an effect.[49] This is for several reasons. First, it has to be proven that the person committed the offense through malice or with culpability.[50] Second, there are various mitigating factors in the law that would either prevent a penalty from being incurred[51] or would cause it to be lessened.[52] Third, since penalties are intended to be a remedy for a situation which has injured the community, if no one knows that the person is guilty of the offense, it is difficult to see how a penalty could remedy a situation which is unknown. Thus c. 915 specifies that the excommunication must be imposed (if it is a *ferendae sententiae* penalty) or declared (if it is a *latae sententiae* penalty) in order for the person to be excluded from receiving the eucharist. Furthermore, the law requires that this be done through a judicial process, if at all possible,[53] so that the rights of the party can be adequately protected, particularly the person's right of defense.

The second instance in which a person is prohibited from receiving the eucharist is if he or she is under an interdict. Like an excommunication, an interdict is a "medicinal penalty" that attempts to remedy a situation adversely affecting the Christian community. However, it is much less severe than an excommunication. Communion with the church is not ruptured by an interdict; nor is the person forbidden to fulfill the duties of ecclesiastical offices, ministries or functions.[54] Like the excommunication, the interdict must have been imposed or declared in order for it to have any effect upon the person's ability to receive the eucharist.

The third instance in which a person is prohibited by law from receiving the eucharist is if he or she is conscious of grave sin.[55] This has been a part of church discipline at least since the Council of Trent, with the Code of Canon Law adding nothing new to the practice. However, it does make the distinction that the person must be "conscious" of grave sin. This implies a decision by the person's conscience, which convicts the person of sin. Obviously, a person who is not conscious of sin cannot be obliged to confess it, and cannot be said to be prohibited from approaching the table of the eucharist.

Finally, the previously quoted c. 915 presents the last category of the Christian faithful who are excluded by law from receiving the eucharist; namely, those who "obstinately persist in manifest grave sin." It is not entirely clear what the drafters of the Code of Canon Law had in mind when using this phrase. However, it is certain that, since it represents a restriction of the rights of the Christian faithful,[56] each word must be considered carefully, lest the application of this canon be extended beyond those cases for which it was intended.

Thus there are three aspects to this phrase.[57] First, the person must obstinately persist in the action. This would imply that the person has been warned that his or her action is sinful, and that the warning has not been heeded. Second, the action must be manifest; that is it must be known by others. This does not mean that it is widely known, however. It simply means that the action is externally knowable by others, without someone having to confide in them or manifest his or her conscience to them. Finally, the action must be gravely sinful. Since for the most part the Code of Canon Law deals with external matters rather than matters of conscience, it might appear that the canon is speaking of "grave matter" in this case. However, since the canon must be interpreted precisely (because it restricts the rights of the faithful), "grave sin" must be taken in its more precise form; namely, knowledge, intention and action, followed by conviction by one's conscience. As such, any description of what precisely constitutes "grave sin" for the individual person would go beyond the scope of the laws of the church. The law can merely say that once a person is obstinately persistent in manifest grave sin, he or she is excluded from receiving the eucharist.

It cannot specify what that sin might be, or provide a list of those things which are considered gravely sinful for the individual person.

Those Excluded from Reception of the Eucharist by Church Practice

In addition to those who are excluded from the reception of the eucharist by church law, there are those who are excluded by church practice. Included in this category would be those Catholics who have not married according to the Catholic canonical form of marriage and those who have remarried while the previous marriage bond is still presumed to exist.[58]

Those in Civil Marriages Only

Although the church teaches that the marriage bond is created by the consent of the parties, church law adds a further stipulation for Catholic members of the Christian faithful: Their exchange of consent must take place before a priest, deacon or designated lay person who has the necessary jurisdiction and in the presence of two witnesses.[59] (In marriages involving a Catholic and a non-Catholic, the Catholic party's bishop can issue a dispensation so that the marriage may take place without the presence of a priest, deacon or designated layperson.) If the consent is not exchanged in this manner, the church does not recognize the marriage as valid.

This has certain consequences for the Catholic party. The church feels compelled to urge Catholics in the strongest manner possible to observe church law regarding the manner in which they enter into marriage. While acknowledging there are many reasons Catholics enter into civil unions, Pope John Paul II clearly reiterated the church's practice of excluding such Catholics from the reception of the eucharist when he stated:

> There are increasing cases of Catholics who for ideological or practical reasons prefer to contract a merely civil marriage and who reject or at least defer religious marriage. Their situation cannot of course be likened to that of people simply living together without any bond at all, because in the present case there is at least a certain commitment to a properly defined and

probably stable state of life even though the possibility of a future divorce is often present in the minds of those entering a civil marriage. By seeking public recognition of their bond on the part of the state, such couples show that they are ready to accept not only its advantages but also its obligations. Nevertheless, not even this situation is acceptable to the church.

The aim of pastoral action will be to make these people understand the need for consistency between their choice in life and the faith that they profess, and to try to do everything possible to induce them to regularize their situation in light of Christian principles. While treating them with great charity and bringing them into the life of the respective communities, the pastors of the church will regrettably not be able to admit them to the sacraments.[60]

Those in Second Marriages while the First Bond Endures

A second group of people who are excluded by church practice from receiving the eucharist are those who have entered into a subsequent marriage while a first marriage bond is still in existence. This would include those who themselves were married previously, as well as those whose current spouse had been married previously. For Catholic members of the Christian faithful, because the previous marriage bond is presumed to be valid until proven otherwise,[61] they would not be able to enter into another marriage in the Catholic church; hence, any subsequent marriage would be invalid because they could not follow the form prescribed for the marriages of Catholics. Other members of the Christian faithful, however, would not be allowed to receive the eucharist, even if they were permitted to do so according to c. 844, or even if they wish to be received into the full communion of the Catholic church according to the Rite of Chrisitian Initiation of Adults.[62] Furthermore, the non-baptized would not be allowed to receive the sacraments of initiation if they were in a subsequent marital union while the prior bond of marriage was presumed to still be in existence.

The reason for this practice does not have to do with the Catholic form of marriage; it has to do with Catholic theology of marriage. Pope John Paul II has stated:

The church reaffirms her practice, which is based upon sacred scripture, of not admitting to eucharistic communion divorced persons who have remarried. They are unable to be admitted thereto from the fact that their state and condition of life objectively contradict that union of love between Christ and the church which is signified and effected by the eucharist. Besides this there is another special pastoral reason: If these people were admitted to the eucharist the faithful would be led into error and confusion regarding the church's teaching about the indissolubility of marriage.[63]

In thus reiterating the practice of the church, Pope John Paul II does not appeal to the laws of the church, but to the theology of marriage. He does not refer back to c. 915 or 916 as justification for the church's exclusion of people from the eucharistic table. Instead, he appeals to the theology of marriage, and the possibility of scandal in the Christian community.

Re-invitation to the Table of the Eucharist

The Code of Canon Law is consistent, however, in providing ways in which people can vindicate their rights in the church. Through penalties, as we have seen above, the church seeks to repair scandal and to keep a person from engaging in behavior which is harmful to the Christian community. For those who have entered into merely civil marriages, the church offers the possibility that couples can enter into marriages that *are* canonically recognized by the church, either through the *convalidation* of the marriage or its *sanation*.[64] For those who have divorced and remarried, the church offers two possibilities: the prior marriage bond could be dissolved[65] or it could be declared null.[66]

Marriage Dissolution

Marriage bonds that can be dissolved are those that are not sacramental bonds or that have not been consummated. While the church teaches that no human power can dissolve a sacramental marriage bond, the church has traditionally claimed authority over non-sacramental marriage bonds, dissolving these bonds for the good of the faith through either the Pauline Privilege or the Privilege of the Faith (sometimes known as the Petrine Privilege).[67]

A non-sacramental marriage bond occurs when one of the parties to a marriage is not baptized. Since baptism is the gate to the other sacraments, in the absence of baptism there can be no sacrament of marriage. Since the marriage bond is one, it cannot be sacramental for the baptized party and non-sacramental for the non-baptized party. Thus, only two baptized people can receive the sacrament of marriage. In marriages where one or both parties are unbaptized, the church recognizes those marriages as valid, since they involved an exchange of marital consent. But it also considers them non-sacramental marriages, which are capable of being dissolved for the good of the faith. In both the Pauline Privilege and the Privilege of the Faith, the church is dissolving a previous marriage as a privilege to an individual person. Ordinarily, marriage is a matter of the public good, since it is given for the good both of the individual and society as well.[68] However, in granting a dissolution of marriage by the Pauline Privilege or the Privilege of the Faith, the church recognizes that at times there is a higher good, namely, the good of the faith. In dissolving a prior non-sacramental marriage bond, the church considers both the faith of the individual who will now be free to enter into a sacramental marriage, as well as the faith of the entire church which will benefit from an increase in membership and the more complete eucharistic participation of its members.

The Pauline Privilege, which was first used in the fourth century and is based upon Paul's first letter to the Corinthians,[69] can be granted when a prior marriage involved two non-baptized people. One of the parties now wishes to be baptized and enter into a new marriage, and the other party does not wish to be baptized and does not wish to reconcile with the other party. Normally, the person who wishes to be baptized wishes to enter into marriage with another Catholic,[70] but in certain circumstances, the bishop can allow the marriage to be with a non-Catholic member of the Christian faithful, or even with an unbaptized person.[77] This privilege is granted by the local bishop, following the procedures outlined in cc. 1143–1147.

The Privilege of the Faith or the Petrine Privilege is of much more recent vintage, with the first cases dating from the 1920s.[71] It is not based upon any text of scripture but upon the church's desire to provide for the spiritual good of the faithful. W. Woestman summarizes the rationale for this privilege when he states that it was

> brought about by three factors: frequent marriages between the baptized and the unbaptized; divorce becoming commonplace; and the desire of divorced persons to celebrate a valid marriage in the Catholic church. Faced with this situation all the popes since Benedict XV have personally intervened to dissolve valid non-sacramental marriages or natural marriages in favor of the faith of one of the parties, or even in favor of the faith of a third party.[72]

It was seen as something that the Roman pontiff was able to do based upon his authority as Vicar of Christ and pastor of the entire church, which conferred on him full, supreme and universal authority.[73]

Prior valid but non-sacramental marriage bonds which are dissolved by the Privilege of the Faith normally involve one baptized party and one non-baptized party, although they may also involve two non-baptized persons if there is no desire for baptism on the part of either party. There are several possibilities which have developed over the years: the unbaptized party may now wish to be baptized and enter into a sacramental marriage; the already baptized party may now wish to enter into a sacramental marriage with another Christian; or a Catholic party who had previously been in a non-sacramental marriage now wishes to enter into a new marriage with a baptized Christian.

This privilege is granted by the Roman Pontiff, with the cases being prepared locally and sent to the Congregation for the Doctrine of the Faith according to norms that were issued in 1973.[74] Since this procedure is of such recent origin and was developed in response to a pastoral need, it might be expected that its use will continue to develop as the church is presented with future pastoral needs. For, at its best, the procedure can be seen as a way in which the church provides pastoral care for the Christian faithful and finds ways of applying the teaching of the church to the realities of the present.

A third type of marriage bond that is dissolved by the church involves marriages that were never consummated.[75] Although this might seem to be a rare phenomenon in North American society, W. Woestman points out that there were 519 such cases worldwide in 1991.[76] As with the Privilege of the Faith, the dissolution of non-consummated marriages was seen as an extension of the power of the Roman Pontiff. It had its origin in the 12th century and originally involved cases where one or both of the spouses, after having exchanged consent but never having consummated their marriage, now wished to enter religious life. Over the centuries the church extended the reasons for dissolving such marriages to cover more and more cases, with the 1983 Code of Canon Law simply stating that the Roman Pontiff can dissolve non-consummated marriages for "a just reason."[77] In summarizing those reasons that are considered "just," Woestman states:

> The cause must be proportionate to the gravity of the dissolution of a ratified marriage. In general, all just causes are ultimately the salvation of souls *(salus animarum)*. According to the practice of the Congregation, the following are considered to be just causes (although this should not be considered a complete list): serious aversion or dislike of the couple without hope of reconciliation and a successful marriage; fear of probable future scandal; discord and quarrels among the relatives; one of the parties had contracted a civil marriage with a third party; civil separation or divorce with the danger of incontinence; contracting an incurable disease after the marriage; partial proof of defect of consent or of an impediment.[78]

The dissolution of non-consummated marriages is done by the Roman Pontiff, following cc. 1142, and 1697–1706 and norms issued in 1986 by the Congregation for the Sacraments.[79] Like the Privilege of the Faith, this form of marriage dissolution can still be seen to be in a state of development, since the church has not precisely defined what is meant by a consummated union in light of the church's teaching on marriage at the Second Vatican Council.

Marriage Nullity

A second way that the church provides for those who are in second marriages not canonically recognized by the church is through the marriage nullity process, which declares that a prior bond of marriage was invalid and that therefore the person's natural right to marry is still intact. This process could be administrative, as in cases where the prior bond of marriage is invalid because the proper canonical form was not followed for marriages of Catholic or Orthodox members of the Christian faithful.[80] Or it could be an abbreviated or summary judicial process, as in cases involving the presence of a matrimonial impediment or where there was a defect in the canonical form that was attempted.[81] Or it could be a formal judicial process, as in cases involving a lack of capacity, knowledge or intention for entering into marriage.[82]

Regardless of which procedure is followed, it is important to keep in mind that marriage nullity processes are not moral judgments; they are legal judgments. They are not attempting to discover whether God has joined this couple together or not, since no tribunal can presume to speak for God. Instead, marriage nullity processes are cases that involve both the status of persons and the rights of persons in the church. In petitioning for a declaration of nullity—whether due to lack of canonical form, or the presence of an impediment, or the lack of capacity, intention or knowledge—a person is saying, in effect, "I do not believe my previous relationship was marriage as the church understands marriage." If an affirmative decision is reached at the end of the process, the church confirms that opinion, based upon the evidence that the person has presented. In declaring a marriage null the church makes a statement that, due to the circumstances of the prior marriage—circumstances that rendered that marriage null—the person's natural right to marry is still intact.

Cases involving the nullity of marriage are normally heard by a diocesan tribunal, followed by a appellate tribunal, although the parties always have a right to appeal their case to the tribunal of the Roman Rota. Tribunals follow procedures that are established in the Code of Canon Law, as indicated above, as well as the directives of the Supreme Tribunal of the Apostolic Signatura, which oversees the administration of justice in the church.[83]

Despite the processes which the church has established for remedying the situations which might prevent a person from receiving the eucharist, there is still a more fundamental question which needs to be answered: Why does the church single out a prior marriage bond as the principal reason for a person not being admitted to the eucharist? It is to this question that we now turn.

Why Marriage?

There are numerous sources of sin and division in our world today and numerous sinful situations that the church has identified. The Second Vatican Council has identified the presence of sin in the world and indicated its effects when it stated:

> The varieties of crime are numerous: all offenses against life itself, such as murder, genocide, abortion, euthanasia and willful suicide; all violations of the integrity of the human person, such as mutilation, physical and mental torture, undue psychological pressures; all offenses against human dignity, such as subhuman living conditions, arbitrary imprisonment, deportation, slavery, prostitution, the selling of women and children, degrading working conditions where [people] are treated as mere tools for profit rather than free and responsible persons; all these and the like are criminal: they poison civilization; and they debase the perpetrators more than the victims and militate against the honor of the creator.[84]

The *Catechism of the Catholic Church* has spoken of "sins that cry to heaven,"[85] and the sin of sexual abuse, which is "compounded by the scandalous harm done to the physical and moral integrity of the young, who will remain scarred by it all their lives" (n. 2389). It has condemned participation in institutions, structures and ways of life that are sinful: the acceptance of famine in the world and the refusal to use all means to remedy hunger (n. 2269); the use of "usurious and avaricious dealings" that "lead to the hunger and death of their brethren in the human family" (n. 2269); the denial of a person's inalienable right to life (n. 2273), or those things that a person needs for adequate health, education, employment, and social assistance (n. 2288); those who abuse their own bodies through excessive use of food, alcohol, tobacco, medicine or drugs (nn. 2290–2291); those who cause scandal among the Christian faithful (nn. 2284–2287);

those who engage in hostage-taking, kidnaping, terrorism or torture (n. 2297); those who participate in the extermination of a people, nation or ethnic minority (n. 2313); those who participate in the arms race (nn. 2315–2316); and those who through "injustice, excessive economic or social inequalities, envy, distrust and pride . . . threaten peace and cause wars" (n. 2317).

In other places the church has condemned racism as seriously sinful, whether the racism be institutional, religious, ethnic, social, spontaneous or eugenic.[86] Furthermore, Pope John Paul II has spoken of three types of social sin: First, he identifies what he calls "a communion of sin," which, in contrast to the communion of saints, "drags down with itself the church and, in some way, the whole world."[87] Second, he speaks of social sin as a sin against the love of one's neighbor, which applies to

> every sin against justice in interpersonal relationships, committed either by the individual against the community or by the community against the individual. Also *social* is every sin against the rights of the human person, beginning with the right to life and including the life of the unborn, or against a person's physical integrity. Likewise *social* is every sin against others' freedom, especially against supreme freedom to believe in God and adore him; social is every sin against the dignity and honor of one's neighbor. Also social is every sin against the common good and its exigencies in relation to the whole broad spectrum of the rights and duties of citizens. The term *social* can be applied to the sins of commission or omission—on the part of political, economic or trade union leaders, who though in a position to do so do not work diligently and wisely for the improvement and transformation of society according to the requirements and potential of the given historic moment; as also on the part of workers who through absenteeism or non-cooperation fail to ensure that their industries can continue to advance the well-being of the workers themselves, of their families, and of the whole of society.[88]

Finally, Pope John Paul II speaks of the social sin that exists in "the relationships between the various human communities. These relationships are not always in accord with the plan of God, who intends that there be justice in the world, and freedom and peace between individuals, groups, and peoples."[89] While admitting that these situations, particularly when they "become generalized and reach vast proportions as social phenomena, almost always become anonymous, just as their causes are complex and not always identifiable," nonetheless John Paul II has issued "an appeal to the consciences of all, so that each may shoulder his or her responsibility seriously and courageously in order to change those disastrous conditions and intolerable situations."[90]

With the identification of all of these sources of sin in society— all of which may be forgiven through the sacrament of penance that allows the penitent to approach the table of the eucharist again— why is a second marriage the one thing that cannot be forgiven? In order to answer this question, it will be necessary to examine more closely the church's understanding of marriage.

The Nature of Marriage

The church's understanding of marriage is found in the *Pastoral Constitution on the Church in the Modern World (Gaudium et spes)*, 48–52. This is reflected in the 1983 Code of Canon Law, particularly canons 1055–1057. In these two documents, which are based upon the scriptures, marriage is seen as being for the good of the spouses and for the generation of life. God is seen as the author of marriage, since God was the one who led the woman to the man. And marriage is seen as an equal partnership, since only the woman was found to be the equal or the suitable partner for the man.

The personal good of the spouses and the generation of life does not exhaust the church's understanding of marriage, though, since marriage is also seen as something that was established for the good of the community. Especially through the writings of the prophets, marriage was seen as a sign of God's relationship with the community. It was not simply for a personal good; it was also for the community's good. When people would see the love of a husband and wife, they would come to know what the love of God was like. When people would see how a husband and wife related to each other, they could see how God related to their community. Thus, marriage became a sacrament, not only from the point of view of how two people related to each other, but also from the point of view of how they related to the community of God's people. Through marriage, they were established as a sign among God's people of God's faithful, fruitful, abiding, loving presence.

Like the sacrament of holy orders, the sacrament of marriage indicates how people stand in relation to the Christian community. In holy orders, people stand as a sign of the shepherding love of God, who leads and guides people on their way to the kingdom. In marriage, people stand as a sign of the relational love of God, who remains faithful to his people and who gives them life.

It is for this reason that marriage is sacramental for all the baptized, not just for baptized Catholics. It is the sacrament of baptism that creates the sacrament of marriage, not the place where the marriage was performed. If people are baptized, then they marry "in the Lord." They form a sacramental marriage bond. They are established within the community as signs of God's faithful, fruitful, abiding, loving presence. Thus marriage is seen as total way of life, not simply as a particular moment in a person's life.

What Happens in Divorce and Remarriage?

Because the marital sacrament is not merely a moment, but a whole way of life, and because that way of life indicates something greater than just two people joining themselves together in love, those who leave that way of life behind and enter a new union are seen as objectively contradicting the sign of marriage. This was the reasoning of Pope John Paul II in his apostolic exhortation, *Familiaris consortio*, noted above. Since then, this notion of "objective contradiction" has been the primary reason given for not allowing people to receive the eucharist if they are in second marriages that are not canonically recognized.[91] While others have associated the situation of the divorced and remarried with the presence of sin in their lives,[92] neither the Holy Father nor the Congregation for the Doctrine of the Faith have done so. They have merely pointed to the objective contradiction between the way the person is living and the demands of the sacrament of marriage as a symbol of faith.

That is, those who have established a second union while the first union is presumably still in existence live in a way that contradicts the symbol of Christian marriage. They live in a way that does not testify to the abiding presence of God in the community, since they have left one union to form another one. Objectively speaking, their way of life says that God's gift and call are not irrevocable, and that God can turn his back on his own. It is this objective reality of their lives, and not any personal sinfulness, which keeps people from receiving the eucharist. Personal sinfulness is subjective and can be forgiven; a way of life is objective and can only be changed. And the church teaches that until it is changed the person is unable to receive the eucharist. Their life is lived contrary to what the church believes about Christian marriage. Hence they do not exemplify the church to the world. Because they are this "living contradiction" they should not approach the table of the eucharist.

Thus the new marriage is sacramentally inappropriate, rather than being morally unacceptable. As such, it falls under the realm of sacramental theology rather than moral theology.

However, the denial of the eucharist to the faithful in these instances represents a conflict of rights in the church. Church law states that anyone who is baptized and not prohibited by law must be admitted to the eucharist (c. 912), and is bound to receive the sacrament at least once a year (c. 920.1). Church practice, on the other hand, has restricted that right by establishing categories of people who cannot receive the eucharist, including those who have entered a second marriage while the prior bond is presumed to exist. Church authority is able to place such restrictions since it is responsible for the regulation of the sacraments. But in the case of the eucharist, it must also ensure that all participants receive the greatest benefit from its celebration (c. 899.3).

Therefore, the question must be asked: Is there sufficient reason for restricting the rights that a person is granted under the universal law of the church? From time to time, the church has reiterated the affirmative answer to that question, based upon the symbolic nature of the sacrament of marriage. It is doubtful, however, that the issue has been closed, given the fact that the question continues to be raised. The continuing discussion of the question, however, will have to take into account both Catholic and Orthodox theology of the sacrament of marriage, as well as the church's role in the economy of salvation.

Exclusion from the Eucharist and Exclusion from Life

Having discussed the concepts of inclusion and exclusion from the viewpoint of church law regarding the reception of the sacraments and church practice regarding the reception of the eucharist, it is now possible to turn to a more fundamental question that lies at the root of the question: Why do we exclude people at all from receiving the eucharist? To answer this question, we will have to look at the meaning of the eucharist, not as a private celebration of an individual or a quasi-public celebration of a particular community, but as a universal celebration of the whole church and indeed the whole world. In other words, we must examine not just this particular eucharistic community, but this eucharistic community in the context of the church in the world.

The Liturgy of the World

Karl Rahner, in presenting what he termed the "liturgy of the world," has written:

> The world and its history are the terrible and sublime liturgy, breathing of death and sacrifice, which God celebrates and causes to be celebrated in and through human history in its freedom, this being something which he in turn sustains in grace by his sovereign disposition. In the entire length and breadth of this immense history of birth and death, complete superficiality, folly, inadequacy and hatred (all of which "crucify") on the one hand, and silent submission, responsibility even to death in dying and in joyfulness, in attaining the heights and plumbing the depths, on the other, the true liturgy of the world is present—present in such a way that the liturgy which the Son has brought to its absolute fullness on his Cross belongs intrinsically to it, emerges from it, i.e., from the ultimate source of the grace of the world,

and constitutes the supreme point of this liturgy from which all else draws its life, because everything else is always dependent upon the supreme point as upon its goal and at the same time sustained by it.[93]

This view of the "liturgy of the world" causes us to rethink our own vision of liturgy, which tends to be too narrow, since it often concentrates on what this community is celebrating here and now. Occasionally our liturgies are punctuated with prayers for various "disaster points" around the world; occasionally a special collection may be taken up for "the missions" or for a "sharing parish" across the city or in another part of the world; and perhaps each Lent a parish may participate in Operation Rice Bowl. However, aside from these passing nods to the rest of the world, our liturgies are mostly self-contained. The "prayer *of* the faithful" becomes the "prayer *for* the faithful," as we place our individual concerns for our sick, our dead and the upcoming parish festival before our God.

When we do this, two things occur: We concentrate on our own wholeness rather than on the wholeness of the world, and we fail to recognize our own brokenness as part of the brokenness of the world. We do not allow our individual liturgies to be symbols of the liturgy of the world. Rather, they become divorced from the larger reality in which we exist. For as M. Skelley has pointed out, "The various ritual forms of worship are symbolic manifestations of this liturgy of the world."[94] We celebrate in our liturgies what we live in our lives. If our liturgies are to be authentic, there must be no dichotomy between those two things. For, as Karl Rahner has noted:

> This ecclesial worship is important and significant, not because something happens in it that does not happen elsewhere, but because there is present and explicit in it that which makes the world important, since it is everywhere blessed by grace, by faith, hope and love, and in it there occurred the cross of Christ, which is the culmination of its engraced history and the culmination of the historical explictness of this history of grace. To anyone who has (or might have had) absolutely no experience in his own life of the history of grace of the world, no experience of the cosmic liturgy, the church's liturgy could only seem like a strange ritualism.[95]

Thus we must look to our own lives, and to our experience of life in the world, to understand what it means to participate in the eucharist.

The Wholeness of the World and the Wholeness of our Lives

The opening words of Vatican II's *Pastoral Constitution on the Church in the Modern World* proclaim:

> The joy and hope, the grief and anguish of the [people] of our time, especially of those who are poor or afflicted in any way, are the joy and hope, the grief and anguish of the followers of Christ as well. Nothing that is genuinely human fails to find an echo in their hearts. (#1)

This, for Karl Rahner, was the liturgy of the world: the drawing together of all human experience in light of the redeeming power of Christ. Our primary goal in life, and hence our primary goal in liturgy, is to create that wholeness which is the kingdom of God. For this reason, M. Skelley, in explaining Rahner's link between the liturgy of the world and our own acts of worship, states, "Worship is not primarily what happens when we gather to celebrate the eucharist; it is primarily what happens when we cooperate together with God in history."[96] Since God in history is seeking the oneness of all creation, our liturgies must also indicate that same oneness. Because, as noted above, the *Constitution on the Sacred Liturgy* reminded us that our liturgies are public celebrations, not private ones, and that they represent the entire church, not just one particular community, our goal when we gather for liturgy is not personal wholeness, but the wholeness of the world.

In order to achieve that wholeness, however, we must come to recognize that we ourselves are broken to the same extent that the world is broken; we are divided to the same extent the world is divided; we hunger to the same extent that the world hungers. This realization is not something that comes easily to North Americans. We tend to perceive ourselves as whole — or at least as deserving of wholeness. And then it is from this perception of wholeness that we seek to draw the rest of the world into what we have gained for ourselves. We minister to others not because we recognize our own neediness, but because it makes us feel good about ourselves. We give to the poor not because we recognize in them our own poverty, but because it makes us feel enriched. We do much of what we do from a position of perceived wholeness, rather than from a position of our solidarity with the brokenness of all of humanity. We stand apart from humanity, then, seeking to bring it to the fullness we have gained for ourselves.

For Rahner, this is the exact opposite of what occurs at liturgy. As Skelley has pointed out, "First and foremost, liturgy has to do with the ways we give our lives over to the transforming self-communication of the absolute, holy mystery,"[97] not when we engage in the self-communication ourselves. It is something that relies on God's initiative, not our own, because it is "first and foremost something that God celebrates. It takes place at the absolutely free and gracious initiative of God," even though we are called to respond to that initiative in a positive or a negative manner.[98] It is something that accepts that which is less than whole, because it recognizes and affirms that all things are being brought to fulfillment through the transforming power of God. For this reason, Skelley notes:

> The liturgy of the world is celebrated not only by those who rejoice in the beauty of life but also by those who persevere in all its ugliness. In fact, the trusting self-surrender of those who are broken-hearted achieves the deepest communion in the life of God because it requires the greatest act of faith. The worship they give by bearing their suffering is the most profound witness to the gracious presence of the absolute mystery. They do what we would never imagine could be humanly possible and so give eloquent testimony to the transforming power of God. That does not make their misery any less painful, nor does it justify the evils they are forced to endure. It does mean, though, that even our darkest moments can be taken up into the liturgy of the world.[99]

In order to achieve oneness with a world that is often broken, hungry, and divided, then, we must first and foremost recognize the brokenness, hunger, and division within ourselves. Jean Vanier, in discussing the world from which we emerge after childhood, describes it as a world of walls that have been erected because of our experiences in life. It is these walls, he claims, that make us "hide and forget the reality of our wounds and our fundamental poverty."[100] The wounds, and the walls that enclose them, are the things that keep us from entering into relationship with others. We are afraid that others will discover our woundedness, and will either exploit our weaknesses or view us negatively because of them. Vanier believes, however, that:

> The road to inner unity or wholeness begins as soon as we start to recognize this broken and chaotic world in the depths of our being. We no longer deny our past mistakes, our share of responsibility for things, and our infidelities. We begin to open the door of our hearts in a desire for truth and reconciliation. . . . Inner healing and peace come gradually as we penetrate these shadow areas without being completely overwhelmed by them, as we learn to live with anguish without falling into depression or self-hatred, anger, or guilt.[101]

In a similar vein, Monika Hellwig speaks of the experience of hunger as forming the basis for our solidarity with the world. She states: "The simple, central action of the eucharist is the sharing of food— not only eating but sharing. The simple, central human experience for the understanding of this action is hunger."[102] Furthermore, she points out that it is only out of our own experience of hunger that we can ever begin to understand the hunger of others, since "one who is never hungry is unlikely to have compassion or concern for those who are constantly hungry and never satisfied."[103] Unfortunately, for many North Americans, this experience of real, physical hunger is lost. We may say that we hunger for acceptance, or hunger for peace, or hunger for justice, or hunger for love, but what we receive in the eucharist is not a mere concept; it is real food. Unless we experience that real, physical hunger for real, physical food, we will not understand fully the meaning of the eucharist and will never be in solidarity with the hungry of the world. It was for this reason that the church instituted periods of fasting during the liturgical year and prescribed a period of fasting before receiving the eucharistic bread. Fasting creates a hunger that can only be satisfied by God. It also creates a oneness with those for whom hunger is a way of life.

It is by the recognition of our own brokenness and our own hunger that we come to lessen the divisions that exist between ourselves and the world. We no longer stand apart from the world, seeking to bring the world up to our standards, or to gift the world with what we have gifted ourselves with. We recognize instead the gift of God's self-revelation in the world, and find as the basis of unity the fact that all people are receivers of that gift. It is first of all our identification with the world that first allows us to celebrate the sacrament of our unity. For we can never hope to be united when we insist on standing apart.

The Exclusions That We Create

To the extent that we fail to recognize our own brokenness and hunger, we will also maintain the divisions that are present in our world. We will continue to exclude people from our lives, even unconsciously, simply because we are not aware of their presence. Our celebrations of the eucharist will be divided and exclusive because the divisions and exclusions exist within ourselves. And we will end up asking questions like, "How can people be excluded from receiving the eucharist?" rather than asking, "How does the exclusion of people from the reception of the eucharist reflect the ways that we have excluded people from our lives?" When we have solved the problem posed in the second question, perhaps there will no longer be a need to ask the first. For we exclude people from the eucharist to the same extent that we exclude people from our lives. The question is not limited to the mere reception of the eucharistic bread and wine. It is part of a more pervasive pattern of exclusion that exists within ourselves and which keeps us apart from one another.

Until we recognize that, the way that we celebrate the eucharist will always reflect the way that we live our lives. The eucharist will not be communion for us until our lives are communion for us. The eucharist will not be unity for us until our lives are united to the rest of life in the world. The signs disunity are all around us; people are excluded from our communities and from our lives all the time. Our world is often experienced as fractured and fracturing. At times we do the fracturing and the excluding without even knowing it. If we celebrate the eucharist as one, and pretend that there are no divisions, that there is no disunity, that there is no fracture, and that there is no exclusion in our world, then we delude ourselves. We fail to admit the existence of that which is within us. If we attempt to celebrate in the eucharist a unity that is not pervasive in our lives, then we have failed to recognize the brokenness that is within us, and the brokenness that is before us. That can be dangerous, since then we will have made the present the end of our journey. We will pretend that we have arrived, which is the worst possible scenario.

Rather than pretending, we must instead come face-to-face with the reality of our lives, understanding how the brokenness of our lives is a reflection of the brokenness of the world and how the lack of wholeness in our lives contributes to the lack of wholeness in the world. In describing the eucharist as the sacrament of our unity, we must ask ourselves difficult questions about unity and division in our lives. We must ask ourselves how the eucharist can be the sacrament of unity for us, not just when people are excluded by church law or church practice, but at other times of exclusion as well. We must ask ourselves how we can celebrate the eucharist as the sacrament of unity when our actions so clearly demonstrate that we are not united with the rest of humanity:

- when we build our houses farther and farther out in the suburbs so that we can escape what we perceive as the decay of the inner city and get away from what we see as its dirt and its crime

- when our sexual encounters, which are meant to express our deepest communion with another person, are fleeting; when our marriages, which are meant to be permanent commitments that exist as a sign to the community of God's own love for us, are discarded when they are not found to be personally fulfilling; when our friends are chosen by how much they are like me, and how much they can do for me; when we do good for others not because the gospel calls us to, but because it makes me feel good about myself

- when we drive alone in our cars every day so that we do not have to take public transportation, which puts us in touch with a "public" that we would rather avoid. Or when we demand "private public transportation," which can take us right where

we want to go, without the inconvenience of meeting someone
who is not like me

- when we shy away from people who are not like me because
they are people with disabilities, because their skin is a different
color, because they are infected with HIV or sick with AIDS,
because they are black or white or brown, because they speak
a different language from me, because they have a different
idea of what is important in life, because they have a different
concept of time or space, because they have a different sexual
orientation

- when we discard people when they are no longer useful to us
by putting our elderly in nursing homes, aborting our children,
downsizing our companies, gentrifying our neighborhoods

- when we allow children to be mistreated and abused, when the
elderly die of the heat in our cities because they have to keep
their windows closed for fear of violence; when these same people die because a neighbor does not know that they live there;
when we do not know the people who live down the hall or
down the block, and believe that the right to privacy is an
absolute right

- when we get angry at people who panhandle us on the street,
who interrupt our reveries on public transportation, who create a disturbance by their loud talk or shouting in public places,
who create a disturbance in our lives because of their smell

- when there is still violence between Arab and Jew in the Middle
East, between Catholic and Protestant in Northern Ireland,
between Muslim and Christian in the Balkans, between Tutsi
and Hutu in Rwanda

- when we exploit the world's oil reserves for our own gluttonous
engines, encourage the cutting down of our rain forests to sat-
isfy our need for natural wood, leave vast regions of our country barren through strip-mining, destroy trees and wildlife in the
acid fallout from our industries, endanger citizens through the
dumping of nuclear waste, contribute to the flooding of our

Patrick R. Lagges

cities and suburbs because we demand more and bigger houses that are built over natural flood plains

- when we come to church wearing athletic shoes made by workers receiving substandard wages and working under substandard conditions

- when we drive to church in cars made in countries that do not allow workers the right to organize, and then take our children to soccer practice where they kick around soccer balls made by 11-year-old Pakistanis who sit cross-legged 12 hours a day, holding the ball between their feet and stitching it with their hands.

How do we find ways to celebrate the eucharist as the sacrament of our unity when we find our lives so divided, so fragmented and so depersonalized? That is the larger question that we have to ask ourselves. The exclusion of people from eucharistic communion is just an illustration of the exclusion of people from human communion.

The question, though, suggests two answers. On the one hand, it means we have our work cut out for us. We must find ways to make our liturgies more inclusive in the same way that we must find ways to make our lives more inclusive. We cannot do one without also doing the other. On the other hand, we must realize that the unity of all creation is the work of God who oftentimes works in spite of us. It is not up to us to make all creation one. It is up to us to cooperate with God in making all creation one. To the extent that we are able to do that, we will find that our celebrations of the eucharist become much more inclusive.

In his book, *An African Prayer Book,* Desmond Tutu recalls the story of an elder of the village of Mogopa in South Africa:

> Mogopa, a village to the west of Johannesburg, was to be demolished and its inhabitants forcibly removed at gunpoint to a homeland in apartheid's forced population removal schemes. On the eve of their departure, a vigil with church leaders from all over South Africa was held in Mogopa. The village clinics, shops, schools and churches had already been demolished. At about midnight an elder of the doomed village got up and he

prayed a strange prayer that I will never forget. He said, "God, thank you for loving us so much."

Several years later, apartheid is dead and the people of Mogopa have returned to their village, which they are rebuilding. God did indeed love them very much, it seems.[104] When we gather for the eucharist, we gather as broken people from a fractured world. We bring our brokenness, our disunity, our fractured world to the Lord. And we see in the eucharist what God can make out of what is broken, and what it poured out. For we do not celebrate in the eucharist who we are at this moment. We celebrate instead what God can make of us. Not everything needs to be the "most perfect" or the "most complete" in our lives. We do not have to do everything "more fully." We simply must cooperate with God in history, as M. Skelley has written, immersing ourselves in the abiding, absolute mystery.[105] When we do that, and if our understanding is like that of the Mogopa elder, then we will realize that God indeed loves us, very much.

1. J. P. Beal, "To Be or Not To Be. That Is the Question: The Rights of the Accused in the Canonical Penal Process," in *Canon Law Society of America Proceedings* (hereinafter referred to as CLSA Proceedings) 53 (1991), p. 77.

2. 1983 *Code of Canon Law*, c. 897. It is interesting to note that this canon describes the eucharist as the summit and source of all *Christian* worship and states the it signifies and effects the unity of the *People of God* rather than referring simply to *Catholic* worship and the unity of the *Catholic church.* Canon 204 identifies the people of God as all the Christian faithful who have been incorporated in Christ through baptism; the term Christian similarly includes all those who have been baptized in Christ. When speaking of the eucharist, then, the laws of the church are more inclusive than exclusive.

3. Vatican II, *Constitution on the Sacred Liturgy (Sacrosanctum Concilium),* in *A.A.S.* 56 (1964), n. 48, p. 113. English translation in A. Flannery (gen. ed.), *Vatican II: The Conciliar and Postconciliar Documents* (hereinafter referred to as Flannery)(Collegeville, MN, The Liturgical Press, 1975) p. 16.

4. John Paul II, *Allocutio,* 3 February 1983, in *A.A.S.* 75 (1983), p. 463.

5. See c. 849: Baptism, the gate to the sacraments, necessary for salvation in fact or at least in intention, by which men and women are freed from their sins, are reborn as children of God, and, configured to Christ by an indelible character, are incorporated in the Church, is validly conferred only by washing with water together with the required words.

6. This is not without restrictions, however. For example, the reception of the anointing of the sick is limited to those who are sick (c. 1004.1); those who establish the sacrament of marriage must be a man and a woman (c. 1055.1); those who receive the sacrament of penance must first have sinned, repented of that sin and resolved to amend their life (c. 987); and, as has been most recently re-emphasized, those who receive the sacrament of orders must be male (c. 1024).

7. This follows from the more fundamental right of the Christian faithful that can be found in c. 213: The Christian faithful have the right to receive assistance from the sacred pastors out of the spiritual goods of the church, especially the word of God and the sacraments.

8. See c. 841: Since the sacraments are the same for the universal church and pertain to the divine deposit, it is for the supreme authority of the church alone to approve or define those things which are required for their validity; it is for the same supreme authority of the church or other competent authority in accord with the norm of c. 838.3 and 4 to determine what pertains to their lawful celebration, administration and reception and also the order to be observed in their celebration.

9. See c. 18: Laws which establish a penalty or restrict the free exercise of rights or which contain an exception to the law are subject to a strict interpretation.

10. The exception to this, of course, would be if there were subsequent official interpretations of a law or subsequent laws established which further specified the rights of the faithful with regard to the sacraments.

11. See note 6.

12. See c. 856: Although baptism may be celebrated on any day, it is recommended that ordinarily it be celebrated on a Sunday or if possible at the Easter Vigil.

13. See c. 1010: Ordination is to be celebrated within the solemnities of Mass on a Sunday or on a holy day of obligation; for pastoral reasons, however, it can take place on other days, even on ordinary weekdays.

14. See c. 843.2: Pastors of souls and the rest of the Christian faithful, according to their ecclesial function, have the duty to see that those who seek the sacraments are prepared to receive them by the necessary evangelization and catechetical formation, taking into account the norms published by the competent authority.

15. The canon purposely uses the term *licit* when speaking of the administration and the reception of sacraments. Since the remaining paragraphs will discuss exceptions to the first paragraph, the general rule could not be given for the *valid* administration or reception of the sacraments. Canon law has two concepts for church order. For those things which are absolutely necessary, without exception, the law states that they are needed for the *validity* of an action. For those things which ought to be done for the sake of church order, the law states that they are needed for the *liceity* of the action. This does not mean that the latter need not be done. Things should be done both *validly* and *licitly*, since both are obligations considered necessary for church order.

16. See c. 205: Those baptized are fully in communion with the Catholic Church on this earth who are joined with Christ in its visible structure by the bonds of profession of faith, of the sacraments and of ecclesiastical governance.

17. See *Lumen gentium,* n. 8: The one mediator, Christ, established and ever sustains here on earth his holy Church, the community of faith, hope, and charity, as a visible organization through which he communicates truth and grace to all [. . .] but, the society structured with hierarchical organs and the mystical body of Christ, the visible society and the spiritual community, the earthly Church and the Church endowed with heavenly riches, are not to be thought of as two realities. On the contrary, they form one complex reality which comes together from a human and divine element. For this reason the Church is compared, not without significance, to the mystery of the incarnate Word. As the assumed nature, inseparably united to him, serves the divine Word as a living organ of salvation, so, in a somewhat similar way, does the social structure of the Church serve the spirit of Christ who vivifies it, in the building up of the body.

18. See C. 844.2: Whenever necessity requires or genuine spiritual advantage suggests, and provided that the danger of error or indifferentism is avoided, it is lawful for the faithful for whom it is physically or morally impossible to approach a Catholic minister, to receive the sacraments of penance, eucharist, and anointing of the sick from non-Catholic ministers in whose churches these sacraments are valid. See also the *Code of Canons of the Eastern Churches,* C. 671.2, and Pontifical Council for Promoting Christian Unity, the 1993 Directory for Ecumenism, in *Origins* 23/9 (July 29, 1993), n. 130, p. 148. This latter document also allows Catholic members of the Christian faithful to receive the sacraments of penance, eucharist, and anointing of the sick from anyone who is known to be validly ordained according to the Catholic teaching on ordination. This slightly expands the notion of non-Catholic ministers in whose churches these sacraments are valid.

19. The Catholic church recognizes as valid the sacraments of penance, eucharist, and anointing in all of the Eastern non-Catholic churches (the Orthodox, the pre-Chalcedonian churches, etc.). It also recognizes as valid the sacraments in the Polish National Church.

20. See C. 844.3: Catholic ministers may licitly administer the sacraments of penance, eucharist, and anointing of the sick to members of the Oriental churches which do not have full communion with the Catholic church, if they ask on their own for the sacraments and are properly disposed. This hold also for members of other churches, which in the judgement of the Apostolic See are in the same condition as the Oriental churches as far as these sacraments are concerned. See also the 1993 Directory for Ecumenism, n. 125.

21. See Vatican II, Decree *Unitatis redintegratio,* n. 4: The term "ecumenical movement" indicates the initiatives and activities encouraged and organized, according to the various needs of the Church and as opportunities offer, to promote Christian unity. These are: first, every effort to avoid expressions, judgments and

actions which do not represent the condition of our separated brethren with truth and fairness and so make mutual relations with them more difficult. Then, "dialogue" between competent expert from different churches and communities. . . . Through such dialogue everyone gains a truer knowledge and more just appreciation of the teaching and religious life of both communions. In addition, these communions engage in that more intensive cooperation in carrying out any duties for the common good of humanity which are demanded by every Christian conscience. They also come together for common prayer, where this is permitted. Finally, all are led to examine their own faithfulness to Christ's will for the church and, wherever necessary, undertake with vigor the task of renewal and reform.

22. See c. 844.5: For the cases of paragraphs 2, 3 and 4, neither the diocesan bishop nor the conference of bishops is to enact general norms except after consultation with at least the local competent authority of the interested non-Catholic church or community. See also the *Code of Canons of the Eastern Churches,* c. 671.5, and the 1993 Directory for Ecumenism, nn. 106 – 107 (regarding non-Catholic churches in general) and 122 – 124 (regarding a special concern for the Eastern or Oriental non-Catholic churches).

23. The Southern African Catholic Bishops' Conference recently drafted such guidelines, entitled *Directory on Ecumenism for Southern Africa.* It is not clear from the document, however, what dialogue took place with the non-Catholic churches. With regard to non-Catholic members of the Christian faithful receiving the sacraments of penance and the anointing of the sick, the South African bishops state, "The mere request for such sacraments can be taken as evidence of pressing spiritual need (vi, b, 2)"; and with regard to the reception of the eucharist, the bishops state, "A special need can be said to exist on occasions when Christians from other churches attend a eucharistic celebration for a special feast or event. On these occasions eucharistic sharing may be both meaningful and desirable, expressing the degree of unity that the participating Christians already have with each other (vi, b, 3)". For the full text of the document, see *Origins* 27/36 (February 26, 1998), pp. 606 – 610.

24. See Vatican II, Constitution *Sacrosanctum Concilium,* n. 14.

25. *Idem.*

26. Canon 899.2.

27. Canon 899.3.

28. 1993 *Directory for Ecumenism,* n. 116.

29. See 1993 *Directory for Ecumenism,* nn. 108 – 135.

30. John Paul II, Apostolic Exhortation *Familiaris Consortio,* n. 84. English translation in *Origins,* 11/28 – 29 (December 24, 1981), pp. 437 – 468.

31. See c. 1331.1: An excommunicated person is forbidden: 1. To have any ministerial participation in celebrating the eucharistic sacrifice or in any other

ceremonies whatsoever of public worship; 2. To celebrate the sacraments and sacramentals and to receive the sacraments; 3. To discharge any ecclesiastical offices, ministries or functions whatsoever, or to place acts of governance.

32. See cc. 872–874 and 892–893.

33. See c. 1108 and 1993 *Directory for Ecumenism*, n. 136.

34. See cc. 511–514 and 536.

35. See cc. 492–494 and 537.

36. See c. 135.2: [. . .] a law which is contrary to a higher law cannot be validly enacted by a lower-level legislator.

37. See c. 98.2.

38. See c. 97.2: Before the completion of the seventh year a minor is called an infant and is held to be incompetent; with the completion of the seventh year one is presumed to have the use of reason. See also c. 99: Whoever habitually lacks the use of reason is held to be incompetent and is equated with infants. Thus children in the law would appear to be those who have reached the age of reason (seven), but have not reached the age of majority (eighteen). They remain subject to their parents (c. 98.2). For those who habitually lack the use of reason, diocesan bishops and conferences of bishops have often provided guidelines for the reception of sacraments by the developmentally disabled.

39. See c. 914: It is the responsibility, in the first place, of parents and those who take the place of parents as well as of the pastor to see that children who have reached the use of reason are correctly prepared and are nourished by the divine food as early as possible [. . .].

40. See c. 913.1: For the administration of the most holy eucharist to children, it is required that they have sufficient knowledge and careful preparation so as to understand the mystery of Christ according to their capacity, and can receive the body of the Lord with faith and devotion.

41. See c. 913.2: The most holy eucharist may be given to children who are in danger of death, however, if they are able to distinguish the body of Christ from ordinary food and to receive communion reverently.

42. See C. 920: 1. All the faithful, after they have been initiated into the most holy eucharist, are bound by the obligation of receiving communion at least once a year. 2. This precept must be fulfilled during the Easter season, unless it is fulfilled for a just cause at some other time during the year.

43. See C. 11: Merely ecclesiastical laws bind those baptized in the Catholic church or received into it and who enjoy the sufficient use of reason and, unless the law expressly provides otherwise, have completed seven years of age.

44. For example, see *Sacrosanctum Concilium*, n. 55: The more perfect form of participation in the Mass whereby the faithful, after the priest's communion,

Patrick R. Lagges

receive the Llord's body from the same sacrifice, is warmly recommended. See also Sacred Congregation for Rites, Instruction, *Eucharisticum Mysterium,* nn. 12, 31. English translation in Flannery, pp. 110–111 and 120–121. Sacred Congregation for Divine Worship, *De Sacra Communione et de Cultu Mysterii Eucaristici Extra Missam,* n. 13. English translation in Flannery, pp. 244–245.

45. For example, see *Eucharisticum Mysterium,* n. 3e.

46. See *Eucharisticum Mysterium,* n. 39.

47. See c. 915: Those who are excommunicated or interdicted after the imposition of the penalty and others who obstinately persist in manifest grave sin are not to be admitted to holy communion.

48. In the revision of the Code of Canon Law, a conscious decision was made to reduce the number of automatic penalties, and to keep all penalties to a minimum. The 1967 Synod of Bishops, in establishing principles for the revision of the Code of Canon Law, stated: As an external, visible, and independent society, the church cannot renounce penal law. However, penalties are generally to be *ferendae sententiae* and are to be inflicted and remitted only in the external forum. *Latae sententiae* penalties are to be reduced to a few cases and are to be inflicted only for the most serious offenses. See *Code of Canon Law,* preface, p. xxii.

49. See c. 1331.2. This canon refers to what a person is forbidden to do, and what happens when the excommunication is imposed or declared.

50. See c. 1321: 1. No one is punished unless the external violation of a law or a precept committed by the person is seriously imputable to that person by reason of malice or culpability. 2. [. . .] 3. Unless it is otherwise evidence, imputability is presumed whenever an external violation has occurred.

51. See cc. 1322 and 1323.

52. See c. 1324.

53. See c. 1342.1: As often as just causes preclude a judicial process a penalty can be imposed or declared by an extra-judicial decree [. . .].

54. See c. 1332.

55. See c. 916: A person who is conscious of grave sin is not to celebrate Mass or to receive the body of the Lord without prior sacramental confession unless a grave reason is present and there is no opportunity of confessing; in this case the person is to be mindful of the obligation to make an act of perfect contrition, including the intention of confessing as soon as possible.

56. See c. 917.

57. For a more complete discussion of these three aspects, see P. J. Travers, "Reception of the Holy Eucharist by Catholics Attempting Remarriage after Divorce and the 1983 Code of Canon Law," in *The Jurist,* 55 (1995), pp. 198–202.

58. In common American terminology, these are referred to as the divorced and remarried. Although this is not a precise term, it is the one that will be used here. However, it should be kept in mind that church law does not require a couple who has separated to civilly divorce. Rather, civil divorce is seen as a last resort to be used by a person only to ensure that personal rights or the rights of the children are protected. See *Catechism of the Catholic Church*, n. 2383.

59. See c. 1108.

60. *Familiaris Consortio*, n. 82.

61. See c. 1060: Marriage enjoys the favor of the law; consequently, when a doubt exists the validity of a marriage is to be upheld until the contrary is proven.

62. In a 1976 reply to the conference of bishops in Scandinavia, who had asked if non-Catholics who were in second marriages could be received into full communion with the Catholic church and admitted to the sacraments, the Congregation for the Doctrine of the Faith replied that such persons could be received into full communion with the Catholic church, but could not be admitted to the sacraments. For the full text of the question and the reply, see J. I. O'Connor, ed., *The Canon Law Digest*, vol. 9, pp. 506–508.

63. *Familiaris Consortio*, n. 84.

64. A *convalidation* occurs when the two parties exchange consent anew before a priest, deacon or designated layperson and two witnesses (see cc. 1156–1160). A *sanation* occurs when it is not possible for the parties to exchange their consent in the manner prescribed by cc. 1156–1160, either because one of the parties is unwilling to exchange consent in this manner or does not see the purpose for doing so. Thus, a sanation is a convalidation of the marriage without the giving of consent (see cc. 1161–1165).

65. See cc. 1141–1150.

66. See cc. 1400–1655 and 1671–1691.

67. For a fuller explanation of the Pauline Privilege, see W. Woestman, *Special Marriage Cases* (3rd ed.)(Ottawa: Faculty of Canon Law, 1994) pp. 33–46. For a fuller explanation of the Privilege of the Faith, see Woestman, pp. 53–66.

68. See *Gaudium et spes*, nn. 48–52.

69. See 1 Corinthians 7:12–15.

70. See c. 1146.

71. See c. 1147.

72. See Woestman, pp. 53–60 for a more complete history of this procedure.

73. Woestman, p. 53.

74. See *Lumen Gentium*, n. 22.

75. See *Canon Law Digest,* vol. 8, pp. 1177–1184 or Woestman, pp. 129–134.

76. For a more complete description, see Woestman, pp. 13–31.

77. See Woestman, pp. 14–15, note 10.

78. See c. 1142: A non-consummated marriage between baptized persons or between a baptized person and an unbaptized party can be dissolved by the Roman Pontiff for a just reason, at the request of both parties or of either party, even if the other is unwilling.

79. Woestman, p. 19.

80. Congregation for the Sacraments, Circular Letter *De Processu Super Matrimonio Rato et Non Consummato,* in *Monitor Ecclesiasticus* 112 (1987), pp. 423–429. English translation in Woestman, pp. 121–128.

81. See cc. 1066–1067 and the Pontifical Council for the Interpretation of Legislative Texts, response, 26 June 1984, in *A.A.S.* 76 (1984), p. 747. English translation in E. Caparros, M. Theriault, J. Thorn, eds., *Code of Canon Law* (Montreal: Wilson and Lafleur Limitee, 1993) p. 1295.

82. See cc. 1073–1094 for a listing of the impediments that invalidate marriage, and cc. 1686–1688 for the process for declaring such marriages null.

83. See cc. 1095–1107 for examples of lack of capacity, intention or knowledge that would render a marriage null, and cc. 1400–1655 and 1671–1691 for a description of the process.

84. See John Paul II, Apostolic Constitution *Pastor Bonus,* 28 June 1988, in *A.A.S.* 80 (1988), articles 121–125. English translation in Caparros, Theriault, and Thorn, pp. 1237–1238.

85. *Gaudium et Spes,* n. 27.

86. *Catechism of the Catholic Church,* n. 1867. In the remainder of this paragraph, the catechism will be referred to by paragraph number within the text.

87. See Pontifical Commission *Iustitia et Pax, The Church and Racism: Towards a More Fraternal Society* (Washington: United States Catholic Conference, 1988) nn. 9–16.

88. John Paul II, Post-Synodal Apostolic Exhortation, *Reconciliatio et Penitentia* (Washington: United States Catholic Conference, 1985), n. 16.

89. *Idem.*

90. *Idem.*

91. See, for example, the pastoral letter of the bishops of the Upper Rhine, "Pastoral Ministry: The Divorced and Remarried," in *Origins* 23 (1993–1994), pp. 670–676; the reply to this letter by the Congregation for the Doctrine of the Faith, "Reception of Communion: Divorced and Remarried Catholics," in *Origins* 24/20

(1994–1995), pp. 337–341; and the reply of the bishops of the Upper Rhine, "Response to the Vatican Letter" in *Origins* 24/20 (1994–1995), pp. 341–344.

92. See, for example, a pastoral letter entitled, "In Truth and Love," issued by the Pennsylvania bishops, and reprinted as "Pastoral Care of Divorced Catholics Who Remarry," in *Origins,* 24/11 (1994–1995), pp. 205–208.

93. K. Rahner, "Considerations on the Active Role of the Person in the Sacramental Event," in *Theological Investigations* 14 (New York, Seabury, 1976), pp. 161–184.

94. M. Skelley, *The Liturgy of the World: Karl Rahner's Theology of Worship* (Collegeville, MN: The Liturgical Press, 1991) p. 102.

95. K. Rahner, "On the Theology of Worship," in *Theological Investigations* 19 (New York, Crossroad, 1983), p. 146.

96. Skelley, p. 93.

97. Skelley, p. 95.

98. Skelley, p. 99.

99. Skelley, p. 98.

100. J. Vanier, *Our Journey Home: Rediscovering A Common Humanity Beyond Our Differences,* trans. M. Parham (Maryknoll, NY: Orbis Books, 1997) p. 62.

101. Vanier, p. 209.

102. M. Hellwig, *The Eucharist and the Hunger of the World* (2nd ed.) (Kansas City, MO: Sheed and Ward, 1992) p. 2.

103. Hellwig, p. 3.

104. D. Tutu, *An African Prayer Book* (New York: Doubleday, 1995) p. 66.

105. Skelley, pp. 95–96.

Gilbert W. Ostdiek, OFM

The Future of Parishes as Eucharistic Communities

I n major pastoral letters on liturgy, Cardinal Joseph Bernardin and Cardinal Roger Mahony have addressed the future of Sunday eucharist in parishes in the archdioceses of Chicago and Los Angeles, respectively. The task here is to take a critical look at the two letters and the revitalization of parish liturgy and the planning that they call for. Part One will situate and comment on the two letters. Part Two will examine five practical steps called for in building eucharistic communities.

Two Pastoral Letters

Guide for the Assembly

Context.

In 1984, Cardinal Bernardin issued a pastoral letter entitled *Our Communion, Our Peace, Our Promise,* to mark the 20th anniversary of the Second Vatican Council's *Constitution on the Sacred Liturgy.* In 1995, he set in motion plans for a second pastoral letter on the liturgy intended to implement the vision of the first, but these plans never came to fruition because of his illness and death. The first letter was reissued posthumously in 1997 under the title of *Guide for the Assembly* [GA].[1]

Recalling the state of the reform in 1984 will help place the letter in context. By that time, all the major rites had been reformed and in use in English translations for ten to fifteen years. ICEL's program of preparing a second generation of revised texts in the light of pastoral experience to date was just underway, with the completion of the revised *Pastoral Care of the Sick* in 1983. Enthusiasm for and investment in the renewal of the liturgy were still at high levels. The archdiocese of Chicago was particularly noted for the energy and resources marshaled around the task of providing the kind of celebration the Council had envisioned. Most people had settled into the new way of celebrating the liturgy and were generally happy with it.

In that atmosphere, Bernardin saw that it was time to take stock of the renewal. He stated the pastoral's aim directly and clearly: "A few decades is very little time for so profound an experience to take hold, but at this point it is useful to ask ourselves how we are doing" (GA, 9). He also voiced his own assessment of the progress made to date: "During these years, much of the liturgical renewal seems to have been concerned with external changes . . . . Now we need to make the liturgy ours, to be at home with it, to know it deeply, to let it shape our everyday lives" (#85).

The picture, however, was not all serenity. A number of factors had begun to make their impact on the renewal. Among these were the allied questions of inclusive language and women's ordination. Discussion of inclusive language was underway, but the more contentious debates were still to come. There were also serious warnings about the declining number of priests; a downward trend had begun in the 1940s, but its effects were not yet being felt in most dioceses. Multicultural communities had also become a reality,[2] but the implications for liturgy were not yet being addressed. Bernardin's pastoral letter does not touch directly on these issues.

Content.

Bernardin addressed this (his first) pastoral letter to all the people of the archdiocese of Chicago. His words are truly pastoral in tone, written from the heart in accessible language. One needs only sample the opening paragraphs to catch the spirit of his words. In his introduction, Bernardin lifts up the familiar goal that Vatican II had set down as primary for liturgical renewal: full, conscious and active participation. This is critical for the future of eucharistic communities. "The liturgy is not an 'extra,' something nice that may give us good feelings. It is our life, our very spirit. It is the source of our identity and renewal as a church" (#13). But the focus is not inward only. The liturgy shapes us to put on Christ.

> Yet liturgy is also a humble reality, and participation in liturgy does not exhaust our duties as Christians. We shall be judged for attending to justice and giving witness to the truth, for hungry people fed and prisoners visited. Liturgy itself does not do these things. Yet good liturgy makes us a people whose hearts are set on such deeds. Liturgy is our communion, our strength, our nourishment, our song, our peace, our reminder, our promise. (#15)[3]

And again: "We need to gather, listen, give praise and thanks, share communion. Otherwise we forget who we are and whose we are; we have neither the strength nor the joy to be Christ's body present in today's world" (#18). Liturgy cannot be divorced from life and the doing of justice.

In the major portions of the letter, Bernardin then goes through the Sunday eucharist, describing it part by part in response to a series of questions: On Sunday, how do we gather? How do we listen to the word? How do we give praise and thanks? What is our communion? What does our dismissal mean? His answering description of the Sunday eucharist, however, is not so much a technical exposition as a mystagogical reflection on the meaning of the Mass. Concrete illustrations of this mystagogical approach will be given in Part Two.

His strategy is to engage people in imagining the liturgy afresh: "I ask you to read what follows in a very practical spirit, thinking of your own parish and the Sunday eucharist there, and especially of your own participation in that Mass" (#21). The letter concludes with his assessment of our progress in the renewal.

Assessment.

In retrospect, Bernardin's pastoral letter is a compelling piece of mystagogy. It consistently stresses the action of the assembly as it moves from the vision of well-crafted celebrations to the deeper meaning within them. It is always concerned with connecting that meaning to daily life and to action in the world for justice and peace. The impact of the letter is hard to measure; 80,000 copies have been sold locally and nationally, suggesting a wide reading. But it should also be noted that the letter provided no organized way to implement the vision presented. To remedy this, a companion study guide was soon published by the archdiocesan Office for Divine Worship and a revised version is now bound with the letter. In particular, the pastoral — perhaps relying on the general commitment to the reform — did not press presiders, preachers and other ministers to improve their skills and style. The projected second letter was to remedy those lacks. It should also be noted that inculturation and multiculturalism seem not to have been at forefront of awareness then, nor was the connection of liturgy to catechesis or other ministries developed. But perhaps the stage was not yet fully set for full treatment of issues such as these.

Gather Faithfully Together: Guide for Sunday Mass

Context.

Cardinal Mahony issued his pastoral letter on the liturgy, entitled *Gather Faithfully Together: Guide for Sunday Mass* [GSM],[4] in a bilingual edition in September 1997. He wrote this pastoral in response to the Holy Father's call to make the year 2000 a Jubilee Year and time of renewal in the spirit of the Second Vatican Council. Mahony chose, as did Vatican II, to place the liturgy on the top of his agenda.

More than a dozen years had passed since Bernardin's pastoral letter on liturgy, and the reform had continued to progress. For the most part, there was an increasing sense of the liturgy being "ours" now, as well as a noticeable deepening of corporate prayer, for example, in the Easter Vigil. The second generation of revised rituals prepared by ICEL[5] and the growing list of pastoral resources[6] reflect a maturing of the reform. Conversations among liturgy, catechesis and pastoral workers were also on the increase.[7]

But issues that were more muted in the mid-1980s had now come to the fore. The declining number of priests was fully documented[8] and more apparent. The decline felt earlier in rural dioceses had spread to the more populous dioceses, where diocesan officials began to establish norms for lay persons to qualify as pastoral associates and administrators of parishes. Ritual revisions originating from and confirmed by Rome provided for lay leadership of various rites.[9] By 1997, there had also been a dramatic increase in the number of lay people seeking preparation for professional ministry. Mahony's pastoral letter does acknowledge this decline in the number of priests, but his response to the phenomenon is limited. He simply notes that this reality "cannot be a reason to delay the renewal of the liturgy" (#86), and asks that parishioners pick up some of the priest's other responsibilities to free him for better homily preparation.

In the dozen years between the two pastoral letters, two other developments converged to raise more serious questions for the renewal. First, public debate over the liturgy grew; polemicized voices became more strident and disagreements more adamant. The ICEL revisions of the *Order of Christian Funerals* and the sacramentary triggered extended debate and led to widespread lobbying efforts addressed to bishops' conferences and Roman officials. The main topics have been inclusive language for the assembly, God language and the loss of "sacral language." But the struggle has not been only over the language of prayer; it has also extended to issues such as kneeling and reverence, the placement of the tabernacle and the need to restore eucharistic devotions. Second, to mark the 25th anniversary of the *Constitution on the Sacred Liturgy* and of centers founded to support the conciliar renewal, several conferences and symposia have taken retrospective and prospective looks at the renewal. In the published proceedings of these gatherings,[10] as in the language debates, there have been competing calls for revitalizing the reform, reforming it, declaring it over or restoring the pre-conciliar liturgy. This latter option, a restorationist option, has received a favorable hearing in Vatican circles. Without a doubt the reform of the liturgy is at a critical juncture.

This turmoil was one of the express reasons that Mahony chose to focus precisely on the liturgy in his Jubilee Year pastoral letter. He writes: "I want to be clear: I believe we are at a crucial place in the Church's liturgical renewal. We can abandon it, believing that what we have now is what the renewal intended, or we can learn from the past—mistakes and successes—and go forward. I want to invite all of us to go forward together" (#116).

Content.

In his introduction, Mahony firmly espouses the vision of the Council and the promise it holds out: "[I]t seems to me that only now are we getting glimpses of that wondrous experience when a parish lives by that full, conscious and active participation in the liturgy by all the faithful" (#17). He invites to the faithful to share his passion for the renewal: "Liturgical renewal is a matter of passion, of catching some glimpse of the way strong Sunday Liturgy makes strong Catholics, and of how these Catholics make their Sunday Liturgy" (#38).

In the introduction he also addresses the question of multiculturality, so much in the fore in Los Angeles. His words are worth heeding:

> [W]e want liturgy with sounds and gestures that flow from the religious soul of a people. . . .Yet we have a Catholic soul. We are in need of witnessing to that soul . . . we need to be the Body of Christ, sisters and brothers by our Baptism. Every one of us needs to know by heart some of the music, vocabulary, movement, and ways of thinking and feeling that are not of our own background. The larger society we are part of needs this witness. . . . We have to accomplish two results: to let the prevalent liturgy take on the pace, sounds, and shape that other cultures

bring; and to strive in our parishes to witness that in this Church there is finally no longer this people or that people, but one single assembly in Christ Jesus. (#29 – 30)

The pastoral approach proposed here steers a course between the two extremes in Sunday worship in multicultural parishes, extremes that Mark Francis has named cultural apartheid and liturgical esperanto.[11]

The first major section of the pastoral letter, addressed to all Catholics of the archdiocese, describes in concrete detail what Mahony hopes will mark the parish liturgy of the year 2000. Two samples suffice to give a flavor. Envisioning a new understanding of the eucharistic prayer resulting from effective celebration and mystagogy, he writes:

> Now the parishioners can talk about the experience of standing and singing God's praise together; they can see how much their lives need to be filled with thanksgiving; and they recognize that their presence to one another at this table witnesses to the breadth of the Church in place and time, a holy communion. They can talk about solidarity with one another across all dividing lines. They can talk about sacrifice and the mystery of Christ's passion, death and resurrection that is remembered and realized here in a powerful shaping of their own lives. Above all, they can talk about the way the Holy Spirit is invoked to transform these gifts and themselves. And so they are talking about the presence of Christ in the simple gifts of bread and wine, and in the mystery that is this Church. (#66)

And commenting on the communion rite of the future, he says:

> People are intent on the hard work of liturgy, caught up in singing, procession and even silence. To be with them is to know deeply that we are the Body and Blood of Christ. To be with them is to learn how to be in this world with reverence, with a love of God that is incarnate in how we speak to others, how we move amidst the holiness of matter and time. (#75)

In words such as these, Mahony reveals his deeply passionate and pastoral bent: "I want to kindle a passion for a vital Sunday Liturgy in every parish of our Archdiocese" (#81). His strategy for moving "from here to there" starts with forming the clergy for better presiding,[12] preaching and leadership (#83, 87; Part II) and all members of the assembly for active participation. He urges the faithful to take several specific steps: "become people who worship in the midst of the Sunday Liturgy" (#106); "become people who prepare themselves for Sunday Liturgy and people for whom Sunday Liturgy is preparation for the week" (#107); "at the Liturgy, be the Church" (#108); "apart from the Liturgy, be the Church" (#109); and "give thanks always" (#110). And to insure that liturgy is connected with life, he counsels them:

> Look at the liturgy as a remote preparation for your week. Listening to God's Word on Sunday morning is preparation for the listening we do for God's Word in our lives all week. The thanks we proclaim at the Eucharistic Prayer is a preparation for thanks over all tables and all meals, and also over all. The common table of Holy Communion is a preparation for looking at the whole world. (#109)

The second major section of the pastoral is addressed to priests and others who have responsibility for the Sunday liturgy. Here, too, his question is: "How do we move from where we are to something more like the intense, nourishing and life-rehearsing Sunday Mass I described in Part One?" (#122) To meet that challenge, he focuses on the need for leaders who embrace the assembly, the qualities of the presider and catechesis for the liturgy. And lest liturgists think renewal is their burden alone, he writes: "We have learned that the renewal of the liturgy cannot take on its own course apart from the renewal of catechesis, the building up of our Churches as places where justice is done, and the strengthening of our parishes as communities" (#117). And again: "Seek and discover how the assembly —and not just the dedicated few—can be about evangelization and catechesis, justice and outreach, the ministering to each other in community" (#119). He therefore calls for fuller collaboration among all ministries, but especially between catechesis and liturgy (#155). Part II concludes with a series of challenges—regarding the homily, the eucharistic prayer, the communion rite and the assembly—and a detailed schedule for implementing the vision for the Jubilee Year.

Assessment.

With Bernardin's pastoral letter, Mahony's shares several passionate convictions: The vision of Vatican II remains in force and its program of liturgical renewal is to be pursued; the liturgy itself has a deeply formative power; and the formation of liturgical ministers is crucial for the renewal. Both letters espouse pastoral practices for a renewed Sunday celebration that liturgists will welcome. Mahony's letter goes beyond that of Bernardin in several ways: It proposes a very concrete, detailed plan for implementation; it wrestles expressly with the issue of multiculturalism; and it devotes significant space to the task of catechesis for liturgy. Of the two, Bernardin's letter seems to provide a more compelling mystagogy of the liturgy and its interplay with life. Since the two pastorals have chosen to focus on the Sunday assembly, pastoral practitioners will find that little if any attention is given to the liturgical seasons, the broader ritual life of the parish and the increasingly vexing issue of the loss of eucharistic celebration in parishes without an ordained presider.

Do parishes have a future as eucharistic communities? Both Bernardin and Mahony leave no doubt that their answer is positive. To accomplish that end, they endorse the Vatican II determination that the full participation of the assembly must be the primary pastoral norm for all liturgical praxis. It is perhaps too early to assess what impact these pastoral letters might have in their dioceses and beyond.[13] It hardly seems coincidental, however, that other bishops have begun to issue pastoral letters on the liturgy as well. The two cardinals have set an example for others to follow at this crucial time. One can only hope and pray that future letters of this kind will also take up the problem of how parishes can remain eucharistic communities without Sunday eucharist.

Some Practical Steps for Building Eucharistic Communities

The two pastoral letters have restated the vision of Vatican II with clarity and commitment. They have drawn on that conciliar vision and the subsequent Roman and NCCB guidelines for the renewal of the liturgy to describe for us the shape of a pastorally effective celebration of the Sunday eucharist for the future. Those areas need no further comment here. Cardinal Mahony's question remains, however: How are we to get from here to there? How are we to prepare for that future? It might be helpful, then, to lift out and build on some of the themes and directions expressed or implied in the pastoral letters. Five such directions will be considered. Expressed as imperatives, they represent five steps that liturgists can take to prepare parishes for their future as eucharistic communities. There is a twofold goal behind these imperatives: to deepen people's participation in the celebration of Sunday eucharist, and to form them in a eucharistic way of living that will sustain them outside the times of such celebration.

1. Reflect on the Deeper Meaning of the Celebration

The *Constitution on the Sacred Liturgy* provides a helpful prelude for the first three imperatives. Paragraph 14 reads:

> In the reform and promotion of the liturgy, this full and active participation by all the people is the aim to be considered before all else. For it is the primary and indispensable source from which the faithful are to derive the true Christian spirit and therefore pastors must zealously strive in all their pastoral work to achieve such participation by means of necessary instruction. Yet it would be futile to entertain any hopes of realizing this unless, in the first place, the pastors themselves become thoroughly imbued with the spirit and power of the liturgy and make themselves its teachers. A prime need, therefore, is that attention be directed, first of all, to the liturgical formation of the clergy.

What should be noted at this point is the need for catechesis and formation in the liturgy woven through this paragraph.

What this first imperative asks, then, is that we as ministers do our own mystagogical reflection on the eucharist as part of our ongoing formation in the liturgy. Bernardin and Mahony offer us a wealth of materials to cue our reflection on the Mass, part by part. A sampling follows.

The gathering rite is more than simply the performance of its component parts. "[Assembling] means gathering together many individuals as one community at prayer, but it also means recollecting ourselves personally — not by leaving behind the cares and distractions of home and work, but by bringing them into the gospel's light" (#22). The liturgy begins not with the entrance rite, but in life beyond the church's doors. "In houses and apartments all through the neighborhood, the true entrance procession of this Mass has been in full swing, sometimes calm, sometimes hectic." (GSM, 40). If participants are asked to check their lives at the door and retrieve them on leaving, liturgy will have little if anything to say to daily life in the world.

To probe the deeper meaning of the liturgy of the word, several images from ordinary experience are used in the letters. The first is that of conversation, which necessarily involves listening. "Listening is a skill that grows dull in the barrage of words one hears all day long. In the liturgy we are schooled in the art of listening. What we do here, we are to do with our lives — be good listeners to one another, to the Lord, to the world with all its needs" (GA, 37). These words are worth pondering in our hearts. A second image is that of story. "Lectors, deacons, and priests must read as the storytellers of the community . . . capable of holding the attention of the assembly through their mastery of technical skills and also through their deep love for God's word and God's people" (#42). The interplay of telling and listening, of biblical stories and life stories, peaks in the homily. "The homily is the assembly's conversation with the day's scripture readings. Only by respecting both scripture and the community can the homilist speak for and to the assembly, bringing it together in this time and place with this Sunday's scriptures" (#49).

Regarding the presentation of the bread and wine, Bernardin's reflection takes a surprising turn. Rather than stressing the requirement that the bread should appear to the senses as real bread, he starts his mystagogy from the impoverished form of bread we normally have before us.

> The unleavened bread is obviously not our usual bread but a simple bread, a bread of the poor. In this bread we cast our lot with the poor, knowing ourselves — however materially

188

The Future of Parishes as Eucharistic Communities

affluent—to be poor people, needy, hungry. Unless we acknowledge our hunger, we have no place at this table. How else can God feed us? (#54)

Even though practices may at times be less than ideal, in mystagogy such as this fresh insights can still be broken open for us to savor.

Mahony's vision for the eucharistic prayer has already been quoted. Praise and thanks, self-offering and transformation—these classical themes from the eucharistic prayer cited by Mahony are given fresh, graphic restatement in Bernardin's pastoral:

> We are called to the Lord's table less for solace than for strength, not so much for comfort as for service. This prayer, then, is prayed not only over the bread and wine, so that they become Christ's body and blood for us to share; it is prayed over the entire assembly so that we may become the dying and risen Christ for the world. Participation in this great prayer of praise, as meal and sacrifice, transforms us. By grace, we more and more become what we pray. (#61)

Or again:

> There is nothing narrow, selfish or blind in our Sunday worship. We give thanks not so much for personal favors from the Lord as for the earth itself, for the goodness of creation and the wonder of our senses, for the prophets and the saints and for our sisters and brothers throughout the earth, for God's saving deeds recorded in our scriptures and visible in our world. Only in such thanksgiving can we look on this world, embrace its sorrows and troubles, and confront the mystery of evil and suffering. (#77)

The pastoral question for us, then, is: "How are we to make our own this prayer which is the summit and center of the church's whole life? How are we to see that this prayer is the model of Christian life and daily prayer?" (#63)

Regarding the communion rite, we have already cited Mahony's vision. Bernardin's reflection draws us one step deeper.

> This communion is why all prejudice, all racism, all sexism, all deference to wealth and power must be banished from our parishes, our homes and our lives. This communion is why we will

not call enemies those who are human beings like ourselves. This communion is why we will not commit the world's resources to an escalating arms race while the poor die. We cannot. Not when we have feasted here on "body broken" and "blood poured out" for the life of the world. (#70)

Reflections such as these truly connect liturgy and life and find a perfect echo and completion in Bernardin's comment on the inner meaning of the sending rite:

> The dismissal of the assembly is like the breaking of the bread. We have become "the bread of life" and "the cup of blessing" for the world. Now we are scattered, broken, poured out to be life for the world. What happens at home, at work, at meals? What do we make of our time, our words, our deeds, our resources of all kinds? That is what matters. (#79)

These stirring words bring our reflections back to where we began. Gathering and sending are the bridges between life and liturgy. Liturgy and life are intertwined; each flows into and out of the other. Mahony sums it up with this simple advice:

> Look at the liturgy as a remote preparation for your week. Listening to God's Word on Sunday morning is preparation for the listening we do for God's Word in our lives all week. The thanks we proclaim at the Eucharistic Prayer is a preparation for thanks over all tables and all meals, and also over all. The common table of Holy Communion is a preparation for looking at the whole world. (GSM, 109)

If our parishes are to be eucharistic communities, we who are its ministers need continuing formation in the liturgy. Only thus can we become mystagogues of the eucharist to the assembly. But before this mystagogy can take place, a second imperative must be heeded.

2. Attend to the Formative Power and Potential of the Liturgy

Return to the words quoted above from the *Constitution on the Sacred Liturgy:* "For [liturgy] is the primary and indispensable source from which the faithful are to derive the true Christian spirit." (#14) Since those words were written, liturgists and catechists have become accustomed to speaking of the formative power of the liturgy, or to put it another way, that we learn by doing.

A catena of such expressions can be drawn from the two pastoral letters: good liturgy makes us a people whose hearts are set on such deeds [of justice]" (GA, 15); we learn to pray by praying" (#88); we need to let [liturgy] shape our everyday lives" (#85); strong Sunday Liturgy makes strong Catholics" (GSM, 38); "These memories of deeds we have done together are a common language . . . we learn the language by doing the deeds" (#149, 152); "Doing their symbols, Christians form Christians" (#141).

In preparing and celebrating the liturgy, then, it is not enough to meet the usual criteria of good performance; we must also ask what potential our celebration of the Sunday eucharist will have to form Christians whose lives are eucharistic. The celebrations are to school us not only in the ways of liturgy, but more importantly in the ways of Christian living. What we have come to understand about the eucharist through our own mystagogical reflections must in turn inform our practice of liturgy if it is to be a source from which the faithful derive the true Christian spirit. That fully formative liturgy is indispensable for the next step.

3. Provide Mystagogy for Liturgical Ministers and for the Assembly

Return once again to the quotation from paragraph 14 of the *Constitution on the Sacred Liturgy* and parse its logic. The ultimate goal of the renewal is a fully participative liturgy with power to form the assembly to live as Christians. But such celebrations will not happen unless pastors (and, *a pari*, all liturgical ministers) are themselves thoroughly imbued with the spirit and power of the liturgy. And finally, only then can they, in a moment of mystagogy, lead the assembly in reflecting on what it has experienced in the eucharist, opening up in turn the way to fuller eucharistic celebration and living. Thus, a "ripple principle" might well shape our pastoral strategy: Form presiders and ministers so that the celebration becomes more powerful and prayerful; celebrate eucharist in this way so that the assembly can be formed by it and reflect on it. Both ministers and people are now experiencing a readiness and hunger for a new, mystagogical catechesis.

How might this begin to be met? Here I wish to focus only on the catechetical-formative dimension of the liturgy. It is the bridge between liturgy and catechesis, the necessary prelude to mystagogy in the fuller sense.[14] The section in Mahony's letter on "catechesis for liturgy" gives some useful leads. Catechesis, he says, must be part of the efforts at renewal of the liturgy. "The primary form of catechesis I want to call forth . . . involves preaching" (GSM, 147). Drawing on the example of Saint Augustine, he goes on to describe a "kind of catechetical preaching [which] invites the assembly to join with the preacher in reflecting on what has been their experience so far" (#151). But keep in mind what Mahony had said earlier: "More than catechisms or homilies, the symbols, when they are respected and done fully, are the teachers of the Church" (#141). The liturgy itself, then, must begin the process of mystagogy. This is accomplished not so much by intrusive explanatory words, but by the evocative language of prayer and homily that open up to us the mystery of God's presence here and in our lives. Renewal is accomplished most of all by the "opening up of our symbols, especially the fundamental ones of bread and wine, water, oil, the laying on of hands, until we can experience all of them as authentic and appreciate their symbolic value."[15]

If this kind of "opening up" has already begun in prayer, homily and symbol, the explicit mystagogy that follows will be much easier. Such mystagogy, however, normally involves other ministries in the parish, such as RCIA or adult education. We liturgists need to work in collaboration with them, as Mahony insists (#155).

4. Integrate Ministry Connected with Liturgy with all the Ministries

Several considerations urge this kind of collaboration. First, the task of identifying and preparing the many ministers needed for the renewed liturgy is massive and has required a concentration of energy that can subtly turn ministry connected with liturgy inward and separate it from other pastoral concerns. Second, compartmentalization of ministries can leave them uncoordinated or even at cross purposes. Third, there is a danger that ministry can become an end in itself, rather than a service to God's pilgrim people to help them mark a particular moment on their integral journey as Christ's disciples.[16]

The goal of liturgy, then, is not to form people just for eucharistic celebration, but for a eucharistic way of life. Now that the renewal has settled in, it is time for liturgy to establish fuller contacts with the other ministries to further this common goal.

With which ministries should liturgists be in partnership? Mahony lists three: evangelization and catechesis; justice and outreach; and ministering to each other in community (#119, also 117). The last involves many forms of pastoral caring for others, including the works of mercy.

Concretely, how might such collaboration begin? An intriguing practical suggestion can be found in an article by Thomas Morris.[17] Speaking of how one prepares a catechetical session during the catechumenate, Morris recommends that we learn to ask not only the catechetical question, but also the liturgical question, bringing the perspective of formation in the liturgy to bear on the catechetical preparation for liturgy. Taking that about, should we not ask the catechetical question when we prepare the liturgy, asking ourselves how this celebration builds on the previous catechetical formation and what potential it will have for further mystagogy? And even more broadly, should we not also factor in the questions of all the other ministries? One practical technique might be to invite representatives from the other ministries to take part in our meetings when we make key decisions regarding the liturgy, or at least to assign one of our number the task of raising their kind of questions.[18] Celebrations of the liturgy that are attentive to such questions will be well on the way to forming people more integrally for a eucharistic way of life.

5. Help Parishioners Connect Liturgy and Life

What liturgy must do, as the pastoral letters insist, is help people form connections between liturgy and life. We are accustomed to hearing the Vatican II dictum that the liturgy, and in particular the eucharist, is "summit and fount" (CSL, 10). That is spoken from a point of view within liturgy. What if our viewpoint is rather from within life? Our questions then are reversed. In the liturgy our lives are to be brought into the light of the gospel (see GA, 22). How can God's voice, spoken so softly in others and in the world around us, find a hearing in the scriptures of the day? The eucharistic prayer is to be the model for Christian life and prayer (GA, 69). How is God's presence and companionship on the way, so subtly hidden from us in the immediacy of daily experiences of brokenness and healing, to be brought in and named in that moment of recognition at the table? Does our thankfulness at eucharist spring not only from the story of Jesus we remember on Sunday, but deep from within our experience patterned on his? Where do that mindfulness and thankfulness lie hidden and unspoken in our days? To share the bread of the eucharist at the table is to know deeply that we are the body of Christ (see GSM, 75). Does it also help us to know that our lives are bread being transformed, broken and given for the nourishment of others?

Karl Rahner offers useful language for this perspective when he differentiates the liturgy of the world and liturgy in the more technical, narrow sense.[19] A faculty colleague, Anthony Gittins, names these more graphically as "eucharist" with a small e and "Eucharist" with a capital E. The former includes all of life, wherever the mystery of dying to sin and self and rising to newness of life is lived out by the Christian. In biblical terms, this is the "living sacrifice," the "spiritual worship" (see Romans 12:1; 15:15–16; Philippians 4:18; 1 Peter 2:5; Hebrews 13:15) that Christians offer by their lives in the world, just as Christ offered himself in his life and death.[20] In liturgy—in the usual technical sense—then, we gather to remember, to keep the anamnesis of that mystery in the life of Jesus and to unite our dying and rising, whether in little ways or in large, to his.

The implications this perspective has for our question of the future of the parish as a eucharistic community are clear. A careful performance of the rite, no matter how well done, cannot guarantee that we will be a eucharistic community in the full sense of the word. An attitude of self-offering suffusing all of Christian life is fundamental to the Sunday celebration of eucharist.[21] Eucharist with a capital E is incomplete if it does not flow from and return to a eucharistic life.

Conclusion

The pastoral letters of Bernardin and Mahony give us cause for hope. From them we learn that we need to work together, through powerful celebration and effective mystagogy, to form ourselves in this deeper understanding of the eucharist we celebrate. Without that, we cannot be fully eucharistic communities.

1. Cardinal Joseph Bernardin, *Guide for the Assembly* (Chicago: Liturgy Training Publications, 1997). Hereafter cited in text as GA.

2. Commentators were noting a shift in the image of U.S. society from "melting pot" to "salad bowl."

3. The descriptive names in the last sentence became the touchstones for a study guide published soon after the pastoral letter.

4. Cardinal Roger Mahony, *Gather Faithfully Together: Guide for Sunday Mass* (Chicago: Liturgy Training Publications, 1997). Hereafter cited in text as GSM.

5. The *Rite of Christian Initiation of Adults* and the *Order of Christian Funerals* were published in their U.S. editions in 1988 and 1989 respectively, and the ICEL revision of the sacramentary was completed in 1996.

6. See, e.g., the *Font and Table* and *Sourcebook* series from Liturgy Training Publications, as well as their *Sunday Mass* Video Series.

7. See, e.g.: Edward Foley, ed., *Developmental Disabilities and Sacramental Access: New Paradigms for Sacramental Encounters* (Collegeville, MN: The Liturgical Press, 1994); Robert Kinast, *Sacramental Pastoral Care* (New York: Pueblo, 1988); Gilbert Ostdiek, "Unfinished Conversations: Vice-Presidential Address," *Proceedings of the North American Academy of Liturgy* (Valparaiso, IN: North American Academy of Liturgy, 1992), 3–14; Elaine Ramshaw, *Ritual and Pastoral Care* (Philadelphia: Fortress, 1987).

8. Richard Schoenherr, *Full Pews and Empty Altars: Demographics of the Priest Shortage in the United States Catholic Dioceses* (Madison, WI: University of Wisconsin Press, 1993).

9. To wit: the Congregation for Divine Worship, *Directory for Sunday Celebrations in the Absence of a Priest,* 1988; the revised *Order of Christian Funerals,* 1989; the revised *Order of Marriage,* 1991, now awaiting approval in English; the National Conference of Catholic Bishops, Sunday Celebrations in the Absence of a Priest, 1994; and the Canadian Conference of Catholic Bishops, *Sunday Celebration of the Word and Hours,* 1995.

10. See: Lawrence Madden, ed., *The Awakening Church: 25 Years of Liturgical Renewal* (Collegeville, MN: The Liturgical Press, 1992); Eleanor Bernstein and Martin Connell, eds., *The Renewal That Awaits Us* (Chicago: Liturgy Training Publications, 1997); *Traditions and Transitions* (Chicago: Liturgy Training Publications, 1998); Timothy Fitzgerald and Martin Connell, eds., *The Changing Face of the Church* (Chicago: Liturgy Training Publications, 1998); Martin Connell,

ed., *Eucharist: Toward the Third Millennium* (Chicago: Liturgy Training Publications, 1997).

11. Mark Francis, "Multicultural Worship: Beyond Cultural Apartheid and Liturgical Esperanto," in *The Renewal That Awaits Us*, 39–56.

12. Mahony labels the church's failure to provide a pastoral plan to form pastors in the spirit and power of the liturgy as "a primary obstacle" that must be faced head on in the renewal (GSM, 126).

13. The public reaction in the media to Mahony's letter seems to have been based on a misreading or an earlier version. See Paul F. Ford, "Arguing against Renewal," *Liturgy 90* 29 (May–June, 1998): 4–13.

14. It is helpful to distinguish catechesis done in preparation for the liturgy, the catechetical-formative element within the liturgy itself, and mystagogical catechesis after the celebration.

15. NCCB, *Environment and Art in Catholic Worship* 15, in Elizabeth Hoffman, ed., *The Liturgy Documents: A Parish Resource* (Chicago: Liturgy Training Publications, 1991).

16. For a fuller reflection, see my article on the Emmaus account in the response to the Mathis Award in this volume.

17. Thomas Morris, "Liturgical Catechesis Revisited," *Catechumenate* 17 (May 1995): 13–19.

18. For further commentary, see my "Liturgy as Catechesis for Life," *Liturgical Ministry* 7 (Spring 1998): 76–82.

19. Karl Rahner, "Considerations on the Active Role of the Person in the Sacramental Event," in his *Theological Investigations* XIV (New York: Seabury, 1976), 161–184. For a simpler version, see Karl Rahner, "How To Receive a Sacrament and Mean It," *Theology Digest* 19 (1971): 227–234.

20. See also Edward Schillebeeckx, "Secular Worship and Church Liturgy," in his *God the Future of Man* (New York: Sheed and Ward, 1968), 91–116. Schillebeeckx speaks of Christ's life and death as "secular worship" and concludes: "On the basis of Jesus' self-sacrifice, the Christian's life in this world can now become worship" (100).

21. The *General Instruction of the Roman Missal* says as much: "Offering: in this memorial, the church—and in particular the church here and now assembled—offers the spotless victim to the Father in the Holy Spirit. The church's intention is that the faithful not only offer this victim but also learn to offer themselves and so to surrender themselves, through Christ the Mediator, to an ever more complete union with the Father and with each other, so that at last God may be all in all." (55f)

Richard S. Vosko

Worship Spaces to House the Many Presences of Christ

Introduction

H.S. is a dear friend of mine. She is 83 years old and still has an inquiring mind and a healthy body. She reads two or three books a week, the *New York Times* and the *National Catholic Reporter*. She works out at the gym with a personal trainer, has a season ticket to the Metropolitan Opera and regularly attends lectures on church-related topics. One could say that H.S. has little patience for Catholic troglodytes.

Unless she is in New York City for an opera, H.S. faithfully goes to the four o'clock liturgy every Saturday in her neighborhood parish church. It is an important part of her routine. Not long ago, that worship space was renovated. The altar was brought forward and the seats were placed on three sides of the table. Surprisingly, instead of liking the changes, H.S. was quite upset because they moved her seat! But that was just the half of it. Her friends' seats were moved as well. Confusion loomed large the first time they came to Mass in the renovated space.

H.S. goes to Mass not only to fulfill an obligation but also to check in with her cronies, to see how everyone is doing and to share some gossip. The regularity of this rendezvous is just as important as the familiarity of the liturgy. For H.S., accepting the changes caused by the Second Vatican Council was pretty easy. Moving her seat at liturgy was simply asking too much.

When I heard H.S. talk about the renovation, I wondered why she complained. The church building was newly painted; the lighting and sound systems were greatly improved; the new altar and ambo were made of the finest materials; an elegant tabernacle was placed in its own beautiful chapel; and all of the artwork was refurbished and kept in place. What went wrong? Apparently, for H.S., the furnishings and objects in the worship space were not as important as making connections with her friends. What can we learn from this story?

In this article we will investigate how a worship environment can help us experience the presence of Christ. What is it in a church that makes the experience of Christ possible? Is it the art? Is it the altar or tabernacle? Is it the building? Is it the people gathered there? Is it the ritual action of the people?

Where is Christ Experienced First of All?

This question is important because over the past thirty years Catholics have focused on the rearrangement of the interiors of their cathedrals and parish churches in order to accommodate the reformed liturgy. The reorganization of these spaces has not been an easy task. We have debated what are the best locations for the altar table, the font and the seats for the assembly. We have fought over kneelers, images of saints and the location of the tabernacle. With all the commotion over these things one would think that the experience of God is dependent upon them.

I am now convinced that while we have paid a lot of attention to building and renovating our worship spaces we have not given enough attention to the reformation of the church itself. After all, the experience of Christ's presence is first of all found in the very body of Christ, the church. Although we have been taught that Christ is present in the people of God in many ways, some people still confine this presence to the reserved eucharistic bread. A renewed understanding of the church as the primary symbol of Christ is essential if one is to understand the reasons for making physical changes in the church building.

In 1965, Pope Paul VI explained in his encyclical *Mysterium fidei* that the "real" presence (in the eucharistic element) is called real not to exclude the other kinds as though they were not real but because it is real *par excellence* (39 and *passim*). This same teaching is reiterated in the rite of *Holy Communion and Worship of the Eucharist Outside of Mass*, 6.

Further, both the *Constitution on the Sacred Liturgy* (CSL) and the *General Instruction of the Roman Missal* (GIRM) remind us that Christ is present in four ways at Mass: (1) in the ordained minister; (2) in the proclamation of the scriptures; (3) in the consecrated bread and wine; and (4) in the assembly (CSL, 7; GIRM, 7). There is no mention of art, furnishings and architecture as the dwelling places of Christ. Pastoral explanations of this doctrine were not required for H.S. and her friends. They knew it in their hearts.

The Function of the Worship Space in Experiencing Christ

If Christ is experienced in the gathered assembly and in its actions at liturgy, why do we need buildings at all? Although frequently called the "house of God," Christians were never taught to build temples for God. In the Christian tradition God does not dwell in buildings. There are no instructions found in the New Testament for erecting structures for the worship of God. The early Christian writers never spoke of such blueprints. For example, Minucius Felix (c. 200) would say "we have no need for altars or temples." Origen (c. 248) would add that "each Christian is a temple, each heart is an altar."

However, Christians were indeed taught to feed hungry people, to build houses for homeless families, to care for sick persons and to work for peace and justice. In fact, the expenditure of time, energy and resources on church buildings, works of art and furnishings without first tending to these "corporal works of mercy" would be considered an awful scandal. What we have learned from history is that the eucharist in the early years of the young church was celebrated in the homes of the faithful. For 300 years the church not only survived but flourished without power, property or church buildings as we know them today. When churches were built, Saint John Chrysostom (d. 407) would remind the faithful that it is not the building that makes the people holy. Rather, he said, it is the people who make the church holy.

A church is the place where Christians meet to proclaim stories of faith (in the scriptures). It is where they ponder how to respond to the challenges of the gospel (in the homily and in intercession). It is also where they share the sustenance of the sacrament (in the eucharist), which is required to do good works. It is in such a gathering of people who share a common bond that the presence of Christ can be experienced. We will see later in this article that the architecture and art of the worship space do matter. However, they must always be considered secondary to what is absolutely essential for worship: uncompromising faith in God and a steadfast commitment to work for peace and justice.

So what is the role of our church buildings, objects of art and furnishings for the worship space? Beautiful parish churches and cathedrals, like art and music, can inspire people to commit themselves to some effort or endeavor. However, it must be understood that church buildings and the objects in them are servants to the community and not the objects of our devotion. Certainly houses of prayer, works of art and furnishings should be treated with care and respect, but they themselves are not the focus of our worship. They are not what create the experience of the presence of Christ. They should be things of beauty but they should not be valued only for that reason. Rather, these things are important to the Christian assembly precisely because they are useful in facilitating the act of worship. This is the primary function of worship spaces.

In this sense, Catholic places of worship should not be thought of merely as containers for religious art and furnishings. While these things are helpful, the significance of spaces set aside for the worship of God cannot be measured solely in terms of the style of architecture, the art and the furniture. Although some museums have been thought of as sacred spaces, cathedrals and churches cannot be compared to them for museums exist to pay homage to architects, artists and their work. Houses of prayer, on the other hand, are crucibles that cradle stories of faith; they are avenues that mark the Christian journey; they are banquet halls where sustenance for the pilgrimage is shared.

Buildings such as churches, synagogues and mosques should be more like resonators of the stories of the faithful. They are the arenas where these stories are remembered and acted out. This unique purpose is what makes them truly sacred spaces. Over time they acquire a patina indicative of the spirit and identity of the culture. The community feeds meaning into the rituals; the rituals feed back and nourish that community. The holy ground for these events is called sacred.

This is why it is important to respect older buildings and their contents. But it would be misleading to say that only certain styles of art or architecture or music are appropriate for Catholic worship. We may cherish an object of art from the Renaissance but we do not live in the 14th century. We may listen to "oldies" music from the 1950s but we do not live in that era. While a particular religious artifact may be maintained because it is part of our heritage, one must ask if it is appropriate in contemporary liturgy.

Some cathedrals and parish churches look like museums where the objects in them dominate the environment. Others look like worship centers where the actions of the community are the focal points. The former may be more decorative on some level, but are they appropriate places for celebrating the current rituals of the church? The latter may not "look like churches" but they may have been designed using the rites of the church as a basic blueprint. After all, Catholic church buildings should be designed and arranged according to the requirements of our rites.

How is Christ Experienced in Church Buildings?

Before we discuss how a worship space can resonate with the stories of the church, we must examine the activity that occurs in the building. The primary purpose of a house of prayer is to accommodate the worship of the community of faith. It is by the celebration of our

Richard S. Vosko

rites that the basic stories of our faith are kept alive. This is what is essential to the life of the church. One could say that a secondary purpose of a worship center is to foster the piety of individuals and their personal devotions (which of course must always harmonize with the liturgy, be derived from it and lead back to it).

At liturgy, rituals are celebrated that memorialize the myths held close to the heart of the community. The whole assembly is invited to participate in the liturgies in an active and conscious manner. Through enacting the ritual the presence of Christ is experienced and the participants are transformed. One can be a spectator at a rite by watching it and remaining outside the experience, or one can participate fully in the rite and be regenerated by its power. It is a little like going to a wedding and choosing to dance or not.

What are the stories that are remembered and enacted in the liturgies? Why are they so important? First, there are stories that deal with the lives of the prophets and saints as well as the personal testimonies of fellow believers. Many of the stories celebrated are myths. They are real and most meaningful for the believer but more often than not they cannot be proven. In fact, these stories (myths) are so important to the life and survival of the believing community they must be remembered and acted out frequently. This is why images of members of the communion of saints should be thought of as important, organic components in the worship area. They are there not so much as objects of devotion (although they may be considered as such). Rather, their presence is important because these saints and prophets are worshiping God in communion with the church on earth. The *Catechism of the Catholic Church* asks, "What is the Church if not the assembly of all the saints?" (946)

However, the paschal mystery is the premier story (myth) remembered and celebrated in the rites of the church. The engagement with this mystery of faith is what makes it possible for faithful persons to experience and embody the presence of Christ today. The rite of the eucharist is the premier memorial of the paschal event. Catholics, like other Christians, keep this story alive by remembering it. It is remembered or memorialized by enacting it in a ritualistic way. This ritual is usually carried out in a manner that is familiar to all; that is, it is done in a somewhat repetitive way. The rites are made up of verbal and non-verbal symbols that bear pre-arranged meanings for the assembly. For example, water is a natural symbol of life and death. Thus, water qualifies as a good element to use in the rites of Christian initiation. Immersion in the water gives one a powerful experience of being immersed in and regenerated by the life and death of Jesus Christ.

Active, conscious participation in the rites draws one deeper into the mystery of the ritual event and the presence of God. One could say that, when the rite is enacted, the myth is further revealed but never fully understood. That is why it is a mystery of faith. The church is a called a sacrament because it is the body of Christ. This is why the assembly is called the primary symbol of Christ. As a sacrament, the church, the gathered assembly, is what it does and does what it is (which is what authentic symbols do). The church is not *like* Christ. It is the *body of* Christ. This is why it should be very difficult for the church to be divided against itself or for any member of the body to offend or hurt or abuse another member.

Truly, the assembly is an outward sign instituted by Christ to give grace. Thus, the sacrament of the eucharist is a celebration of the sacrament of the church, the body of Christ. One cannot be more deeply immersed in the presence of Christ than in the memorial celebration of the paschal mystery — the Mass. In fact, active, conscious participation in the liturgy is active, conscious participation in the paschal mystery remembered.

A chapel, parish church or cathedral is the normative place to house our liturgies. What constitutes an appropriate environment for our celebrations? In discussing how Christ can be experienced in the sacred space, certain factors that make up the environment for worship must be recognized.

The Environment for Worship and the Presence of Christ

Every time I participate in the Rite of Dedication of a Church and an Altar, I am reminded that the celebration is not really about dedicating a building or the things in it. Rather, it is all about dedicating or rededicating the people of God—the body of Christ. The prayers, the scriptures, the ritual actions bear this out emphatically. As the building is sprinkled with the baptismal water, we remember our own call to priesthood. When the walls are anointed, we remember that we are God's chosen people. When incense is used, we remember that we should fill the world with the fragrance of Christ. When the building is lighted for the first time, we remember we are the beacons to the whole world. When we approach the newly anointed altar table for the eucharist, we recall Augustine's statement, "Be what you celebrate."

The connections are beautiful and obvious. The church building itself, then, is a metaphor or architectural resonator for the people of God. As a symbol of the faith community, the building is what it does. This is why we can call the sacred space sacramental. In order to accomplish this, the environment for worship must be a place of movement, mingling, memory, myth, mystery and moderation. These characteristics help to identify the faith community as it continues to seek the experience of the holy one. Worship spaces must be designed as resonators of these characteristics. We will examine two of these features: movement and mingling.

Places of Movement

Christians are pilgrim people who are still on the move. The journey is not over and we have not yet arrived. Passages and crossings are commonplace in our story. Consider the Israelites and their search for the promised land. They escaped captivity only to be confronted by one challenge after another. Some wanted to return to captivity just so they could keep their bellies full. Others wanted to stand still because they were afraid to go further. Only a remnant pressed on and journeyed into the future. Every human being has a similar story, a similar journey.

In the Christian tradition, the life of Christ and his way of the cross are models for the pilgrimage. To commit to the journey is to experience and embrace the life, death and resurrection of Christ. The image of Jesus as the sheepgate is another good reference. One can experience the fullness of God by going "through" Jesus Christ and entering the sheepfold.

This is why portals and doors are such important symbols in the worship environment. Passing through an outdoor gateway leading to the church grounds, or pushing and pulling a door, speaks about the crossings and tensions that are experienced in life. On the other side of the gateway is the sheepfold, the promised land, the field where the lion and lamb lie down together. Christians strive to reach this place.

While some worshipers still walk to church, most arrive by automobile or some means of mass transportation. Fast cars and rapid transit have confused our sense of pilgrimage. The tensions in the parking lot on Sunday morning are a good indicator of this loss. Parking as close as possible to the church building is just as important as being able to exit quickly. It seems that no one wants to walk anymore. Walking requires endurance and patience and, one might add, training.

Imagine church properties with pathways, gardens and a series of thresholds all designed to make the walk to church one that engages the senses and triggers the memory of pilgrimage. Parking areas would have to be kept as far away from the building as possible. Pathways to the front door would be pedestrian-friendly. Even with urban churches, the approach to the building would be planned to foster a sense of gathering and walking together. This engagement can create an experience of Christ even before arriving inside the meeting place. Where two or three are gathering, Christ is there.

Places of Mingling

Prior to Vatican II, it was often the case that piety was fostered through the practice of private devotions. The Baltimore Catechism, for example, taught Catholics to "assist at Mass with great interior recollection and piety, and with every outward mark of respect and devotion." Post-conciliar instructions describe private devotions as important, but subordinate to the celebration of the eucharist.

Personal piety is important for any person of faith in any religious tradition. The practice of private devotions can be an important part of someone's daily routine. Fingering rosary beads, meditating on scriptures, visiting a church or chapel along with doing some good works constitute what many believe to be good practices of faith.

For many Catholics, the time of Mass was set aside as private time to connect with God in a very personal way. The setting was conducive to contemplation. That is why many Catholics are still uncomfortable with the social side of the liturgical life of the church. Efforts to promote active, conscious participation and notions that the assembly is a primary symbol are considered distractions. Other people understand socializing or mingling as necessary parts of going to church.

The environment for worship can be a resonator of the church as the body of Christ when it provides pathways and gathering areas for the people. Imagine churches with one common entrance, an ample gathering place and convenient amenities like a parish parlor, child-care rooms and barrier-free restrooms. These features of hospitality can help affirm the church's teachings about charity and evoke the presence of Christ in the gathered assembly. They are also reminders that, while personal piety is important, the time set aside for the public liturgy of the church may not be the best time to engage in one's private devotions.

The arrangement of the assembly at the altar table is another way for the building to resound with the beliefs of the church. If the sacrament of unity, the body of Christ, the church, is the celebrant of the Mass, then the seating plan for the assembly will also matter. While some will argue that such things do not matter, research in the area of proxemics suggests that the built environment can affect the behavior patterns of people using a space.

The arrangement of seats in many churches still suggests the assembly is an audience. In most situations the worshipers are gathered in fixed and often uncomfortable and crowded pews facing the stage-like sanctuary. They can feel and behave like spectators called to watch the ministrations of the clergy (and a host of new liturgical ministers). One midwest bishop observed, while sitting anonymously in the back row of a parish church, that out of a 60-minute liturgy, the congregation did, sang or recited something for only seven minutes!

Imagine more centralized seating plans in worship places. In these plans the focus would be on the actions of the whole community at the font, the ambo and the altar table. Imagine gracious and wide processional paths to and from these centers, which themselves are wide-open and spacious areas. There would be no fenced-off spaces for the furnishings. There would be no place of honor for certain members of the assembly. Every worshiper would be seated equally at the table of the Lord. The altar table would be placed in the midst or in a more centralized location. Bishops, presbyters, deacons and laity—every worshiper—would participate according to his or her office or ministry in the church. The ministry of the entire assembly would be celebrated. The liturgy would be perceived as the work of the whole people. Such arrangements of the space would not only conjure memories of the seating plan in the upper room *(triclinium)*, but could also remind everyone that the act of celebrating the eucharist is not a private act but one that belongs to the whole church.

The Presence of Christ Par Excellence

At the conclusion of every liturgy some eucharistic bread is saved so that it may be taken to the sick and dying members of the faith community. It is a beautiful tradition in the church to watch over and pray in the presence of this reserved sacrament.

The location of the tabernacle in which the sacrament is reserved has oddly become a point of some controversy in some quarters of the Catholic church in the United States and Canada. (I personally do not know if Catholics in other countries are so emotionally involved in this issue.)

A brief overview of the history of our practice regarding the reservation of the eucharistic bread outside Mass may be helpful here. We know for sure that the celebration of the eucharist began at a table in the context of a meal. From then on the celebration of that meal was the memorial of the paschal event. The ritual kept the myth, the story, alive. Everyone who attended the meal would partake of the elements as a gesture of belief in and commitment to the standards of living taught by Jesus Christ. It was a symbol of their common bond. Members who were absent or distant from the memorial were not forgotten. The eucharist was saved and carried to them.

We know also that the understanding of the eucharistic meal changed over time for various reasons. Those reasons included lapses of memory, clericalism, power, plagues, millenialism, limited access to the sacrament, reactions to heresies, philosophical debates over what constitutes real presence, Thomistic categorization of doctrine, developing devotional practices and a host of allegorical explanations. All of these collectively affected the understanding of the Mass.

Eventually, the Mass was perceived as a dramatic reenactment of the passion and death of Jesus Christ, a frightful mystery. The altar was no longer recognized as a banquet table. Instead, gradually, it became an ornate backdrop for making the sacrament present to the people. The Mass was something that the priest did for the gathered faithful. It was his private prayer and he uttered it quietly while everyone watched.

Soon, the laity developed their own private prayers and devotions, including gazing at the elevated host. Over time, more attention was given to the eucharist as an object of adoration rather than as spiritual food and drink. Only the clergy took communion. The notion of a shared meal and participating in the paschal event was lost.

The location of the reserved sacrament also changed with time. In house churches, the remaining eucharistic bread was kept in cupboards. When churches were built, the reserved sacrament was kept in various places. It may have been hoisted high in the corners of the building or maybe even over the altar. The containers also varied. Some looked like pelicans, others like doves. When adoration of the host became popular, the containers became more unique, often resembling reliquaries used to house bones of martyrs and saints.

Later in history some tabernacles were freestanding towers. Others were ambries mounted on walls. After the Council of Trent, when the church was gearing up to maintain power and presence in the face of the Reformation, the tabernacle and its contents became an even more important symbol for Catholics. It was in this post-Reformation period that legislation ordered the tabernacle to be placed in a central location—on the main altar. From this period on, all Catholic places of worship included an elaborate setting for the altar that included central placement of a tabernacle.

The traditions and current teachings of the church remind us that the original and primary reason for reserving the sacrament is to take it to sick and dying people. The secondary reasons are related to private prayer and adoration. Such private devotions in the presence of the reserved sacrament are important for many Catholics. Because of this, the church wisely instructs that the tabernacle should be placed in its own chapel that is distinct and separate from the main body of the church where the public liturgy occurs.

The setting that is prepared for the reserved eucharist must be one that takes these teachings seriously. The chapel should be designed to be spacious and beautiful. There should be enough room to accommodate individuals and even small groups gathered for adoration and prayer. A location that is removed from the more public areas of the church will make it possible to create spaces that are more contemplative. People should know from practice the location of the chapel. A single candle signals the presence of the sacrament. The tabernacle, fixed and unbreakable, is the focus point of the chapel. It does not have to be very large for it is not a dispensary for the eucharistic elements. Images of saints and other works of art are not required.

The location of this chapel should not create confusion nor should it compromise the nature of the eucharistic celebration. The reserved sacrament should be perceived as the fruit of the sacrificial banquet. However, there is no requirement that the tabernacle be seen or accessed from the community's worship space.

Conclusion

In this article I have recalled the teaching of the church regarding the many ways that Christ is present in our liturgies, and the teaching that the assembly is the primary symbol of Christ. I reviewed why the active participation in the rites of the church by the community is essential for memorializing the paschal mystery. I have discussed the difference between private devotions and the liturgy of the church. I have also shown that the reserved sacrament, the object of private devotion, is not required for the celebration of the eucharistic mystery.

I have indicated that the primary function of a worship space is to house the body of Christ as it engages in its ritual actions. Further, I have stated that church buildings are not just containers for furnishings and art, but should be considered as metaphors or architectural resonators for the church. I have spoken to the point that the chapel for the reserved eucharist be designed to honor the private prayer and adoration of the sacrament and that a space more removed from the nave of the building would be more conducive for this purpose.

The post-conciliar church is in a time of transition. Old habits are hard to let go of and any new reading of time-honored stories is often met with suspicion. It is a time when respect for ancient traditions and customs must be balanced with new possibilities. Will the church step backward, will it stand still or will it move forward?

A Living Prayer

*Throughout our time together at the conference, Teresita Weind spoke
as we gathered for prayer. Here are the thoughts she shared with us
on Thursday, June 18th.*

*Scripture readings: Sirach 48:1–14: Blessed they who shall have seen you
before they die, O Elijah, enveloped in the whirlwind! Then Elisha, filled with
a twofold portion of his spirit, wrought many marvels by his mere word.*

*Matthew 6:7–15: This is how you are to pray: Our Father in heaven,
hallowed be your name.*

About a month ago, I was working in the yard around the neighborhood house of prayer where I live in Saginaw, Michigan. It was late in the evening, although in this time of the season, light endures until almost ten o'clock in Saginaw. I was trying to take advantage of the last moments of daylight. And as I worked toward the end of that evening, three girls approached me and said, "Are you the prayer lady?" I said, "Well, I do live here and this is a house of prayer and I try to pray. What can I do for you?" I said. One child said, "Would you pray for us?"

I pursued that request, trying to get more specific with them. And they answered most of the questions I asked, but not the way I expected them to answer. One child said, "My relatives live in Chicago and my mother is down there right now because my cousin was killed." When I asked the age of the cousin, I found this was a teenager. Another child asked me to pray because a relative of hers was in a hospital in Saginaw. That seemed expected, age-wise and reason-wise. Another child—the youngest of the three—said, "I would like to live to be eighteen or twenty." I said, "How old are you now?" She said, "Eight."

We talked a little longer and I learned more about their lives in the street. And when they first approached me I would have guessed they were in their teens, so worn by their lives in the streets. But an eight-year-old, a ten-year-old and a twelve-year-old were wandering the streets on the east side of Saginaw, requesting prayer so they might live to be young-aged—not middle-aged, not old-aged.

I think today, as I stand here with you in prayer, of the oldest sister in the congregation of sisters that I belong to, the sisters of Notre Dame. Sister Immaculata is 101 years old. I doubt that Sister Immaculata worried about reaching 100 when she was eight years old. I don't remember ever worrying about that when I was eight years old. I worried about getting home before my mother got home, I worried about getting in before the neighbors had something to tell her about me. I worried about other children stealing my marbles, especially my steely. And I worried about things that children usually worry about, but I did not worry about reaching 18, 20, 30, 40, or this tender age of 55 that I have finally arrived at.

If these girls had known about Elijah, they might have asked for a show of strength as they stood in my yard, or they might have asked for some wonder of a whirlwind to assure a timely deliverance from the destruction that was impending in their experience. If these girls could have recounted the marvelous deeds of Elisha, they may have requested some portion of his power and told me how they could stand sure in the face of any intimidation because the word from a prophet like Elisha could not be daunted. But knowing what they did about God, all they asked was that I pray for them.

I assume and imagine that they knew enough about God to know that God provides, that God protects, that God lifts up and that God leads. I assume and imagine that these three young ladies knew enough about God that they had a sense of belonging to the family that cries out "Our Father." And it was translated to me that night that they knew that God can help us; in their plea I heard them say, Would *you* help us? It's their request translated into, God cares enough about us to provide for us and protect us; will *you* do that here at the house of prayer? God cares enough about us to deliver us from the entanglement of destruction and death; do *you* care that much, prayer lady? God cares and God's care can get us through our fears and tears, so that we might live through a few more years; will *you* keep time with us, prayer lady?

"Pray for us," is all they said. Not measured in words but "Pray for us" by investment of interest in us. By the choices that you make of the foods you eat. By the choices that you make of the clothes you buy. By the choices that you make when you read the labels and rest with relative assurance that another group of children are not going to die before their time because they are making garments that you can wear inexpensively, at their cost.

Would you pray for us, prayer lady, and for all the children in the world so they can get to be as old as you are? Will you pray for us by the way you respond to disappointment and frustration, always with gentleness and compassion, not with your dukes up and ready to wipe out anyone who disagrees with you? Pray for us, prayer lady, pray for us. Do it and show it in the way you live your life.

No, they did not know Elijah, at least they would not have known to recount what we heard here today. I doubt they could even pronounce Elisha, but they were caught up in the power of these prophets and even more so they are held in the loving embrace of the Father that we name and claim as our Father.

So, my sisters and my brothers, let us pray, truly confident that our familial relationship with each other here and with children and men and women all over the world will continue to reveal the glory and the honor that is rightfully due to God whom we call *our* Father. May our lives in word and action be a living prayer for the children and for the human community all over the world.

O Lord, hear our prayer! Hear us, Lord! Hear our prayer!

Authors

John Baldovin, SJ, is professor of history and liturgy at the Jesuit School of Theology, Berkeley, California. He is an author, teacher, scholar and past president of North American Academy of Liturgy.

Michael J. Begolly is a presbyter and pastor of the Blessed Sacrament Cathedral, Greensburg, Pennsylvania. He teaches liturgy at St. Vincent Seminary, Latrobe, Pennsylvania. He is author of *Leading the Assembly in Prayer: A Practical Guide for Lay and Ordained Presiders.*

Michael S. Driscoll is a presbyter of the diocese of Helena, Montana. He is assistant professor of theology and liturgy at the University of Notre Dame. He has served as an advisor to the NCCB's Bishops' Committee on the Liturgy.

Dorothy Dwight, BVM, is an author, liturgist and musician. She is on the faculty at Loyola University, Chicago.

Joseph A. Favazza is an author and assistant professor of religious studies at Rhodes College, Memphis, Tennessee. He is a coeditor of LTP's A Reconciliation Sourcebook.

Timothy Fitzgerald, a presbyter of the diocese of Des Moines, Iowa, is associate director of the Notre Dame Center for Pastoral Liturgy. His writings include *Infant Baptism: A Parish Celebration and Confirmation: A Parish Celebration.*

Maxwell E. Johnson is an ordained minister of the Evangelical Lutheran Church in America and associate professor of theology at the University of Notre Dame. He is editor of *Living Water, Sealing Spirit: Readings on Christian Initiation.*

Theresa F. Koernke, IHM, is an author and assistant professor of theology at Washington Theological Union, Washington, DC. She has served as an advisor to the NCCB's Bishops' Committee on the Liturgy and to the Faith and Order Commission of the World Council of Churches in the area of ecclesiology.

Patrick R. Lagges is a presbyter of the archdiocese of Chicago, where he serves as judicial vicar of the archdiocese. His articles have appeared in *The Jurist, Studia Canonica, Marriage and Family* and *Catechumenate.*

Gilbert W. Ostdiek, OFM, is professor of liturgy at Catholic Theological Union in Chicago. He has served as a member of the Advisory Committee of ICEL since 1986. His writings include *Catechists for Liturgy: A Program for Parish Involvement.*

Richard S. Vosko is a presbyter of the diocese of Albany, New York. He is an award-winning designer and consultant for worship environments in the United States and Canada. He serves on the planning committee for Form/Reform Conferences on church architecture.

Teresita Weind, SNDdeN, is the director of the Neighborhood House of Prayer in Saginaw, Michigan. A musician and author, she serves as a retreat director and preacher across the United States.